OFF THE BEATEN PATH® SERIES

FIFTH EDITION

OFF THE BEATEN PATH®
QUÉBEC ➡

A GUIDE TO UNIQUE PLACES

KATHARINE AND ERIC FLETCHER

gpp®
travel

Guilford, Connecticut

All the information in this guidebook is subject to change. We recommend that you call ahead to obtain current information before traveling.

To buy books in quantity for corporate use
or incentives, call **(800) 962-0973**
or e-mail **premiums@GlobePequot.com.**

Editor: Amy Lyons
Project Editor: Lynn Zelem
Layout: Joanna Beyer
Text design: Linda R. Loiewski
Maps: Equator Graphics © Morris Book Publishing, LLC

ISSN 1540-2142
ISBN 978-0-7627-5987-3

Printed in the United States of America
10 9 8 7 6 5 4 3 2 1

To our dear parents, who encouraged us both, from our earliest years, to explore the paths least trodden, to celebrate the differences among all Earth's peoples, and to wonder at our natural world.

About the Authors

Katharine and Eric Fletcher are award-winning freelance writers, editors, and publishers who live in the Pontiac region of Québec. Their company is Chesley House Publications. They live on a hundred-acre farm, Spiritwood, adjacent to the wilderness sector of Gatineau Park. From there they file travel, environment, nature, and gardening stories as well as photographs to their editors and publishers. They grow organic vegetables and fruits and are mostly successful at keeping wild turkeys, white-tail deer, and black bears from devouring their apples and grapes.

Sharing a keen love of adventure, nature, and travel, they travel often and as extensively as possible. In early 2010, for instance, they left Spiritwood on a year-long trip—for the second time. (In 1983–84 they backpacked for 14 months, being intrigued with extended explorations of India, Australia, Nepal, Burma, and China.)

They believe sustainable tourism—tourism which promotes and supports local communities and which is environmentally responsible—is key. Katharine is chair of sustainable tourism for the Canadian Chapter of the Society of American Travel Writers. In this capacity, she seeks to live and travel "like a local" as much as possible. As you'd expect, Eric shares her philosophy. And that's why, here in this guide, they showcase local traditions, culture and foods as much as possible.

In 1988, Katharine's self-published book, *Historical Walks: The Gatineau Park Story* launched her career as a professional writer. And, when The Globe Pequot Press invited her to write the first edition of this book in 1999, Eric became co-author. Today, both are professional members of the Society of American Travel Writers and they write articles, books, and contribute to many anthologies. The couple offer self-publishing workshops and their course, *Publish Yourself: The Basics of Self-publishing,* is popular. Katharine also leads custom hikes, bus tours, and both lectures and gives slide shows on Canada's National Capital Region, and is frequently interviewed on television and radio stations.

Eric is also a computer guru who specializes in e-publishing and document management. He teaches *Publish Yourself Part Two: Electronic Publishing and Software Essentials.*

Books: *Historical Walks: The Gatineau Park Story,* 3rd ed. (Fitzhenry and Whiteside: 2004); *Capital Walks: Walking Tours of Ottawa,* 2nd ed. (Fitzhenry and Whiteside: 2004); *Promenades historique dans le parc de la Gatineau* (Chesley House Publications: 1998); *The Canadian Writer's Guide, 13th ed.*

(Fitzhenry and Whiteside: 2002). **Columns:** *The Equity* (weekly environment column since Oct 1989), *Forever Young* and *Capital Parent* (ecotourism columns since 1998). **Magazines:** *Canadian Wildlife, Arrival, VIA Destinations, Ottawa City Magazine, Canadian Living.*

We enjoy hearing from our readers. Send an e-mail with your comments or suggestions to us at quebecbook@chesleyhouse.com.

Acknowledgments

We are delighted to present you with our updated fifth edition to our home province of Québec. Our insiders' introduction reflects not only the human and natural history of Canada's largest province, but also offers you a glimpse into its vibrant culture.

Since this guide was first published in 1999, we've heard from many readers who have followed our routes—and who have enhanced four new editions with their feedback. As all travelers understand, hotels, destinations and events sometimes close or change. And that's where these acknowledgements really become genuine: We could not keep *Québec Off the Beaten Path* as current as possible without some outstanding support.

So we thank visitors to *la belle province* who have contacted us with recommendations. We salute our fellow Québecers who love this province and who have told us about legends, history—as well as suggestions of destinations which we have subsequently researched and often included. Both of us are particularly grateful to friends, neighbors, and fellow residents of the Pontiac region in which we live whose opinions over the years have proved insightful.

Finally, thanks to Tourisme Québec whose representatives are always helpful. Merci à tous!

We also want to acknowledge the team at Globe Pequot Press who produced this book—again—so successfully. It's a great pleasure to work with you all.

—Katharine and Eric Fletcher
Quyon, Québec

Contents

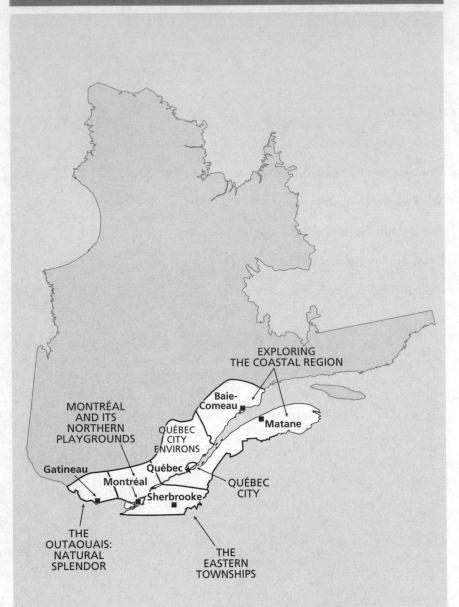

EXPLORING
THE COASTAL REGION

Baie-
Comeau

Matane

MONTRÉAL
AND ITS
NORTHERN
PLAYGROUNDS

QUÉBEC
CITY
ENVIRONS

Gatineau

Montréal

Québec

QUÉBEC
CITY

Sherbrooke

THE
OUTAOUAIS:
NATURAL
SPLENDOR

THE
EASTERN
TOWNSHIPS

Welcome to Québec

We live in *la belle province* (the beautiful province) and—well, that says it all, in our opinion. We moved here in May 1989 and now live in the *Outaouais* (pronounced *OOO-tah-ways*) region of West Québec. Our farmhouse is a mere forty-five minutes north and west of Ottawa, the capital of Canada, located in the neighboring province of Ontario. The border between the provinces is the Ottawa River, known in French as *la Rivière de l'Outaouais*.

In fact, if you look at a map of the province, water defines it, both inside and out. The Ottawa is a tributary of the St. Lawrence—or *Saint-Laurent en français*—which in turn flows into the Atlantic Ocean. Québec's Gaspé Peninsula—or *Gaspésie* in French—juts into the Gulf of St. Lawrence. Farther north, Québec touches on Hudson and James Bays.

And wait until you check out the interior watersheds. Where we live in spectacular Pontiac County, we are fortunate to have what's known as Québec's triple play of rivers: the Noire (Black), the Dumoine, and the Coulonge. For whitewater canoeing, they are unrivaled. Northeast of the province's capital, Québec City, there's the mighty Saguenay River, forming a true glacial fjord. There is world-renowned whale watching here, notably at the Saguenay's confluence with the St. Lawrence. Meanwhile, down in the Gaspé we'll discover the Restigouche, the Matapédia, and the Cascapédia, celebrated salmon rivers.

Finally, coursing north from the New England states is the Richelieu River and Lake Champlain, a historic trading route between the Thirteen Colonies, now the United States of America, and Canada.

Which brings us rather neatly to politics. Ever since the fateful conquest of Québec City, on the Plains of Abraham in 1759, and the ensuing fall of New France (*Nouvelle France*) via the Treaty of Paris in 1763, Québecers have gnawed at the bone of independence. Truly marking the Conquest of New

meaning of québec

Québec is an Algonquin First Nations word meaning "place where the river narrows" and was first used in 1601 on a map depicting the present site of Québec City. By 1763 it was used to describe the province.

France, the French king ceded all of French North America to Great Britain except for the twin islands of Saint Pierre and Miquelon, which to this day remain French. There was the famous uprising against British rule, known as the Rebellion of Lower Canada, in 1837–38, led by a hero of Québec, Louis-Joseph Papineau. In 1967 the president of France, General Charles de Gaulle, stood on the balcony of Montréal's City Hall to shout the unforgettable rallying call *"Vive le Québec Libre!"* ("Long live a free Québec!") to thousands of Québecers on June 24—the special holiday of Saint-Jean-Baptiste Day in this still predominantly Catholic province. His cry annoyed Canada's then prime minister Lester B. Pearson and terrified federalists throughout Canada. Even today the words are a rallying call for separatists who want the province to secede from Canada.

Past injustices, real and perceived, and the deep conviction that the Québécois are "a people" have kept the desire for separation—or for the perplexing "sovereignty association"—a life-sustaining force in the hearts of roughly 30 percent of residents. Throughout the 1960s and into the twenty-first century, Québecers have rallied to yet another call, to be *maîtres chez nous* (masters of our own house), eschewing the official bilingualism policy introduced by the late prime minister Pierre Elliott Trudeau in the 1970s.

400thanniversary

In 2004 Québec celebrated 400 years of permanent French settlement in North America, with special events throughout the province. In 2008 Québec City celebrated its own personal 400th anniversary: when in 1608 Champlain founded Québec, at a habitation located in today's Place Royal.

Former Québec premier Lucien Bouchard—whose title, ironically, is *prime ministre* in French—called a referendum on Oct 16, 1995, on the question of whether Québecers wanted to remain a part of Canada. The mandate of his party, the Parti Québécois, is to separate from Canada. Fortunately, from our point of view—we are federalists—that referendum was defeated, but only by a wish and a prayer, with 51 percent voting no. Bouchard's successor, Bernard Landry, kept this separatist dream alive and hoped for yet another referendum (we call these votes "neverendums") but, like Bouchard, he only wanted to call another vote under "winning conditions." In 2003 federalist Jean Charest, leader of Québec's Liberal party, won the provincial election. Fast forward to 2009 and Charest remains the province's head honcho. So enquiring minds ponder: Is separatism on a back burner?

It's never far away, although it's perhaps not front and foremost at the minute. In 2006, Conservative Prime Minister of Canada Stephen Harper introduced a motion in the House of Parliament recognizing that Québecers form a nation within a united Canada. On the 26th of November he said, "Our position is clear. Do the Québécois form a nation within Canada? The answer is yes. Do the Québécois form an independent nation? The answer is no and the answer will always be no."

The brief flirtation Québecers had with the Conservatives ended during the 40th federal election in October, 2008. With the country again returning a minority federal Conservative party, Québecers elected 49 Bloc Québécois representatives, dashing Harper's hopes for a strong showing in the province. They are still strongly represented by Gilles Duceppe on Parliament Hill, who has been leader of this party since 1997. The "Pequistes'" goal is to create a sovereign nation, thus answering the perennial "Québec question" which refers to the province's place in Canadian confederation. Ironically, federal separatist Bloc Québécois politicians are paid handsome salaries by the people of Canada to lobby, in Parliament, for Québec's interests—including sovereign nationhood.

Only in Canada, you say? The separatist presence adds a unique voice if not tension to our politics, that's for sure! Even though Duceppe periodically maintains that separation is not "top of list" on his party's agenda, it remains true that the primary goal of the Bloc Québécois is to make Québec a sovereign nation.

Québecers are savvy to the political game and have a long history of delivering severe warnings to their political leaders on election day. Separation? Personally we don't think it will happen, but who knows? This razor's edge of uncertainty keeps Québec interests firmly in the minds of federal and provincial politicians—not to mention of Canadians throughout the country.

Amid all the political navel-gazing, life jogs along relatively happily among ordinary people, whether they speak English, French, or whatever. That being said, Québec provincial government "language police" wander the cities and countryside threatening shop owners with stiff fines if English or other non-French languages feature prominently on their signs.

But here in Québec there's contagious *joie de vivre*. There are vivid native legends, born from long winter nights when the wind howled in the bush. There are the morality tales, arising from the French and Irish Catholic spirit of sin and repentance. And there's the revelry in March associated with the sugar shacks (where maple sugar is rendered from sap), where old-time music is played while folks lap up pancakes covered in maple syrup and tap their feet to the rhythm. There are the sophisticated, internationally recognized *Cirque du Soleil,* with its incredibly intricate circus acts, and the red-toqued snowman *Bonhomme* (Good Man), mascot of Québec City's Winter Festival.

What are we doing here, you might ask. Eric was born in British Columbia and moved to Ottawa in 1966. Katharine was born in England and moved to Toronto, Ontario, in 1958, then to Ottawa in 1974. We moved together to Québec in 1989. We love Canada passionately, and our Canada includes Québec. In the Outaouais, or West Québec, where we live, residents voted over 93 percent *against* separation and for a unified Canada during the 1995 referendum. Where we live, people hail from Germany, Ireland, Scotland, England,

Lithuania, and Poland. The Outaouais symbolizes Canada: a microcosm of our nation within the bosom of Québec. A model for how we can all get along, if you ask us.

Québec. *La belle province*. It's a complex place that inspires passionate love. Come and visit. Often. Don't shy away from using the French language. Experience the diversity. Revel in our beautiful farmland, our spectacular rivers and woods, our vibrant cities. Explore her ways and you, too, will love enchanting Québec.

Keys to Québec

We thought we'd start by giving some insiders' tips on how best to travel in Québec. Let's address this business of French language right off the top.

Language

American, Australian, British, and other tourists to Québec are astounded at how much French language they see and hear. "It's as if we were in France," they murmur. Most visitors find it intriguing and exhilarating. But sometimes it can be intimidating.

If you don't speak or read French at all, the best way to get around in Québec is to have a completely open mind and to be flexible. Have a smile on your face. Try to master just a few pleasantries, such as the lovely greeting *Bonjour,* which means "Good day."

At the back of this book is a small glossary of French words and phrases. Pronunciation can be mystifying: If you are up for it, buy a French language CD, such as those offered by Berlitz, to listen to and give yourself a feel for this beautiful language's rhythms and inflections.

Many people in Québec speak a little English; if they don't, often someone nearby will. If all seems hopeless (sometimes you're exhausted by the end of the day), smile and see if our French glossary at the back of the book helps. Point to a phrase, smile, and we feel you'll be well looked after. And if you want to start in a region of Québec that eases you into the province, come to us here in the Outaouais, where almost everyone is bilingual to some degree. (We're not biased: the Outaouais simply is one of the loveliest introductions to Québec you'll ever get.)

We were delighted to find that some provincial and local museums had binders available with English translations of major exhibit information panels. In fact, while revisiting destinations for this edition, we found that many more venues now offer English, Spanish, or other translations of exhibit text. But note: the binders may not be displayed, nor are they automatically offered. If you do not see English, and would benefit from it, you should simply ask for them. Many smaller museums, however, still do not have translations.

Federally operated museums, historic sites, and services offer bilingual services. Why? Because the Government of Canada is officially bilingual and all staff are supposedly fluent in French and English. (Interestingly, the only Canadian province that is officially bilingual is New Brunswick.) Places you can usually rely on for bilingual services include post offices, ferry docks, and most tourist information centers. Federally operated locations usually display the Canadian flag or have the flag printed on their signage.

Tourist Information

Follow the distinctive "?" symbol for help at one of Québec's tourist information centers. In fact, we suggest that the first stop you make—no matter which entry point into Québec you use—is at one of these. Whether at a provincial or local center, we've found staff to be friendly and helpful, even if they are not bilingual. Best of all, you can pick up excellent local or regional maps that show even the smallest roads. Information centers at or near the U.S. border have brochures explaining road signage, how to claim reimbursement for sales tax you are charged while visiting Canada, and other details you might find useful.

You'll also find informative tourist guides prepared in English for each of Québec's twenty tourism regions. They are useful, but be aware that they list only the attractions and locations of tourism association members. Many of the places we include in this book are listed in the guides, but we've also discovered many others that are either new or have chosen not to be members of the associations.

askforenglish translations

If you don't read French, you can ask for English translations at such places as museums or restaurants. To inquire if they have translations of informational material, such as guidebooks or menus, the all-purpose phrase is "*Avez vous une guide en anglais s'il-vous-plâit?*" To pronounce the phrase, simply say "*Avayvoo une geed en englay seal voo play?*"

The maps in this book are intended as general guides only, so do plan to use more detailed maps as you travel. You'll find them at the tourist information centers; you can also contact the provincial government for maps. Getting maps before the trip can save you a lot of frustration later.

Do you have access to the Internet? If so, visit the Tourisme Québec Web site at www.bonjourquebec.com, where you will find links to each of the tourism regions in Québec.

Tourisme Québec can be reached by calling (877) 266-5687 (toll-free from Canada and the United States) or (514) 873-2015; or consult your travel agent.

For information on wheelchair access in Québec, contact KEROUL at 4545 ave. Pierre-de-Coubertin, CP 1000 succursale M, Montréal H1V 3R2; (514) 252-3104; www.keroul.qc.ca.

For snowmobile trail maps and information, contact Fedération des clubs de motoneigistes du Québec at 4545 ave. Pierre-de-Coubertin, CP 1000, succursale M, Montréal H1V 3R2; (514) 252-3076; www.fcmq.qc.ca.

Entering Canada and Québec

As of June 2009, U.S. citizens must have a valid passport (or a document that complies with the Western Hemisphere Travel Initiative) to re-enter the United States from Canada. Canadian entry rules are less stringent, but you may be asked for such documents to prevent problems upon your return to the United States. Contact Canada Border Services Agency at (800) 461-9999 or www.cbsa-asfc.gc.ca for current information. Ordinarily, crossing our peaceful borders is not a problem. Long may that last.

Handguns are not welcome in Canada. They will be confiscated at the border, or you will be refused entry. If you plan to bring in a gun for hunting, check with Canada Customs for restrictions before you leave home.

The American Consulate General is at Place Félix-Martin, 1155 rue Saint-Alexandre, Montréal; (514) 398-9695; fax: (514) 398-0973. The mailing address is CP 65, Station Desjardins, Montréal H5B 1G1.

Money

The Canadian monetary system has 100 cents to the dollar. Common denominations of paper currency, in various colors, are $5, $10, $20 and, less commonly, $50 and $100.

Coinage starts with the penny, or 1 cent, followed by the nickel, or 5 cents; dime, or 10 cents; quarter, or 25 cents, and, less commonly, the 50-cent piece (if you find one, keep it, as they're quite rare). Then we come to what Canadians affectionately call the "loonie"—the $1 coin with the picture of a loon on one side. And then, just so the loonie wouldn't be lonesome, the Royal Canadian Mint produced the "toonie," or $2 coin, adorned with a polar bear and Queen Elizabeth II. (Canadians immediately coined the expression "the

Queen with a bear behind" to describe the loonie's new cousin. Now who says Canadians don't have a sense of humor?)

For U.S. visitors, Québec can be a bargain: As we prepared this edition, the Canadian dollar was worth approximately 95 cents U.S.—although it has risen from a low of less than 70 cents several years ago. Many places will gladly take U.S. dollars, but you will usually get a better exchange rate at banks. You probably don't need to change a lot of dollars, however: Québec is well equipped with automatic teller machines (ATMs), and most establishments accept debit cards for payment.

Prices are in Canadian dollars unless otherwise noted.

Holidays in Québec

January 1 and 2; Good Friday; Easter Monday; Victoria Day (third Monday in May); Saint-Jean-Baptiste Day (June 24); Canada Day (July 1); Labor Day (first Monday in September); Thanksgiving (second Monday in October); Remembrance Day (November 11); Christmas Day (December 25); and Boxing Day (December 26).

Road Signs and Rules

If you don't speak or read French, signage—especially on highways—can be challenging. To help you get oriented, we've included some of the more common terms in the glossary at the back of the book.

If you're stuck, ask a police officer for directions. Many are bilingual.

Québec, as in all Canada, uses the metric system. Distances are given in kilometers on road signs, and speed limits are posted in kilometers per hour: 50

Hitch a Ride on the Moose

Don't have a vehicle? Want to explore the back roads? Contact the Moose Travel Network! This service transports Canadian visitors around a figure-eight loop through both Ontario and Québec in a comfortable van. It's a simple, efficient concept that follows the international demand for JOJO—jump on, jump off—tourism. Owner Neil Crawford told us that people jump on at, say, Québec City, and travel to a destination such as Baie-Saint-Paul, spend a day or so exploring, then jump back on and head to Tadoussac. There are several package loops you can buy, all tax-included. The Mohawk Tour is a 3,000-km loop through Ontario and Québec; the 1,500-km Big East covers Ontario but also links to Montréal, Mt. Tremblant and Fort Coulonge. Information: Moose Travel Network, 460 King St. West, Toronto; (888) 816-6673; www.moosenetwork.com.

kilometers is about 30 miles; 100 kph is about 60 mph. You'll find drivers tend to push the limits on the major highways, but the posted speed is safest on secondary roads. Radar detectors are illegal in Québec, and police can confiscate them.

Fuel is sold in metric volume: A liter is roughly equivalent to a quart, with approximately four liters to a gallon. Yes, gas is more expensive than in the United States, but, hey, the taxes embedded in the price pay for our great roads!

Signs that include references to a time of day usually use the twenty-four-hour system or a variant. Instead of 4:15 p.m., for instance, the sign can indicate 16:15 or 16h15. Watch for it especially on parking signs.

NOTE: Although it had been illegal to turn right on a red light anywhere in Québec, the law changed in Sept 2002, allowing drivers to make a right turn on red except in the city of Montréal or where specifically prohibited.

Getting Around

Québec is Canada's largest province. It's almost three times the size of France and more than ten times the area of Maine, New Hampshire, Vermont, and Massachusetts combined! Most of its 7.8 million people live within 100 miles of the U.S. border, with only a few small pockets of industrial sites and native villages in the vast territory to the north.

While Québec's roads and highways are generally excellent in the south, there are still plenty of challenging back roads to explore. A glance at a map will show you that very few roads extend north. The few that do exist have long stretches with no services, may have rough pavement or graveled sections, and often are traveled by lots of big trucks. We've driven all the main routes described here in our Honda Accord without any problems. We've also included a few route suggestions for the more adventurous or for those of you itching to put your sport-utility vehicle to the test. Some really off-the-beaten-path attractions are accessible only by gravel roads, but we'll warn you about that in the text. And because we don't like to backtrack, we've tried to find circuits where you won't need to retrace your path.

That being said, there are some well-known "nightmares," and we'll try to steer you clear of them. First of all, road signage can be perplexing—a fact exacerbated by language. Montréal's road tunnels can be claustrophobic to some: just take a deep breath and relax. And you haven't really driven until you've experienced Montréal's raised auto-routes. The main tip is, try to avoid rush hours, typically 6:30 to 9 a.m. and 4 to 6:30 p.m.

Québecers love to travel. We were told that throughout Québec (with the exception of the Outaouais), about 95 percent of tourists are

French-speaking and upwards of 85 percent are Québecers. The park-like hinterlands of Montréal and the city of Québec can draw astonishing crowds. In summer and on winter weekends, rush hours can be just as vexing as during the normal workweek as people escape from and reluctantly return to their jobs. Québecers also love cycling. Everywhere, bicycle paths are springing up, along old rail beds, highways, and byways. Come winter, rural regions are crisscrossed by snowmobile trails that, on occasion, cross roads. Bikers and snowmobilers are usually respectful of traffic, but

québectrivia

Tip: Buy a phone card, available in different denominations and sold at many stores, even gas stations. As you make calls, the amount is debited from the card and you won't have to fiddle around for change.

as you drive your car, remember that you are handling a potentially lethal weapon. Drive defensively—always.

Montréal boasts a subway system called *Le Métro* (the Metro). It's inexpensive and efficient, and it offers another slice of Montréal culture. Here you'll find an underground city, full of shops and delis, along walkways that protect you from inclement weather. Along the way, you may be entertained by buskers in this underground world. Safe. Convenient. Inexpensive. Try it!

Green Transportation: Bicycling big in Québec

Québecers love their bikes. Not only does Canada boast the Trans Canada Trail (www.tctrail.ca), the world's longest trail network (22,000 km when it's completed), but the province of Québec has its own connecting as well as independent stretches of this trail. The entire "green route" network in Québec is called **La Route Verte** (www.routeverte.com). It was developed in part by a province-wide association, Vélo Québec (www.velo.qc.ca). Browse it online or get a copy of *Cycling in Québec*, Vélo Québec's booklet describing the 4,076 km trail network. It's handy because it contains 176 maps (so far . . .) and describes lodgings as well as bike-friendly campgrounds.

Many cities and villages pride themselves on being bike-friendly, too. Take Montréal, for instance: in 1999 it was voted the most bike-friendly city in North America. Ten years later it introduced **Bixi** (an acronym combining bicycle and taxi, in the summer of 2009 (public bike rental service—see Montréal section). That city's not alone: excellent urban and rural trails are available throughout the province as well as in such parks as Gatineau Park (see Outaouais section).

Staying in Touch

It currently costs $1.11 to send a postcard, a letter, or a greeting card to the United States from Canada, including the pernicious GST (goods and services tax) and QST (Québec sales tax). The overseas rate is $1.86.

Similar to American zip codes, the postal codes you'll see in Canadian addresses help route mail efficiently; please include them.

You'll find telephones everywhere in Québec, and most phone booths accept credit cards and calling cards. Calls are generally less expensive from 6 p.m. to 8 a.m. Many tourist information centers are equipped with phones so that you can more easily call hotels or other lodgings for reservations.

As you'll see from the contact information we provide, many of the attractions and accommodations include Internet addresses. You'll find wired and wireless Internet access in the most unexpected places. And you can access the Internet from most accommodations: if it isn't obvious, ask.

québectrivia

Michel Tremblay is a famous Québec writer/playwright. In 1964 he won first prize in a Radio-Canada (the French wing of the Canadian Broadcasting Corporation) competition for his play *Le Train*. It launched his career. Four years later, *Les Belles-soeurs* established him as one of Québec's literary geniuses. His work has been translated into more than 20 languages.

Stores in major centers often carry the English-language *Montréal Gazette* as well as a selection of other Canadian and foreign newspapers. Check out a French-language newspaper: It'll give you another opportunity to brush up on your French as you follow stock prices or the weather forecast.

Ditto with television. Québec has some excellent English- and French-language television productions that never make it beyond the borders. Pity.

There's another intriguing language twist: the politics surrounding translation. Interestingly—and Québec is ever thus—some English TV programs or films destined for Québec and France can be translated twice into French: once for the province, once for the country of France. Even some French-only Québec TV shows are translated into "International French" which residents of France can better comprehend.

Ostensibly this is because of *joual*, the name given to describe what some call Québec's "street French". Although it has been mocked in some circles because it is an old dialect, it is nonetheless the language of many Québécois. Indeed, in the 1960s, many Québécois writers purposefully adopted it so their works would have authenticity and truly reflect how people speak.

Trust Québec to give us all some serious food for thought—that's a good thing, we believe! Want to explore literary *joual?* Read Michel Tremblay's 1968 two-act play, *Les Belles-sœurs*.

Hospitals and Doctors

We all aim to stay healthy, especially on vacation. So pack your usual medications, and don't forget any special ones you might need. If you do require medical help, Québec offers excellent health services, and all cities and most towns have at least one hospital.

Québec has what are called *Centre Local de Services Communautaire* (CLSCs) to provide health and social services. You'll see signs on roads pointing to them. If you are in a small town, a CLSC should serve your needs for routine health problems. In areas with hospitals, you will see the international sign, H, directing you to the facility.

Weather

Québec enjoys four seasons, with refreshing springs, hot summers, crisp autumns—and cold winters. But don't let the cold scare you. Québec is a wonderful place to visit in winter. With the right clothes, you don't have to feel daunted by the cold, and there is so much to do: skiing, snowshoeing, skating, and snowmobiling. In our opinion, January and February are among the best times of year to visit Québec because blue-sky days are fantastical against a snowy backdrop. Come summer, those frozen lakes you might ski over in February are just the place for cooling off on a hot day. Major newspapers in either language carry daily weather forecasts

Food

Fresh local produce plus regional recipes equal delicious, memorable meals. Delectable *tarte au sucre* (sugar pie) is made from maple sugar, while *la tortière* is the famous meat pie. There's Matane salmon, fresh from the river, or crisp *pommes* (apples) and throat-warming *cidre de pomme* (apple cider)—hard or soft. Tasty microbrewery *bière* (beer). Tangy *chèvre* (goat cheese). Sweet *pain d'or* (French toast). Divine *cassis* (black currant liqueur). Moose, lobster, wild boar, caribou. Blueberries, strawberries, raspberries, and August's golden corn. You name it. *La belle province* serves it up with flair and a flourish.

In fact, we can say Québec has joined the international movement whereby regional producers are being celebrated. It's not simply the growers, but also the entire agri-food industry (including chefs and restauranteurs) which is being scrutinized by consumers. In Québec, *produits du terroir* is the special term for such regional foods, where producers have been certified or registered with such provincial bodies as Québec's Ministry of Agriculture and Fish or Québec's Centre of Animal Health.

Increasingly, the province has become a culinary tourist's haven catering to locavores and "100-mile-diet" aficionados.

What is a locavore? Someone who wants to eat fresh, regional food which has been grown, sold, prepared within a 100-mile (or kilometer . . .) radius of where one is living/visiting. Accordingly, many Québec regions such as Charlevoix (east of Québec City), Abitibi-Témiscaming, and the Outaouais, have agri-food maps of their regions, where tourists and residents alike can visit producers to purchase the freshest of foods. In many cases, food can be purchased at the farm gate itself, at village *dépanneurs* (corner stores), farmers' markets, or even some large grocery chains.

Mind you, you can also chow down on what some declare is the province's real specialty, *poutine*, served up at innumerable roadside *casse-croûtes*, or snack bars. What the heck is *poo-teen* anyway? French fries with gobs of cheese-curd sauce, covered in gravy. "You can't leave without trying it," some say. (Get the drift? We're not keen on *poutine*, but thousands flock to *casse-croûtes* to enjoy it.)

Restaurants

The word *restaurant*, thank heavens, is bilingual and *cafe* and *bistro* are also common English words. But what of the ubiquitous Québécois *casse-croûte*? Perched beside the highway, it's a fast-food joint, really, where you can buy *poutine* as well as the beloved *le hot dog* and *le hamburger*. At the opposite end of the spectrum is the *relais gastronomique*, a fancy gourmet restaurant that usually denotes expensive and memorably delicious cuisine in a wonderful ambience.

The words *apportez votre bouteille du vin* posted on signs at a restaurant indicate you can bring your own wine. This is a really Québécois thing to do in restaurants that don't have a liquor license.

Économusées

As you travel throughout Québec, you will discover *économusées* (economuseums): small commercial operations, specifically designed to demonstrate and showcase both the tools and skills of artisans or specialty tradespeople as well as their final output. There are 32 *économusées* in Québec; as well as several others in the Atlantic Provinces. At these, you can watch the labors of blacksmiths at their forges, weavers at their looms, apiarists extracting honey from their beehives, and so on. Each économusée is owned and operated by the workers themselves and financed by the sale of their products on-site. You may find that only French is spoken, but usually you'll find someone who can help translate. Don't miss these fascinating places depicting traditional artisinal skills. For more information, contact International Economuseum Network Society at www.economusees.com or (418) 694-4466.

Alcohol and Tobacco

In general, Québec has a more cosmopolitan attitude about alcohol than most other Canadian provinces. However, consumption of alcohol is illegal in parks. That means don't brandish it about on your picnics or in the campgrounds.

Which brings us to the subject of our beer. It's stronger than American brew. Beer is usually over 6 percent alcohol. Wine, hard cider (*cidre*), and the French apple liquor called *calvados* are very alcoholic. Beer and wine are widely available at stores, but spirits are sold through the government liquor outlets called Société des alcools du Québec (SAQ). Take care; be sensible and thoroughly enjoy yourself.

Note that some *économusées* produce traditional alcoholic beverages such as at Cassis Monna et Fills. Find their delectable black currant *cassis* at their *économusées* on L'Île d'Orléans east of Québec City. Increasingly, regions of the province feature are starting to feature wine routes, called *la route des vins* (check www.laroutedesvins.ca).

Drinking and driving is a punishable offense and is not taken lightly. There are road checks. If you are caught driving while impaired, you may lose your license and have your vehicle impounded. Don't drink and drive: have a designated driver and make sure that individual does not drink any alcohol.

Smoking in public places such as restaurants and bars in Québec has been banned since 2006, and private smoking areas were eliminated in May 2008. As of 2009, this ban extends to public patios as well as the workplace.

Accommodations

Quick: What's the difference between a *gîte* (pronounced jeet) and an *auberge?* A *gîte* is a B&B operated by a family, at which breakfast is the only meal available. (Some occasionally will serve dinner if pre-arranged, but this is rare and mostly only in remote locations.) An *auberge* usually has a restaurant attached and is a bigger operation.

Gîte du campagne is a country B&B. *Ferme vacances* signifies a farm vacation. You'll see these along the byways.

Hotels and motels are widely available, ranging in price and style from the grandly opulent to the neat and affordable. Our favorites are mentioned in the appropriate chapters.

Forfait is a Québec expression for "package deal." Many auberges and gîtes offer such deals and include anything from a B&B accommodation with a massage, or a whale-watching expedition, or even a tai chi lesson. Watch for this word because, just as in English, package deals are usually your best buy.

Parks

Some parks are federal and thus will be bilingually interpreted, with brochures and signs in both French and English. Other parks are provincially operated and are French only. Confusingly for non-Québecers, "provincial" parks are *parcs nationalles*—which is yet another of Québec's political statements. Regardless of whether we're talking about a federal or provincial park, sometimes services and guides are available in French and English, as well as in Japanese, Spanish, and German. Ask. Don't be surprised, however, if some of the guided nature walks are not interpreted by bilingual guides: although leaders will genuinely try to be helpful, English may not be fluent. It's still worthwhile to hire a guide, however: we always enjoy speaking French and you'll see that any efforts you make, too, will be warmly welcomed, if not admired!

It is illegal to hunt or fish without licenses, and in some cases (notably salmon fishing) you must register, too. Along some rivers, such as the Cascapédia and Matapédia in the Gaspé, fishermen are assigned to a specific pool. Rivers are protected rigorously and wardens actively patrol them. For an English-language booklet on fishing regulations, call Tourisme Québec toll-free at (800) 363-7777. Throughout the back roads, you'll find signs declaring that the territory is a *zec (Zone d'exploitation contrôlée)*, meaning it's a controlled hunting and fishing zone.

As you explore Québec, you'll undoubtedly come across references to *"Sépaq" (Société des établissements de plein air du Québec)*, the government agency mandated to manage, operate, and develop a growing number of recreational facilities throughout Québec. Sépaq works with local partners to protect, conserve, and foster sustainable development. Their Web site is an excellent resource for current information about hours of operation, fees, facilities, and directions to many of Québec's finest wildlife reserves, vacation resorts, campgrounds, and parks.

For information, check www.sepaq.com or contact the sales and reservations office in Québec City for brochures. (Most are available in English.) The address is 2640 Blvd. Laurier, Suite 250, 2nd floor, Québec QC G1V 5C2; (800) 665-6527 or (418) 890-6527.

QUÉBEC CITY →

The words *"C'est magnifique!"* will tumble from your lips as you begin to discover this truly magnificent city. Because it is the only walled city in North America, it was designated a UNESCO World Heritage Site in 1985. Thanks to extensive restoration projects in the old quarter—the Lower Town sector—you can capture the ambience of the city as it must have appeared in the 1700s.

Québec City holds a very special place in our hearts. We explored its cobbled streets and enjoyed many a candlelit dinner during those wonderful, heady days when we were first dating. The capital city of the province of Québec represents Old World charm, history, the birth of our nation—and romance. We spent countless hours wandering the city's streets, hand in hand, personally discovering some of its many restaurants. It's a place we've never tired of, for its many bistros, cafes, museums, parks, antiques alleys, and artists' creations continue to intrigue us.

The most famous landmark of Québec City is the magnificent Château Frontenac, a definite must-see hotel. It towers atop cliffs whose sheer walls formed the strategic defense of the city, which troops led by the canny British officer General Wolfe scaled during his siege of the capital in 1759.

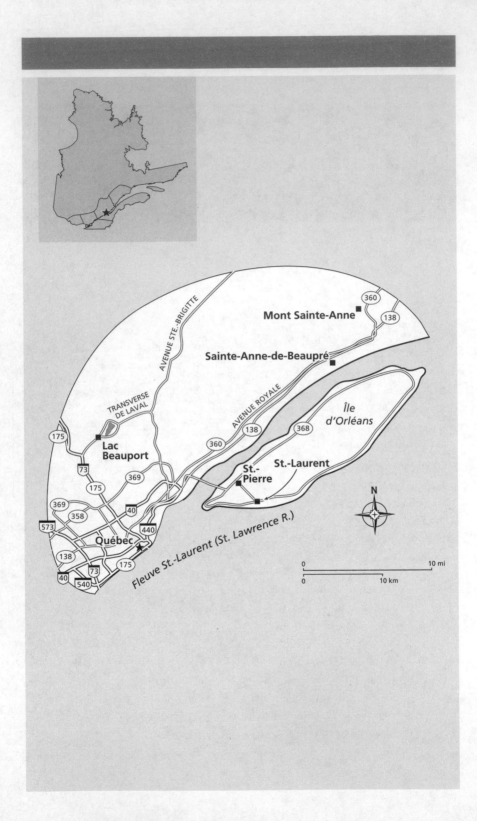

Mont Sainte-Anne

Sainte-Anne-de-Beaupré

Île d'Orléans

AVENUE STE-BRIGITTE

AVENUE ROYALE

TRANSVERSE DE LAVAL

Lac Beauport

St.-Laurent

St.-Pierre

Québec

Fleuve St.-Laurent (St. Lawrence R.)

N

0   10 mi
0   10 km

Stand on the boardwalk called the Terrasse Dufferin, which extends around the hotel, and from it look eastward, down the mighty St. Lawrence River beneath you. Drink in the spectacular views of the river; of a pastoral island, Île d'Orléans, to the east; and of the rugged Laurentian Mountains to the northeast.

The history of the river and the land you survey can be traced back thousands of years. The St. Lawrence River was used as a trade route by Amerindians for upwards of 4,000 years. Of course, in our Eurocentric way, "discovery" of what is now Québec City is attributed first to Jacques Cartier in 1535.

In fact, the Celts were probably the first "Europeans" to land here, before A.D. 1000, and during that millennium, the Vikings are also thought to have claimed all the land along the Atlantic Coast. By 1500 Newfoundland had been claimed by Portugal.

québectrivia

Three times the size of France, Québec is the largest of Canada's territories and provinces, representing 15.5 percent of the country.

The next major French explorer of the region was Samuel de Champlain, the "father of New France." In 1608 he had the first fortified habitation built, Place Royal, in what became Québec City's Lower Town, a site that can still be visited.

Back in the 1600s, predictably, Old World conflicts resulted in New World land grabs. On July 19, 1629, Britain's Sir David Kirke led an attack on Québec City and Champlain surrendered. So began the French-English conflict over the city. Four years later, France won it back and reinstated Champlain as governor.

The most famous conflict, however, became known as the Battle of the Plains of Abraham in 1759. British general James Wolfe led an ambush on the city by having 3,000 men scale the cliffs. On the windswept plains, Wolfe defeated French general Marquis Louis-Joseph de Montcalm—but both

AUTHORS' FAVORITES IN QUÉBEC CITY

Artillery Park National Historic Site	Plains of Abraham Battlefields Park
Château Frontenac	Ursuline Museum
Fêtes de la Nouvelle France	Winter Carnival
Musée de la Civilisation	

leaders lost their lives in this decisive encounter that lasted a mere fifteen minutes.

The defeat also sounded the death knell for the aspirations of New France. By 1763 Britain and France signed the Treaty of Paris, transferring the French lands to the British and enfolding them into British America. Shortly thereafter, American general Robert Montgomery seized Montréal in 1775 and cast covetous eyes on Québec City. Since the British had cannily permitted those of French extraction to retain their language and religion, the two groups worked together to roust the upstart intruders. Québec City remained with the devil it knew, which evolved into the Canada of today.

québectrivia

Before the Conquest of 1759, Québec's population was mostly French. But the early immigration waves of the 1800s turned the tides: By 1861 it was 51 percent British and other groups. However, by the 1981 census, only 4 percent of the city's population was English-speaking.

That's what happened so long ago. Now let's begin our modern-day exploration of this fabulous, romantic city and its rugged hinterland. As our starting point, we'll use the city's principal landmark, the *Fairmont Château Frontenac* (1 rue des Carrières, Québec; 418-692-3861 or 866-540-4460; www.fairmont.com/frontenac). Although it hardly represents an off-the-beaten-path location, it simply must not be missed. It was built in 1893 in the Châteauesque style, which noted architect Harold Kalman says is possibly the only truly Canadian architectural style. Note its sheer baronial castle walls and steeply pitched copper roofline with dormer windows. Whimsical turrets and a stately bearing on the exterior complement the rich opulence of the wood-paneled interior. Château Frontenac resembles a fairy-tale castle of old, furthering the romantic mood of Québec City.

If you book a room here, it'll be pricey—but you expected that, didn't you? After all, such notables as Elizabeth Taylor and Alfred Hitchcock, Winston Churchill and President Franklin Roosevelt, Queen Elizabeth—and even the Harlem Globetrotters have all stayed here.

The Château Frontenac site is situated on an incomparable location, on the actual foundations of the former Château Saint-Louis, which was razed in 1834. (In fact, thanks to some fascinating excavations where its old walls have been revealed, you can explore thee ruins of the Château Saint-Louis yourself, when touring the Dufferin Terrace.) Because of its prominence, the Château Frontenac provides a superb link between Québec City's Upper and Lower Towns.

Downstairs, the Château's beautiful airy dining room serves incredible buffets. We've had breakfasts here that have truly set us up for the day. Whether it's yogurt and fruit, muesli, bacon and eggs, or pancakes and muffins, you'll find exactly the meal you desire. Lunches and dinners are similarly scrumptious and the smorgasbords are famous for serving *les produits du terroir*. Just make sure you bring a hearty appetite.

And what better way to work up an appetite than by a brisk walk? Head outside onto the *Terrasse Dufferin* (Dufferin Terrace) in front of the hotel, where you'll find a statue honoring *Samuel de Champlain*. Founder of Québec City, the explorer built Château Saint-Louis here in 1620—it was the first of four forts occupying this site. His was a wooden construction, protected by a palisade. When he was forty, Champlain wed twelve-year-old Hélène Boullé. His marriage contract stated that he had to wait two years before living with her, as she hadn't gained sexual maturity. She came to New France also in 1620 but was miserable: she hated it here. So the young bride returned to France in 1624, never to return. When Champlain died in Québec City in Dec 1635, she became a nun at the Ursuline convent in Paris.

Next to Champlain's statue, find the plaque commemorating Québec City's designation as a World Heritage site by UNESCO in 1985, in recognition of it being the only walled city north of Mexico on the North American continent. Gaily colored horse-drawn calèches can be found here. A forty-five-minute ride for up to four people costs about $80. Call *Calèches du Vieux-Québec* at 418-520-1555; www.calecheduvieux quebec.com.

Walk along the Terrasse Dufferin, looking across the still-tidal St. Lawrence River (*St. Laurent en français*) south to Laval and east toward Île d'Orléans. It was here that Montcalm planned his strategy for the defense of the city at the time of the Conquest of 1759.

safety in québec city

While attending a conference in 2009, I found myself enervated and not ready to return to my hotel room at the Château Frontenac. Instead, I joined many others who were strolling about, enjoying views from the Dufferin Terrace, exploring the excavated Château Saint-Louis, and wandering streets where people were relaxing with drinks at patios spilling onto the sidewalk. A few times I was greeted by a friendly nod or a gracious *"Bonsoir, madame!"* (Good evening!). I was never bothered; I never felt unsafe. I returned to my room at 1:30 a.m., relaxed after a delightful evening walk *en plein air*.

—Katharine

Here you'll find the ruins of ***Château Saint-Louis*** built under the direction of Governor Frontenac in 1692. There is no fee to explore and the excavations are intriguingly displayed: you descend steps, weave about the old foundations, gaining an appreciation of what the old defences must have looked like.

Here were stationed a garrison of 25 or so men plus 17 of the governor's private guard. Thanks to Parks Canada, bilingual interpretive signs explain what archaeologists have unearthed so far.

In all seasons, continue exploring Terrasse Dufferin, which extends along the cliff's edge, to enjoy the wonderful (free) views of the St. Lawrence and the cliffs. Soon the walkway becomes the *Promenade des Gouverneurs* and starts climbing several sets of stairs.

Are you exploring in winter? If so, don't even think of missing a toboggan ride down the old-fashioned wooden slide, located behind the western edge of the Château Frontenac. *Les Glissades de la Terrasse* operates from Dec to mid-Mar. Buy a ticket ($2 per person; 418-829-9898). The wooden toboggans seat four—and if you're like us you'll scream like a banshee as you hurtle down the tall slide. Your icy run makes deliciously scary bumps, jostles and jolting noises as you descend. Our cries and gasps turned to (relieved?) laughter as sand dust spread on the terrace grab at and stop your sled. Fun? Yes: it's well worth the slippery, icy ascent you'll have to make!

During the summer, consider coordinating your trip with the *Festival d'Été* (www.infofestival.com) or, in winter, the famous *Carnaval (Winter Carnival)* (www.carnaval .qc.ca). Even though the streets are absolutely thronged with visitors during both these festivals, it's really something to share the infectious *joie de vivre* of this friendly city, *en plein air* (in the fresh air).

Generally speaking, you'll usually find the entire walk from the Château Frontenac to the Citadel via this series of boardwalks and staircases remarkably uncrowded. There are many benches *en route* so that you can catch your breath and have a sip of water. We've always felt safe, even quite late at night, for this is a welcoming city that is used to visitors.

steamshipcrossing oftheatlantic

The first steamship to travel from west to east across the Atlantic was made in Québec City. The paddle wheeler *Royal William* was built by Black & Campbell in the winter of 1830–31. Because of the 1832 cholera epidemic, the trans-Atlantic crossing was postponed until 1833. But on August 13 of that year, the *Royal William* left from Pictou, Nova Scotia, bound for Cowes, on the Isle of Wight, carrying 324 tons of coal. Samuel Cunard was one of this ship's investors and, although the *Royal William* was sold to the Spanish navy, this crossing marked the start of Cunard's great steamship line.

At the top of the final rise of stairs, you suddenly emerge at a *belvédère* (lookout) just west of the star-shaped fortifications known as the *Citadel*, built by the British to defend the city against American attack, between 1820 and

TOP ANNUAL EVENTS IN QUÉBEC CITY

JANUARY/FEBRUARY

Québec Winter Carnival; three weeks of *joie de vivre* in the snow capital, with Bonhomme, the snowman who wears a *toque* (woolen hat) and *ceinture fléchée* (hand-woven sash). Activities include ice carving, dogsled races through the streets of the old city, and the extravagant Mardi Gras Ball, which you can attend in rented costumes, while you dine on sumptuous fare and dance the night away. For more information contact:
Carnaval de Québec,
290 rue Joly, Québec G1L 1N8;
(866) 422-7628 or (418) 626-3716;
www.carnaval.qc.ca.

JULY

For more than thirty years, the **Festival d'Été Québec Summer Festival** has transformed Québec City into a wonderful, outrageous international festival of music and street theater. Find out times and who'll be there by calling (888) 992-5200 or (418) 523-4540; www.infofestival.com.

AUGUST

Les Fêtes de la Nouvelle France (Festival of New France) celebrates the era of New France (1608–1759) and residents rent or make period costumes and wander the streets of Old Québec. For more information call:
(866) 391-3383 or (418) 694-3311;
www.nouvellefrance.qc.ca.
Rent costumes from *Créations Face-á-Face,*
225 ave. Lamontagne;
(418) 522-4087;
www.costume123.com.

1831. In the old 1750 powder house, the ***Royal 22nd Regiment Museum*** has an excellent collection of military artifacts. This regiment, located here since 1920, is part of the chain of command that makes this fortification the longest-standing military presence in North America. These days the regiment puts on such shows as the ***Changing of the Guard*** and ***Beating of Retreat*** during the summer. (Côte de la Citadelle, Québec; 418-694-2815; www.lacitadelle.qc .ca; daily fifty-five-minute guided tours; $10 for adults, $9 for seniors and students, $5.50 for ages eight to seventeen, seven and under free, $22 family rate.)

West of the Citadel is a beautiful stretch of grassy parkland. This is the ***Parc-des-Champs-de-Bataille (Plains of Abraham Battlefields Park)***.

The Plains of Abraham take their name from a ship pilot and farmer named Abraham Martin, who owned land northeast of the Plains in 1646. It was near here that Generals Wolfe and Montcalm lost their lives in the battle of 1759, which actually took place near what is now the **Musée National des Beaux-arts du Québec,** at the western edge of the Plains of Abraham. To find the museum, walk westward, with the Citadel at your back, along Avenue Ontario, which becomes Avenue George VI. Follow the latter as it curves to the right and you'll see the museum beside the old prison. The Musée is one of the city's proudest gems, where you can view the history of the province depicted in prints, sculptures, paintings, and religious articles. (Musée National des Beaux-arts du Québec; 418-643-2150 or 866-220-2150; www.mnba.qc.ca; June 1 through Sept 5: daily 10 a.m. to 6 p.m., Wed until 9 p.m.; Sept 6 through May 31: Tues through Sun 10 a.m. to 5 p.m., Wed until 9 p.m., closed Mon; $15 adults, $12 seniors, $7 students, $4 youth [age twelve to seventeen], under twelve free).

In front of the museum is British general **James Wolfe Monument,** which was erected in 1790, supposedly on the very spot where the great general died. Before expiring, he asked for water and his men retrieved some from a well, **Wolfe's Well,** situated just east of the monument.

Many monuments are located on the Plains. Surprisingly, Montcalm is not commemorated here, although a statue, donated by France in 1911, stands in a park bearing his name on Rue Laurier. But here on the 250-acre Plains you can happily wander around, viewing such statues as that of *Jeanne d'Arc* (Joan of Arc) sitting astride her charger.

It's hard to leave the Plains of Abraham. We delight in it and evidently so do Québec City residents,

oldestgrocerystore innorthamerica

While you're outside the walls of the old city, you could take a diversion to **Épicerie Moisan,** which professes to be the oldest grocery store in North America, dating back to 1871 (699 rue Saint-Jean, Québec; 418-522-0685; www.jamoisan.com; open 9 a.m. to 10 p.m. daily). Its old wooden shelves, curved glass display cabinets, and well-stocked shelves harken back to earlier times.

who jog, walk their dogs, bike ride and, in winter, cross-country ski, toboggan, and snowshoe here. We think it's one of the very best spots in the city to learn about the history of Canada while taking in the fresh air and welcome breeze.

But leave we inevitably must. We suggest you walk down Avenue George VI to Rue Grand-Allée Est and turn right. This marvelous street is lined with trendy restaurants and shops—and art galleries.

Grande-Allée Est is also home to some outstanding Victorian and Second Empire (with their mansard roof) homes, now converted to businesses. During the **Winter Carnival** (late Jan through mid-Feb), this street is closed—for a *dogsled race.* Yes, come festival time the road is thronged with people—and, to our infinite amusement, other dogs—who cheer on the canines as they speed past hauling their sleds and human mushers and careen full-speed toward the Château Frontenac. We laughed delightedly at the doggy spectators who honestly seemed just as transfixed as their owners. Many wore jaunty bandanas, and several even wore boots.

Looming on your left you'll soon see the baroque **Hôtel du Parlement (Québec National Assembly),** surrounded by statues of such notables as Samuel de Champlain and Georges Étienne Cartier, one of Canada's fathers of Confederation. There are free tours of Québec's parliament buildings, and there's a good restaurant inside. *Assemblée nationale*, 1045 rue des Parlimentaires; (418) 643-6640; www.assnat.qc.ca.

Find your way to rue Saint-Jean, a fun part of town, full of life, bustling cafes, and inevitably, more history. Check out the **St. Matthew Cemetery and Church**—the latter is a heritage site and now houses the public library (Bibliothèque Saint-Jean-Baptiste; 418-641-6798; open Tues, Thurs, Fri noon to 5 p.m., Mon and Wed noon to 8 p.m., Sat and Sun 1 to 5 p.m.). It's all too easy to forget that Québec City was home to nationalities other than the French. Many years ago it was more than 80 percent English-speaking. The cemetery opened in 1771 and is said to be Québec's oldest burial ground.

With parliament behind you and to the left, at the corner of avenue Honoré Mercier, Grande-Allée becomes Rue Saint-Louis. Watch for a **cannonball** lodged in the base of a tree between 59 and 55½ Rue Saint-Louis. Look down this street:

Sensual Delights

It was a distinct pleasure to discover an award-winning country inn called *Château Bonne Entente.* This charming hideaway located on a 120-acre once-private parkland was the brainchild of Colonel Charles Hugh LePailleur-Jones, who built his retirement retreat here in 1946. Four years later his son converted the residence to an inn. Today the splendid property is abloom with flowers come summertime—but wait until you see the inn! In 2002 a Napa, California–inspired grill bar was opened here, where diners can eat alfresco on a patio. Inside the sumptuously appointed inn are 163 deluxe rooms and suites. Outside are a pool and badminton and tennis courts. In winter there's a skating rink. After all your off-the-beaten-path explorations, why not indulge in a massage, body wrap, or other sensual delight? Colonel LePailleur-Jones's dream of creating a restorative ambience has been fully realized—in unexpected ways! Château Bonne Entente is located west of Québec City, south of Highway 40 and west of Autoroute Duplessis (3400 chemin Sainte-Foy, Québec; 800-463-4390; www.chateaubonneentente.com).

Québec City Ironies

The song that became the Canadian national anthem was first sung on June 24, 1880, to celebrate Saint-Jean-Baptiste Day, an annual holiday that Québec nationalists—or separatists—have adopted as their own. The national anthem, or *chant national*, was not sung in "English Canada" until twenty years later.

On the other hand, you too can partake, for $6.30 and a reservation, of an **English Tea Ceremony** at the **Artillery Park National Historic Site**. Sit down with costumed guides and help reenact a nineteenth-century tea ceremony, which is ended with a joyous "God Save the King!" This all takes place in what's called the Dauphine Redoubt Officers' Mess, built in the 1600s. The entire complex, complete with museum, makes an intriguing spot to visit (2 d'Auteuil St.; 418-648-4205; www.pc.gc.ca/artillery).

In front of you is **Porte Saint-Louis,** one of the six gates to the old Upper Town. Continue straight down until you find Rue des Parloir on your left. Stroll up here to the **Ursuline Convent,** a famous pilgrimage site whose buildings date from the 1600s and 1700s, and on the next street, the **Ursuline Museum** (12 rue Donnacona; 418-694-0694; open May through Sept: Tues through Sat 10 a.m. to noon and 1 to 5 p.m., Sun 1 to 5 p.m., closed Mon; Oct through Apr: Tues through Sun 1 to 5 p.m., closed Mon; $6 adults, $5 seniors, $4 students seventeen and older, $3 for ages twelve to sixteen, free under age twelve).

The Ursulines came to the city in 1639 to administer to the little settlement's urgent spiritual needs as well as to found Québec's first hospital. Under the leadership of Reverend Mother Marie de l'Incarnation, the sisters taught and housed the *filles de roi* (daughters of the king), who were the young women sent to New France to become wives to the mostly male colonists. General Montcalm's body was brought here after his death on the Plains of Abraham. Ironically he was first interred in a crater gouged beneath the altar by a British cannonball.

As an intriguing aside, Donnacona Street commemorates the native Chief Donnacona, who accompanied Jacques Cartier back to France in 1536. One can only speculate as to what the chief must have thought of the Atlantic crossing and of Europe. How we wish he'd kept a journal.

The twisty-turny streets here are something else. Along the way, look for the **Anglican Cathedral of the Holy Trinity** (31 rue des Jardins; 418-692-2193). It's important to recognize that Québec City was home to Protestants and Anglicans as well as to Irish and French-speaking Catholics. The famous Saint-Martin's-in-the-Field Church in London was the architectural inspiration for this cathedral. King George III donated many artifacts here, including a seat in the royal box. Benches are made of oak from Britain's Royal Windsor Forest—a wee bit o' Britain for you, in the heart of *la belle province.*

Return to the corner of Rue des Jardins and Saint-Louis. Look for two important Québécois houses here. The first is now home to **Aux anciens Canadiens** restaurant, which we heartily recommend (34 rue Saint-Louis, Québec; 418-692-1627; www.auxancienscanadiens.qc.ca). The building boasts the typical French Canadian style of architecture: plain white front wall with an inset doorway and a steeply pitched, bright-red tin roof punctuated by three dormers. Its exterior charm is matched by its pleasing interior and simply superb regional cuisine served by costumed servers.

Nearby, watch for **25 Rue Saint-Louis,** the oldest house in the city (1648–50), where the Duke of Kent lived with his mistress, Madame de Saint-Laurent. The lovebirds lived here for three years, after which time the duke returned to England to marry and to eventually father Queen Victoria. This house is important for another reason, though: In 1759 the capitulation of Québec was signed here.

Now descend Rue Saint-Louis and pass the **Place d'Armes,** where troops used to practice their military maneuvers. On your right you'll see Château Frontenac. For now, past the château, descend well-named **Escalier-Casse-Cou (Breakneck Stairs)** to the old Lower Town, whose rooftops so delighted you from Terrasse Dufferin.

Immediately on your right find **Maison Louis Jolliet,** a house named after the explorer who, in 1673, paddled down the Mississippi. The house was built for him ten years later. A plaque identifies Jolliet as the discoverer of this river that used to belong to New France. Intriguing, isn't it, to contemplate that until the 1803 Louisiana Purchase, Québec City ruled that part of what is now the United States?

Want a Running Commentary?

Why not explore while jogging? That's what two entrepreneurs thought—so they started **Québec Jogging Tours** (www.quebecjoggingtours.com; 418-204-0511). So there I was, in the depths of winter, wondering: how can I negotiate all this snow? Fortunately, fluently bilingual guide Martin Thériault advised our mightily relieved group we'd be doing a fast walk through Old Québec. Do it: It's a fun, outdoorsy way to explore the city. Want to go on your own? Join off-street joggers on the Plains of Abraham where, in winter, residents cross-country ski or even snowshoe, in the heart of the city.

Now you're in the oldest part of the city. Wander around and absorb the flavor of the old port (*Vieux Port*) that's home to some of North America's oldest houses, all built of stone. It's charming, despite being jam-packed with tourists come summertime. Lots of restaurants, souvenir shops, and art galleries vie for your attention along the ***rue Petit Champlain*** extending directly ahead at the base of Breakneck Stairs. If you head left on rue Sous-le-Fort and then left again, you'll find historic ***Place Royale*** of ***Notre-Dame-des-Victoires (Our Lady of Victory)*** church. Built around 1688, it's the oldest church in Québec.

churches

The Catholic Church is a dominant feature towering above Québec towns. Early surviving examples are of fieldstone, which was originally plastered to protect the facade from the elements. A good example is Notre-Dame-des-Victoires in Place Royale, Québec City, whose front door is on the short gable-end of the rectilinear structure. Roofs are most often of metal, and the steeples—or clochers (bell towers)—usually pierce the sky over the main doorway.

Step inside (it's free) and look up to see a model of a sailing ship built between 1665 and 1666—*Le Brézé*—suspended from the ceiling.

Outside and directly in front of the church is a bust of Champlain and the site of his 1608 settlement. Stand and look around you. All the buildings are of cut stone and built in the old Norman style. Note the very low doorways and the small-paned windows. Each pane of glass was small because all crossed the Atlantic inside kegs. After successive devastating fires, houses began to be made of stone with raised gable-end roofs, a fire-retardant feature that was enforced by the mid-1700s. Fire was a major problem and this city, along with others like Montréal, suffered from conflagrations in which many lives were lost and businesses destroyed.

Fire regulations also decreed that all roofs had to be constructed of metal, and all had to have ladders affixed to them. Accordingly, in this reconstructed part of the city, you'll find ladders permanently mounted on the roofs. Many of these merchants' houses had ground-floor vaults used for storage of their goods.

Until the mid-1960s, Lower Town was increasingly rundown. Then, with federal and provincial funding, the city looked to its past, examined old engravings that showed the architectural detailing of this part of the city, and restored its former glory. We're glad public funds were put to such superb use, as this is really the cradle of our European-Canadian history.

Walk up Rue Saint-Pierre, passing the ***Auberge St. Pierre*** (79 rue St-Pierre, Québec; 888-268-1017 or 418-694-7981; www.auberge.qc.ca). This old hotel offers lots of forfaits such as ski, cultural, romantic, and adventure packages. They're a good deal. We enjoyed our stay here, deep in the heart of the old Lower Town.

Directly opposite the hotel is the ***Musée de la Civilisation*** (85 rue Dalhousie, Québec; 418-643-2158; www.mcq.org). There's lots to do and see here, including viewing a longboat found on this very site when the museum was being constructed. Plan to linger for at least a couple of hours.

What's particularly unusual is actually outside: from June through October there's a garden to explore, growing on the roof. Climb steep steps leading from rue Dalhousie up into the terraced ***Visionaries Garden*** (www.mcq.org/dragone). This is completely free, being an outdoors, airy garden where you can see innovative garden design through to some rarer sorts of vegetables and herbs. Informative signs explain that basil, for instance, has been cultivated for thousands of years in Mediterranean countries. Egyptians combined it with myrrh, frankincense, sage, and thyme to embalm people who had died and help them on their way to the afterlife. From these steps, enjoy the rooftop view of the old city.

A nearby roof houses ***Auberge Saint Antoine*** (8 rue Saint-Antoine; 418-692-2211; www.saint-antoine.com). It's one of the posh, international "club" of Relais and Châteaux properties—which is also a boutique hotel owned and operated by the Price family. Although it can be expensive, particularly if you select one of their sumptuously decorated suites, very cleverly the family offers affordable rooms too.

And this is important, we think, because it gives more of us the opportunity to sleep, literally, amid historical artifacts. When the Prices expanded their hotel, they unearthed treasures from this eighteenth-century marine warehouse here along the docks of the *Vieux Port* (Old Port). The family incorporated many artifacts into the rooms, wall niches, and there is an excellent display inside the lobby detailing the multilayered stories of the land beneath your feet.

The Auberge's on-site restaurant, ***Panache*** (418-692-1022; www.saint-antoine.com) serves delicious regional cuisine. Even if you don't take a room here, reserving for dinner, then browsing these fascinating artifacts makes an already special evening even more memorable.

Nearby, there is yet another great hotel with a completely different feel. The arty ***Hotel le Priori*** (15 rue Sault-au-Matélot, Québec; 418-692-3992; www.hotellepriori.com) dates from the mid-1800s. The street name means "sailor's jump," referring to how sailors could jump from the street—the natural shore of the St. Lawrence at that time—into their boats. Today's hotel has been completely renovated, with Art Deco furnishings by the Martin family. Wander around Lower Town, exploring the enchanting antiques stores that crowd the streets. Many restaurants in this section of town are frequented by fewer tourists and more local residents. At 79 rue Sault-au-Matélot find leather artisan Guy Levesque's studio (418-694-1298; www.guylevesque.com). His exquisite, unique, organic-looking purses—as well as intriguing masks in the guise of birds, cats, and goodness-knows-what—are captivating.

Continue north along rue Saint-Pierre, watching for rue de la Barricade. Turn left momentarily and look up to read a historical plaque to the memory of American Benedict Arnold and Québec's early defender, British general Sir Guy Carleton. "Here stood her old and new defenders . . . saving Canada, defeating Arnold at the Sault-au-Matélot Barricade on the last day of 1775, Guy Carleton commanding at Québec."

Turn back to rejoin Rue Saint-Pierre, and then left onto Rue Saint-Paul. Here a long string of antiques shops offers everything from antique quilts or hooked rugs to Art Deco lamps. Fun-looking bistros and cafes punctuate the shopping experience, so you can browse, enjoy a *café au lait*, then return to purchase that exciting find. Want an inexpensive, typical meal? Try one of our favorites eateries, the modest, always-packed **Buffet de l'antiquaire** (95 rue Saint-Paul, Vieux-Québec; 418-692-2661). This is a casual "locals-only" spot; try *entrecôte sauce au poivre* (pepper steak) or the *Assiette Québeçoise*. Afterwards, take a left onto Rue Saint-Paul.

This is the *Vieux Port* (Old Port) section of the city, which culminates in the old train station. As you walk, you'll notice that the antiques shops give way to several boutique hotels, including **Hôtel des Coutellier** (253 rue Saint-Paul, Québec; 418-692-9696; www.hoteldescoutellier.com). Only twenty-four rooms, it's tiny and quiet, and most rooms feature exposed, original stone walls of the old building. It's also close to the train station.

Hungry? Whether your visit is in the depths of the old city's snowy winter or in the height of summer, there's a splendid farmer's market awaiting discovery. **Maré du Vieux-Port de Québec;** 160 Quai St-André; (418) 692-2517; www.Marevieuxport.com; Jan through mid-Mar, Thurs to Sun from 9:30 a.m. to 5 p.m.; mid-Mar through Nov, daily 9 a.m. to 5 p.m. (to 6 p.m. July through Sept); Christmas market during Dec, daily 9 a.m. to 6 p.m. Rain or shine, it's lovely to head inside this cheerful indoor market where bouquets of flowers fragrance the air, rows of vegetables gleam, and where you can sample artisinal cheeses, blueberry spreads, or perhaps find a souvenir at one of the many local artists' booths. Purchase *baguettes, poisson fumées* (smoked fish), *pâté* and some *cidre* (cider) for a picnic, else purchase a meal at one of the handy stalls. Outside, find tables, chairs and people-watch to your heart's content.

From here, you can spy the grain silos which dominate this section of the port.

Smuggling Rum?

You may also spot the **Marie-Clarisse**, a two-masted wooden schooner purchased and restored by Loto Québec and now made available for fund-raising efforts. Originally a cargo ship built in 1932 and used for hauling salt cod, it was used for smuggling rum from France's off-shore islands, St. Pierre and Miquelon, to Boston. It saw yet another life, as a training ship, prior to being shipwrecked off the coast of Nova Scotia in 1944. In 1946 it was refurbished—only to sink again in 1974. The schooner was raised, renovated, and saw service as a tourist cruiser until late 1999. Now, after being completely refurbished in Charlevoix, the *Marie Clarisse* sails the St. Lawrence again, her sails and slim line cutting a picturesque image on the river.

During Québec City's 400th anniversary celebrations in 2008, Eric and I joined thousands of spectators who thrilled to the **Image Mill.** It was a fantastical mixed-media audio-visual history of Québec City projected onto the 81 grain silos. We're not surprised to learn that Robert Lepage's creation was so successful that a reworked *Image Mill* will continue to be shown here until (at least, in our view) the summer of 2013. Shown during summer nights, check Québec City's Web site (www.quebecregion.com) to learn of its current starting time and dates when you visit.

What is so special about *Image Mill*? First, the silos are more than 600 metres wide and 30 metres tall. Therefore, creator Robert Lepage had to envision projecting his work onto a screen whose size is the equivalent of 25 IMAX screens. If that's not astonishing enough, figure that he used 27 projectors and roughly 240 spotlights to evoke the varied moods of the historical montage. One minute the silos become gigantic images of nuns gazing down on the city; another, silos are transformed into bullets . . . Don't miss this technical extravaganza from one of Québec's gifted, iconic artists.

While in the Old Port area you might want to check out day trips down the St. Lawrence River as far east as Tadoussac on boats operated by Groupe Dufour (57 rue Ste-Anne, Québec; 418-692-0222 or 800-463-5250; www.dufour .ca). Call or check their Web site for a host of departure times and fares for trips available mid-May through mid-Oct. We had a fantastic time on a sail upriver to Montmorency Falls and can imagine that a longer jaunt would be an insightful way to learn about the river and river settlement while literally on the water!

In fact, while on-river, you can relive the advance of General Wolfe and his troops upon the city in 1759. While onboard and below the fortifications, think of this: A cannonball shot from the river reached rue Saint-Louis, where you have just strolled. It's no wonder that during the British siege of 1759, cannons more-or-less destroyed Lower Town.

Places to Stay in Québec City

L'Hôtel du Capitole,
972 rue Saint-Jean,
Québec;
www.lecapitole.com
(800) 363-4040 or
(418) 694-4040

La Marquise de Bassano (B&B),
15 rue des Grisons,
Québec;
www.marquisedebassano
.com
(418) 692-0316

Château Laurier,
1220 Place George V
West,
Québec;
www.oldquebec.com/
en/laurier
877-522-8108 or
(418) 522-8108

Places to Eat in Québec City

Café de la Paix,
44 rue des Jardins,
Québec;
www.cafedelapaix.ca
(418) 692-1430
Superb French cuisine
served in the heart of
Upper Town's Old Québec.
Intimate, romantic, full of
locals.

Jules et Jim,
1060 ave. Cartier,
Québec;
(418) 524-9570
Well-known for its single
malt scotch, enjoyed to the
smokey voices of Edith Piaf
and Charles Aznavour.

Le Café de la Terrasse,
Château Frontenac,
1 des Carrières,
Québec;
(800) 441-1414 or
(418) 692-3861
The highly regarded Executive Chef of the Château
Frontenac, Jean Soulard,
will inspire you with his
interpretations of regional
gastronomy. This elegant
dining room has, in our
opinion, the best view in
the city, bar none.

Le Lapin Sauté,
52, rue du Petit-Champlain,
Québec;
(418) 692-5325
Truly, this resembles a
charming old country
inn—in the Petit Champlain Lower Town district!
Of course, try the *lapin*
(rabbit), prepared in oh so
many delicious ways.

QUÉBEC CITY ENVIRONS →

Lying just beyond the limits of the old-world charm and romance of Québec City are wonderful treasures to explore in every season. Follow the circuit presented and give yourselves as much time as possible to savor these areas, for there is much to see and do.

Your general route is to leave Québec City heading east on Route 138 Est. Go north briefly on Highway 73 to visit Wendake and Lac Beauport, then return to Route 135 and continue east. Wander through Île d'Orléans, then to Sainte-Anne-de-Beaupré (via *chemin Royal*—"the King's Road"), and veer north to Mont Sainte-Anne. Rejoin Route 138 Est, and at Baie-Saint-Paul go north again to the rugged Parc Grands Jardins on Route 381, then return to Baie-Saint-Paul and continue east past Malbaie to Saint-Siméon. Here you travel north on Route 170 toward Chicoutimi, exploring the fabulous Saguenay Fjord. Then you'll veer north and southeast to visit a wonderful bed-and-breakfast at Saint-Fulgence before returning via Lac Saint-Jean to the east. We suggest staying overnight at the ghost town of Val-Jalbert before heading south on Route 175 back to Québec City.

Some of these places—such as Wendake, Mont Sainte-Anne, Lac Beauport, and Sainte-Anne-de-Beaupré—can be easy day trips from Québec City.

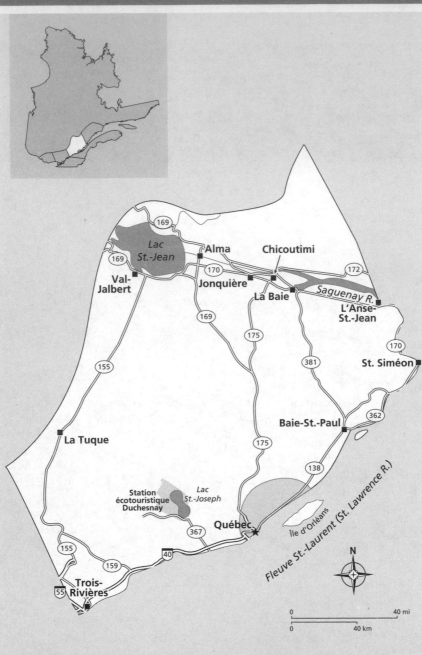

Wendake

Kwe Kwe ataro! (Welcome Friend!—in the Huron-Wendake language.)

Wendake is an exciting tourism venture for the Huron-Wendat First Nation people, who live in a suburb of Québec City approximately 20 minutes northwest of downtown. The enterprising group built a luxury hotel and museum called ***Wendake Hotel-Musée Premières Nations***, (5 Place de la Rencontre, Wendake, Québec; 866–551–9222; www.tourismewendake.com).

Don't miss this site: the architecture alone is stunning, so regardless of whether you stay overnight at this four-star lodge, it's worth visiting. It will become even more of an attraction when the Nordic spa, gardens and other projects are completed.

While the hotel recalls a traditional Huron longhouse, the design of the attached museum takes the form of a smokehouse, while a lowered stockade symbolizes welcome and peace between nations. The structures rise from the embankments of the lazy St. Charles River.

You'll find serenity and peace here along with the Wendake peoples' delightful pride of place and culture. Enter, and you step into a zen-like time and space. The lobby's earth tones are emphasized by hand-hewn tree trunks, while bear and coyote skins adorn leather settees. Taut drum-shaped side-tables further recall First-Nations culture, while two poster-sized Norval Morrisseau black-and-white artworks (which appeared to be originals) make a proud statement of the Wendat-Huron's living culture.

And that's what's truly celebrated here: the two renowned eastern First Nations' cultural families: Algonquin and Iroquois.

Another nice touch: each room's door is decorated with an individualized deerskin piece of art upon which an animal totem has been painted along with the room number. Look for sacred turtles, spirit horses and other animals guarding the doorways. Once inside, every room features natural elements such as white birch bark and twig decorations. Floor to ceiling windows further enhance the natural theme, bringing nature "inside". A glance outside reveals the St. Charles flowing past, snaking its way through a fringe of white birch and maple trees. Effectively, the hotel's architects as well as interior designers have emphasized a feeling of connectedness to the natural world.

This makes a wonderful place to chill out particularly if you've just enjoyed Québec City's Carnaval or other festival. Plan to dine at Wendake's on-site restaurant, *La Traite*. The menu is a contemporary interpretation of authentic native cuisine, where practically everything hails from the regions of Québec. The English translation for the menu, however, may not be accurate.

Bike it!

Next trip to Québec City, we're taking our bikes for sure. That's because the **Corridor des Cheminots** (www.canadatrails.ca/tct/qc/cheminots.html) is a 22 km (double it for a return trip) bike path connecting the old capital to Val-Bé. The easy path courses through such neighborhoods as Charlesbourg, linking them to Wendake and other villages. Another great bike route is **Corridor du Littoral** which links to the Jacques-Cartier/Portneuf bike network. Choose from various levels of difficulty from easy to hilly, as you wish. Trails are well-maintained and especially nice in fall (read: neither humid nor buggy). What a great idea to bike from Québec to Wendake, stay a couple of nights, then return! More info about biking using Québec City as a base—say to bike around L'Île d'Orléans—plus bike happenings can be found at www.quebecregion.com/e/velo.asp.

(Katharine ordered an intriguing-sounding soup supposedly made from local wildflowers. Rather inexplicably, instead it turned out to be scoops of passion-fruit sorbet! Whoops . . .) Not to worry: hopefully this is remedied by the time you visit—but it might be prudent to enquire before ordering.

Venture out on foot to explore the quaint village of old Wendake. There is the circa 1800 **Tsawenhohi House** where archaeological finds are displayed, the 1862 **Nôtre-dame-de-Lorette mission church**, and the **Sagamité Restaurant**. (Find all on Tourisme Wendake's Web site)

But whatever you do, be sure to visit the **Musée huron-wendat** (guided tours Wed through Sun, 10 a.m., 1 and 3 p.m.; www.museehuronwendat.com). The entrance alone is stunning: the floor is illustrated with an illumination of the turtle creation myth. Once inside, interactive exhibits as well as sacred artifacts such as wampum belts await. Photography is selectively allowed—but as do many museums, some cultural sensitivities (photographing sacred objects) as well as preservation concerns prevent the use of flash or even a photograph at all.

tasteaKWE!

While in Wendake, order a Wendat-Huron inspired KWE, an artisinal blond beer made by Archibald *microbrasserie* (microbrewery).

As is usual when learning about indigenous peoples, this museum reminds us all how European contact has been detrimental to (this time) the Wendake peoples' culture and traditions. In fact, as a people, they migrated here from previously held territories near Georgian Bay, a body of water in Ontario that is part of Lake Huron and the Great Lakes watershed. Decimated by disease, famine and conflict after

European contact in the 1600s, they came here because of their trade affiliations with early French coureurs de bois (fur traders).

Wendake is worth visiting to appreciate the living history of a people and culture who aim not only to survive, but also to prosper.

Lac Beauport

Another fun destination is Lac Beauport: from Québec City, head north on Highway 73 and turn right at *sortie 157* (exit 157) onto Boulevard du Lac toward Lac Beauport. This drive of perhaps twenty minutes is part of Québec City's backyard playground, offering summer cottage rentals, golf, water-skiing, swimming in summertime, and fabulous snowmobiling and cross-country and downhill skiing in winter. In fact, you'll be following in the footsteps of holiday-makers who, by the late 1800s, were riding north to Beauport and St. Charles Lakes on horseback and in carriages to take in the country air. Even then, this was a day trip.

Lac Beauport was settled in 1825 by Peter Simons, whose descendant Archibald became known as the "seigneur of Lac Beauport." In fact, the largely English-speaking community clustered around the lake in the 1820s was known as the Waterloo Settlement.

Come winter, there are miles and miles of cross-country ski, snowmobile, and snowshoe trails to explore. Eric had never driven a snowmobile before, so you can well imagine the thrill we had coursing over hill and dale. On Lac Beauport itself, he really let loose and zipped across the completely safe, flat, and frozen surface. Québec has some of the most extensive snowmobile trails in the world.

AUTHORS' FAVORITES IN QUÉBEC CITY ENVIRONS

Wendake	Parc des Grand Jardins
Avenue Royale (the King's Road)	Saguenay Fjord
Baie-Saint-Paul	Station écotouristique Duchesnay (and its Ice Hotel)
Île d'Orléans	
La Maraîchère du Saguenay B&B	Val-Jalbert Heritage Village
Montmorency Falls Park	

Me? On a Snowmobile?

I admit it. I've been negative about snowmobiles in the past: they seemed noisy, polluting, hard to control. But I've had a change of heart. When we went out for what we thought would be a spin around a local trail at Lac Beauport, I was surprised to find that the machine was quiet enough that I could still talk with Katharine. And the machine was comfortable, responsive—and fun. In fact, by the end of the day we had covered almost 100 kilometers and I could have done more. Québec is famous for its network of snowmobile trails—winter highways, actually—which are well groomed and have lanes and signage just like roadways. I still prefer cross-country skiing and snowshoeing, but I can now certainly understand the appeal of snowmobiling. And there probably isn't a better way to see Québec's vast hinterland territory in winter.

—Eric

During our day of snowmobiling at Lake Beauport, we ate at **Manoir Saint-Castin,** a hotel and restaurant overlooking the lake (99 chemin Tour du Lac, Lac Beauport, Québec; 800-561-4764; www.stcastin.com). We watched skaters glide past on the lake's swept rink and dined on excellent fare. You can rent snowmobiles here, too, and there's downhill skiing nearby, plus snow rafting, snowshoeing, and many other activities. The Saint-Castin makes a good base for exploring, and the atmosphere is welcoming. English and German are spoken.

The hotel is named after the Baron de Saint-Castin, a man who arrived in New France in 1670 and, four years later, inherited the title of baron. A swashbuckling swordsman, Saint-Castin was a distant cousin to Aramis, one of the inseparable three musketeers made famous by author Alexandre Dumas. Apparently Saint-Castin had a fiery temper and actively fought the English when Admiral Phipps attacked in 1690.

Although the people Eric rented his snowmobile from are now closed, you'll find a similarly exhilarating experience by driving northeast of Lac Beauport to another small village tucked into the hills, Sainte-Brigitte-de-Laval. Here you can rent snowmobiles for 3 to 8 hours or more from **Nord Expe** (996 Ave. Sainte-Brigitte, Sainte-Brigitte-de-Laval, Québec, G0A 3K0; 418-825-1772; www.nordexpe.com). However, keeners among you can opt for six-day trips where, like Eric, you can zoom into the hinterland, stay overnight in log auberges, and even venture into Labrador, all by snowmobile.

Return to Québec City via Route 73 Sud, or, to get past the city traffic, continue along the south shore of Lac Beauport on Chemin Tour du Lac to Traverse de Laval. Turn right and after about 5 kilometers turn south on Avenue Sainte-Brigette. As you enter the urban area, this road becomes Boulevard Raymond and connects with Route 40 Est. Follow Route 40 to the river, where it becomes Route 440, and you'll see the bridge to Île d'Orléans.

Île d'Orléans

This pretty island has borne several names. Algonquins called it Minigo, meaning "bewitched place." When Jacques Cartier landed here in 1535, there was such an abundance of wild grape vines that he named it Bacchus Island after the Roman god of wine and merriment. Perhaps sadly, he renamed it only one year later, giving it its current appellation, but for many years residents were dubbed "island sorcerers." This island is a haven for bird-watchers (although the Sept hunting season can be a bit daunting, so we're told). It's best to come for the spring migration or to visit later, perhaps during Oct.

TOP ANNUAL EVENTS IN QUÉBEC CITY ENVIRONS

FEBRUARY

La Classique Course de Chiens de L'Isle
Québec's largest dogsled race held on Île-aux-Coudres with participants from across North America;
(418) 438-2930.

JUNE–AUGUST

Chamber Music at Sainte-Pétronille Church
Listen to summer concerts at this pastoral setting on l'Île d'Orleans;
(418) 828-1410;
www.iledorleans.com.

JULY

Mountain Biking World Cup
at Mont-Sainte-Anne;
(418) 827-6600;
www.velirium.com.

AUGUST

Le Festival du bleuet
(Blueberry Festival) in Mistassini;
(418) 276-1241;
www.festivaldubleuet.qc.ca.

AUGUST/SEPTEMBER

**Theme weeks at Wendake:
Visual arts and Handicrafts**
First Nations artisans come to Wendake to demonstrate their crafts, plus in workshops and lectures the Wendat-Huron First Nations share cultural traditions;
www.tourismwendake.com.

The island is home to more than 600 heritage buildings and represents the oldest agricultural settlement in the province. And because of this, it is the ancestral home of 317 of Québec's original French settlers, often referred to as the *pure laine* (literally, the "pure wool") peoples. When you go to the tourist information center, ask for the tourist guide booklet and find a list of all the family names and their original locales on-island. People are still extraordinarily proud of their lineage.

It's only since 1935 that there's been a bridge linking the island to the mainland. Be forewarned: In autumn's harvest time, the bridge can be really backed up because of all the urbanites coming in to pick their own fruit.

First you might like to drop into the Tourist Information Center to pick up maps and postcards and to orient yourself further. Follow the ? sign that appears immediately after you cross the bridge. Ask for the cassette (or CD) for use in your car (or while cycling or walking if you own a portable player), so that you can enjoy the circuit tour while you listen to a history of the island. Afterward, proceed west on Route 368 to **Sainte-Pétronille,** first settled by the French in 1648. A Huron mission was built later, and during the 1759 siege of Québec, it was a British encampment. In the late 1800s it was a popular summer retreat, and today its often English-style architecture reflects both its humble beginnings as well as this early recreational period of cottage construction.

As you drive around the island, you'll see some pretty forests. Many of the trees are sugar maples, and there are a number of wonderful maple sugar "cabins" where you can sample this treat. Early spring is the sugar season, but several cabins are open year-round; check with the information booth near the bridge. In early February we enjoyed a filling baked bean dinner with lively Québécois folk singers followed by delicious *tire-sur-neige* (snow-hardened) maple taffy at **Cabane à sucre l'En-Tailleur** (1447 chemin Royal, Saint-Pierre; www.entailleur.com; 418-828-1269; call ahead for hours—they differ each year due to the temperatures, which control the sap run!).

Do you like chocolate? If you like it as much as we do, you won't be able to resist pausing at the pretty **La Chocolaterie de l'Île d'Orléans** (150 chemin du Bout del' Île, Saint-Pétronille; www.chocolaterieorleans.com; 418-828-2250). We can vouch for the splendor of the dark chocolates filled with the island's very own maple sugar. A small exhibit (in English, too) explains how chocolate is made—from cocoa bean to final delectable product. Also available are locally made jams and jellies with yummy-sounding combinations, such as banana and chocolate spread.

Continue exploring Sainte-Pétronille. Drive to the Auberge and **Restaurant La Goéliche** on chemin du Quai. Its parking lot on the easternmost tip

Island Routes

Speaking of the old families on Île d'Orléans, the Chocolaterie's owner, Marcel Laflamme, can trace his name back to a fellow named Quemeneur, one of the first settlers. The name changed over time to "Laflamme," which means "the light." Marcel told us that this surname indicates that one of his ancestors must have been one of the hardy fellows who used to light buoys on the river at night so that boats wouldn't hit the rocks. Thus, Marcel Laflamme is a *pur laine* Québécois.

of the island provides a superb vantage point from which to view towering Québec City. Imagine how, in 1759, General Wolfe and his troops would have plotted their plan of attack from here.

We visited La Goéliche when the mighty St. Lawrence was chock-full of ice chunks, whose crunching sounds were awesome as the high tide swept floes upstream. (Yes, the river is tidal up to and just west of Québec City. No wonder it's called *la mer*—the sea!)

Although we didn't stay overnight, this tidy inn is a gem. Certainly our luncheon of smoked salmon salad, served up in the glassed-in terrace, was superb. (Restaurant La Goéliche, 22 chemin du Quai, Sainte-Pétronille, Île d'Orléans; www.goeliche.ca; 418-828-2248.)

Continue on Route 368, locally known as the *Chemin Royal* (Royal Road). Past the chocolaterie, look for the 1855 wharf and find Anse au Fort (Fort Cove), also known as Anse au Iroquois (Iroquois Cove), nearby, where the mission used to be home to more than 300 Huron Indians. They sought refuge from the Iroquois here and were sheltered for years by the Jesuit priests until, in 1656, an Iroquois raid destroyed their haven. It was only after the peace treaty of 1701 that colonists were safe from attack.

After leaving Sainte-Pétronille you approach **Saint-Laurent and Le Parc Maritime du Saint-Laurent (St. Lawrence Maritime Park)** (120 chemin de la Chalouperie, Saint-Laurent; www.parcmaritime.ca; 418-828-9672). The interpretation center here has displays depicting the region's shipbuilding era. The name of this street, Chalouperie, is derived from the wooden boats of the same name that the early settlers used to build. In 1908 Ovide Filion founded the Saint-Laurent shipyard, and naval warships were built here during World War II. Between 1908 and 1920 three shipyards existed in Saint-Laurent.

Return to Chemin Royal. On the left-hand side of the road, find the not-to-be-missed *Économusée de la Forge à Pique-Assaut (Pique-Assaut Forge Museum)* (2200 chemin Royal, Saint-Laurent; 418-828-9300). As with almost

TOP ATTRACTIONS IN QUÉBEC CITY ENVIRONS

Montmorency Falls Park
2490 ave. Royale, Beauport;
www.sepaq.com/ct/pcm;
(418) 663-3330;
just east of Québec City, is spectacular
at any time of the year but particularly
impressive in winter, when an ice dome
builds up at the base.

Sainte-Anne-de-Beaupré basilica
10018 ave. Royale,
Sainte-Anne-de-Beaupré;
www.ssadb.qc.ca;
(418) 827-3781;
from 6 a.m. Sept daily, closing times
vary during the year; free. This dramatic
two-steepled Catholic shrine attracts
many people making pilgrimages.

**Grosse Île Parc and the Irish
Memorial Historic Site**
2 rue d'Auteuil,
Québec City,
(418) 234-8841 or (888) 773-8888;
www.pc.gc.ca/grosseile;
Grosse Île is the island where thousands
of immigrants were quarantined
between 1832 and World War I. There's
a guided tour; the western part of the
site can be explored on foot, whereas
the east and central parts of the island

are served by a special tourist train.
Fees vary (from $46 to $70) depending
on where you get the boat and the
duration of your stay (allow about four
hours). The island is in the St. Lawrence
River about 50 kilometers east of
Québec City on Highway 20. Open daily
mid-May through mid-Oct.

**Parc national de la Jacques Cartier
Provincial Park**
www.sepaq.com;
thirty minutes north of Québec City.
This 258 sq mi (670 square km) park
has a wide range of activities year-
round, including interpreted walks—and
howling with wolves programs in winter!
Rent snowshoes here to allow you to
explore the quiet, snow-draped woods
where you'll discover fantastical ice
formations among gorges and along
still-open streams.

Saguenay–St. Lawrence Marine Park
(federal) and Parc du Saguenay
(provincial) cover both the waters of the
Saguenay Fjord and its surroundings.
About 200 kilometers from Québec City,
this area offers unparalleled outdoor
activities, such as kayaking, hiking, and
whale watching.

all the économusées in the province, all the signs are in French. However, this won't prevent you from trying your hand at hammering a red-hot nail on the anvil under the direction of artisan Guy Bel. Many artifacts are on display, and there is an intriguing gift shop.

Also in Saint-Laurent is the restful inn and restaurant *Auberge Le Canard Huppé (The Wood Duck Inn)* (2198 chemin Royal, Saint-Laurent; 800-838-2292 or 418-828-2292; www.canard-huppe.com). It serves splendid food prepared whenever possible from local produce. We thoroughly enjoyed our lunch of game terrine and smoked trout, finished off with an assortment of pastries presented with a flamboyant swirl of confectionery sugar. Nearby is a wonderful beach. The inn's helpful bilingual proprietor, Gaëtan Sirois, says there's great bird-watching, beach strolling, picnicking—and, come wintertime, cross-country skiing—at the water's edge.

Cyclists? Bring your bikes! L'Île d'Orléans is perfect for bicycling. We suggest booking one of the ten rooms at Le Canard Huppé, filling your day pack with water, binoculars, and a camera, and heading off. You can tour all or most of the island during a day—or, take longer, depending upon your speed and inclination.

A few miles past this auberge, you'll approach the hamlet of Saint-Jean. Keep your eyes peeled left for the old ***Manoir Mauvide-Genest*** (1451 chemin Royal). Built in 1734 as a residence for surgeon Mauvide Genest, the facade still shows bullet holes from a British attack in the mid-1700s. Enjoy a fine meal here, with costumed wait staff.

In Saint-Jean find a delightful gallery, ***Ma P'tite Folie Galerie et Café*** (1822 chemin Royal, Saint-Jean; 418-829-3076), showcasing fine art, including the chalk pastels of gallery owner Louise Lainé. Some of her works, notably of animals or birds, are reproduced in affordable prints. Also check out artist Manon Lortie's amazing hats, as well as a woodworker's appealing cheval à bascule (rocking horse) and other local artists' works.

We hope that you do more than we had time for—follow Route 368 around the island through the villages of Saint-François and Sainte-Famille, the island's oldest settlement, dating from 1661. After visiting Saint-Jean, we drove north to Saint-Pierre on La Route des Prêtres

québectrivia

There are more than 350 bird species in the province, of which only 5 to 7 percent are year-round residents.

(Priest's Road), one of only three routes transecting the island. There's a legend about this road. The true story tells how the northern hamlet of Saint-Pierre accused the parishioners of Saint-Laurent of stealing their sacred relic, the preserved arm bone of St. Clement. For thirty years, bickering and strife ensued until, in 1733, the bishop of Québec decreed that the two pastors and their flocks should meet halfway between the villages. At the meeting, the relic was returned, and to commemorate the occasion, a wayside cross was erected. You'll pass it en route and travel in the footsteps of the humbled parishioners.

Turn left onto Chemin Royal to be regaled by Mr. Gaetan Beaudoin, the enthusiastic owner of ***Savons Adria & Antiquités aux Quatre-Épaules***. Here you'll discover a unique combination of exquisite handmade goat's milk soaps, along with antiques and collectibles such as religious art and old hardware! Gaetan reveals the secrets of how he makes his wonderful, soft soaps molded into the shapes of horses, hearts, and all sorts of things. And if you don a hair net, you can accompany him into the room where the soaps are made. Enchanting fragrances emanate from his shop and studio, where such soaps as "Ondine" (lover's soap) and fleurs de Provence (flowers of Provence), made with petals of organically grown flowers fill the air with sweet perfume (Savons Adria, 1551 chemin Royal, Saint-Pierre; 418-828-2644).

roadsidecrosses

Often you'll come across roadside crosses on your travels. Although many were raised to the memory of a loved one who perished on the road, others are Catholic "stations of the cross." Perhaps the best examples of these are along the Chemin Royal to Sainte-Anne-de-Beaupré, a center for pilgrims that draws thousands to the site just east of Québec City. Still others, as on Île d'Orléans, mark a spot where a significant activity took place. We were told that they were also erected by priests so as to remind sometimes forgetful parishioners to pray—and to go to Mass.

When Jacques Cartier landed on-island in 1535 he named it Bacchus Island . . . No wonder, then, that our next destination, a vineyard, takes the name *Vignoble Isle de Bacchus* (1071 chemin Royal, Saint-Pierre; www.isledebacchus .com; 418-828-9562). We were eager to stretch our legs by taking a guided tour of the vineyards, then sample a wine tasting. No wonder their *Le Fleur de Lyse* (French Lily) dessert wine—along with others—has won awards.

Continuing our drive back toward the bridge, we stopped at *La Ferme Monna,* where you can taste and buy *cassis* (black currant) wine and liqueurs (721 chemin Royal, Saint-Pierre; www .cassismonna.com; 418-828-2525). Their 5 hectares of fruit-bearing currant bushes yield 30,000 bottles annually. Enjoy a very short tour followed by the ambrosia of tasting the cassis products. In 1995 they were awarded an international gold medal for their wine.

When returning to Québec City over the bridge, we reflected that prior to the bridge's 1935 construction, the only way the island inhabitants could be connected to the city during wintertime was to cross the ice after freeze-up. We imagined the horse-drawn sleighs crossing the channel and thought about how truly isolated the islanders would have been. Even today with the bridge, summertime's population of 10,000 dwindles to about 7,000 come wintertime.

The Côte de Beaupré (Beaupré Coast)

Back on the mainland, turn right to proceed east on Highway 138. Immediately find the turnoff left to *Parc de la Chute-Montmorency (Montmorency Falls Park).* (The park is 12 km east of Québec City, located at 2490 ave. Royale,

Beauport; 418-663-3330; www.sepaq.com/ct/pcm; open year-round. The $9.25 parking fee Apr through Oct at the lower park is refundable if you eat at the Manoir; cable car $10.50 for adults, return $5.25 children.) Good old Champlain named this falls after the Duke of Montmorency, Viceroy of New France and Admiral of France and Brittany.

This is the famous falls so often depicted with the frozen "sugar loaf" of ice that forms at its base. In the late 1800s, it was a favorite spot to visit in winter. Imagine the scene: horses pulling colorful sleighs, whose occupants were bundled up in gaily colored costumes, kept cozy by glossy bearskins. There were horse races on the ice, and on the sparkling sugar loaf itself, people slid on toboggans. In *A Yankee in Canada* (published in 1850), American author Henry David Thoreau wrote: "In the winter of 1829 the frozen spray of the falls, descending on the ice, made a hill one hundred and twenty-six feet high."

Climb the stairs beside the 83 metre-high falls, or indulge in the cable car. At the top is **Manoir Montmorency**, a reconstruction of the 1780 English-style manor home built by Governor Handimand that was destroyed by fire in 1993 (2490 ave. Royale, Beauport; 418-663-3330). Its reconstruction, built one year later, is true to the original. There's an excellent museum inside. Queen Victoria's father, the Duke of Kent, stayed here from 1791 to 1794, after which the house was nicknamed Kent Lodge. But this was no mere country home. The museum explains how, in 1885, the falls supplied Québec City with electricity—supposedly the first time electrical energy was carried over a long distance (7 miles). By 1897 energy from the falls powered Québec City's first electric train. In addition, there was a cotton factory and sawmill.

The Manoir Montmorency has a superb dining room that affords great views. We had an amazing lunch here: *cuisse de canard confite à l'orange*— duck thigh in orange sauce—as part of

alllitup

For Québec's 400th anniversary celebrated in 2008, the woods around the Manoir Montmorency were illuminated by thousands of LED lights. They remain, so after dark, they twinkle and magically illuminate the night.

their table d'hôte. If you stop for lunch, you might want to return to your car by crossing the bridge over the top of the falls and taking the trail and steps down.

Now take the first left turn off Route 138 onto Côte de l'Église, which takes you up to the old road, **Avenue Royale**, the King's Road. Turn right (east). This was the first road built in the area and is particularly interesting because of the many *maisons anciennes* (old homes) built right "on the road." Building homes right on the street's edge is also reminiscent of old British houses;

the reason is the same, too. Originally the road was much narrower. When expansion and pedestrian sidewalks were built, what front garden there might have been was paved. Also, settlers had to do road maintenance themselves, so it would behoove them to be as close to the road (and to the market of passers-by) as possible. Watch for homes whose ground floors are old shop fronts. The actual residence was on what is the second—or main—floor, often with an overhanging, quite ornate front porch.

You can spot many old root cellars tucked away into the hillside on your left. There are also many bake ovens where housewives have baked their specialty breads for centuries. Such a spot is *Chez Marie* (8706 ave. Royale, Château-Richer; 418-824-4347). The 1652 dwelling is typical Québécois style, with curved roofline and red tin roof. The 150-year-old bread oven where Marie bakes her simply fabulous bread is outside. Get yourself a loaf, and while there don't miss buying a slice and spreading it with the scrumptious maple butter—a divine taste sensation.

Also as you drive, look south, across the channel of the St. Lawrence called Chanal de l'Île d'Orléans, to the island you've just left. You'll see the rise of the landmass and, at the top of the island, the line of dwellings that you passed, reflecting the settlement patterns of the day.

Next stop is the *Atelier Paré Économusée des Légendes (Econo-museum of Legends)* (9269 ave. Royale, Sainte-Anne-de-Beaupré, Québec; 418-827-3992). This is a must-see as inside its doorway you step into the imaginative world of Québec's folk tales. Françoise Lavoie is not only charming and bilingual, but she also animates the carved legends by spinning the tales just for you. We lingered here, admiring the beautiful carvings, and afterward we discovered a book, *Legends of Québec*, written by one of the économusée owners/artisans, Scott Kingsland. If you want an English-language copy of this province's colorful folk tales, buy it here: We never saw it again in all our years Québec travels.

Now enter the pilgrim's world of *Basilique Sainte-Anne-de-Beaupré and Musée de Sainte Anne* (10018 ave. Royale, Sainte-Anne-de-Beaupré; www.ssadb.qc.ca; 418-827-3781). The colossal cathedral and adjacent museum are surrounded by a sea of cars and worshippers. The cathedral has been a celebrated sanctuary since 1665. In that year Marie de l'Incarnation wrote these words about its miracles, to her son: "The paralytic walk, the blind see, and the sick, whatever their illness, are healed." Nowadays more than a million people visit annually.

Outside the basilica, a circular building houses a very rare must-see religious painting—a 360-degree painting depicting scenes in Jerusalem at the time of Jesus' crucifixion. Called cycloramas, these continuous, or panoramic, paintings were extremely popular in the late 1880s—prior to movies! The artist, Paul Philippoteaux, painted it in Chicago in the 1880s. Before it was moved here, just before 1900, the cyclorama was shown in Montréal, where it drew great crowds. It continues to be a pilgrim's delight and an extraordinary sight today. Visit the *Cyclorama de Jerusalem* (unmistakable round building beside a parking lot) daily May through Oct, 9 a.m. to 6 p.m.; $9 adults, $8 seniors, children six to sixteen $6, family $25 (8 rue Régina; 418-827-3101; www.cyclorama.com).

Rejoin Route 138 Est. The next destination is Mont Sainte-Anne, only a few minutes from here. Keep in mind this is a Québec City suburb: It takes only twenty-five minutes or so to drive here from the capital. The view from the top of the mountain, whether you hike up or take the gondola (and ski down, perhaps, in winter) is unforgettable. You are rewarded with a bird's-eye view of the territory you've driven through, and by looking east you will see the widening St. Lawrence River plus the Laurentian Mountains you have yet to explore. We stayed at *Château Mont Sainte-Anne* (500 blvd. Beau-Pré, Beaupré; 800-463-4467 or 418-827-5211; www.chateaumontsainte anne.com).

Winter Fun

When we stayed at the Château Mont Sainte-Anne, we went on a moonlit snowshoe exploration of the forest. We had brought our own torches, but the moon was bright enough to manage without them. The next day, I visited the tiny *Musée de Ski,* which celebrates more than a century of skiing in the region. There's old equipment, photos of the area's first skiers, and wonderful replicas of European woodblock prints depicting skiing in the Old World.

I satisfied a lifelong goal: to drive a team of sled dogs. I adored it! It was all arranged at Château Mont Sainte-Anne, and after a brief stroll up to the dog kennels, the operator—named Bruno—introduced me to my dogs. The leader was an energetic canine named Jack, who even obeyed my (probably irritating) commands to slow down while I got my "mushing legs." With the wind whipping my cheeks to rosy red, I whisked through silent, snow-clad forests with the dogs. Sheer heaven.

Because he's not keen on dogs, Eric bought himself a half-day ski pass and rented the latest gear, just for fun. Although he hadn't been downhill skiing for a few years, his ski legs soon returned, and by the end of the morning he was running the black diamond (most difficult) slopes and marveling at the magnificent view of Québec City from the peak. Note that if you visit in other seasons, there are lots of activities such as mountain biking, hiking, horseback riding, golfing: make your own discoveries.

—Katharine

For summer visits, camping is available only 7.7 kilometers east of the alpine resort. Turn left onto Rang Saint-Julien to find **Mont-Sainte-Anne Camping** (2000 blvd. Beaupré; www.mont-sainte-anne.com/camping; 418-827-5281; 800-463-1568). They have jogging trails, swimming, and cycling paths, as well as showers, picnic areas, washers-dryers, and a playground for kids.

The Charlevoix Region

Continue east on Route 360 to rejoin Route 138 Est to Baie-Saint-Paul, a half hour away. You enter the Charlevoix region of Québec. There were lots of moose signs, although we were sorry not to see any of the ungulates while driving here in August. What we did find, in great abundance, were wild blue-berries for sale. If you hike, just watch for them in early to mid-August. We picked a lot of them for free, on the rocky outcrops beside the road.

Be sure to stop at the Tourist Information Center spectacularly situated on the highway at **Baie-Saint-Paul**, before you descend into the town. It houses the interesting, small **Charlevoix Museum**, which depicts the story of how this region's topography was shaped by an ancient meteor. It illustrates how Charlevoix sits at the crossroads of three significant geological formations: Canadian Shield, St. Lawrence Lowlands, and Appalachian Mountains. In 1988, Charlevoix became a UNESCO Biosphere Reserve, joining more than 325 others that exist in more than seventy-five countries. We also confirmed that caribou once roamed these parts in giant herds. In fact, 10,000 were reported up to the turn of the twentieth century. By 1925 they had disappeared because of habitat loss and overhunting. That's why we wanted to head north, to the Parc des Grands Jardins—the last spot in this area to spy caribou. Ask at the museum entrance for the printed English guide. Admission is free. This is also a good spot to pick up detailed maps and current information about the region. Staff members are friendly and speak English.

Baie-Saint-Paul is a picturesque tourist town full of "Kodak moments." The road sweeps downward into the meteor's crater. The village boasts delight-ful Québécois-style and Victorian homes as well as cafes, many galleries and bookshops, and inns.

Where to eat and even stay in the heart of town? Impossible to miss brightly coloured **Restaurant l'Orange Bistro** (29 rue Ambroise-Fafard; www.orangebistro.com; 418-240-1197). It's a Victorian *ancienne maison* (old home) complete with beautiful terrace where Charlevoix gastronomical delights are served. Why drive anywhere else? Stay here overnight by booking one of the two rooms decorated with Victorian-inspired furnishings.

The Charlevoix Meteor

Much of Québec north of the St. Lawrence River is ancient Canadian Shield, among the oldest rocks on earth, dating back some 2.5 billion years. The St. Lawrence marks the shield's southern edge, where it abuts the sedimentary Appalachian Mountains. Some 350 million years ago, a 2-kilometer-diameter, 15-billion-ton meteor slammed into the Charlevoix region, carving out a crater 28 kilometers in diameter. Like a drop falling in water, the shattered central part rebounded. Over time, the mountains have been eroded by glaciations and the St. Lawrence River. From the information center, you can clearly see the curve of the crater's valley with the rugged mountains on its perimeter.

Armed with new geological knowledge, we turned north on Route 138 toward **Parc des Grands Jardins**, 30 kilometers north of Baie-Saint-Paul. A former Montagnais native hunting ground, the game-rich region became an American private hunting club in 1890. A preserve since 1981, its 310 square kilometers of mountains and lakes offer superb year-round activities. The hills created by the meteor's impact formed a beautiful backdrop to the pastoral farmland we now drove through.

For a local taste treat, cheese-lovers absolutely must not miss the **Économusée du fromage (Museum of Cheese)** at the Laiterie Charlevoix (1167 blvd. mgr. de Laval, Baie-Saint-Paul; 418-435-2184; www.fromagescharlevoix .com). We're delighted to report that since our first visit in 1998, this économusée now has English signs explaining the process and history of cheese-making in Québec. It's particularly appropriate because cheddar cheese (for which this économusée is famous) originated in England, in the town of the same name, Cheddar, Somerset. Ironically, it was American Loyalists who introduced this piquant food product to the Eastern Townships of Québec (which shares a border with the United States) after fleeing their homeland after the War of Independence. We bought delicious three-pepper spicy cheese curds, as well as a raw-milk cheese. A few years ago the Canadian government tried to ban the sale of raw-milk cheeses, raising the ire of souls like us who've enjoyed them for years. Another cheese maker, **Maison d'affinage Maurice Dufour** (1339 blvd. mgr. de Laval, Baie-Saint-Paul; www.fromagefin.com; 418-435-5692; open daily 9 a.m.

québectrivia

Québec boasts Canada's largest dairy industry. The main producer is the Holstein, the large black-and-white cow.

to 6 p.m.; free), famous for its Migneron de Charlevoix and Le Ciel cheese, is nearby.

Soon Route 138 veers right; we drove north on Route 381 toward Chicoutimi. At Saint-Urbain village, the houses crowd the street. We gained elevation and suddenly the landscape became extremely rugged, resembling mountains in British Columbia. Devastation from a recent forest fire dramatically emphasizes the rocky starkness of the first mountains of **Parc des Grands Jardins** (25 Boul. Notre-Dame; 800-665-6527 or 418-439-1227; www .sepaq.com/pq/gr).

Pull off the highway at the *accueil* (ranger station) on the left-hand side of the road after passing through the *Pied de Montagnes* (Foot of the Mountains) sector of the park. If you have reservations, you can continue on to the camping area, but you might want to stop for a more detailed map or to arrange fishing permits. We pressed on to a second accueil 8 kilometers farther along a bumpy gravel road, through extraordinary wilderness scenery. We had reserved a campsite at **Lac Arthabaska** (866-702-9202 for information; 800-665-6527 for reservations). We selected a choice lakeside spot with a shelter over a picnic table, a firepit, and a flat campsite. After pitching our tent, we hiked 1.7 kilometers through taiga to Lac Beaumont. Along the way we passed moose tracks and a "kettle," a deep pit created when a ball of glacial ice melts below the surface.

At Lac Beaumont are photos of the 30 blindfolded caribou the Québec government flew in to replace the decimated herd in 1966. Now the herd has grown to 103 animals. Sightings are usually in winter; the park staff gives you a form to fill out, should you see one, to help them monitor these shy beasts. Guided three-hour taiga walks with a naturalist are available in English for $10, and you can stay in a bed here for $16 plus taxes. Cabins are also available,

Laptop Constellations

The sky was exceptionally clear the night we camped at Parc des Grand Jardins and the stars were brilliant. I remembered that I had a program on our laptop computer that showed the constellations, so after a late dinner we brought it out. Our view from the picnic table looked south over the lake, and we soon identified the constellations. To see the northern sky, we had to walk back behind the trees. We heard some murmuring from nearby campers, who must have been wondering why on earth these people were wandering around a near-wilderness campground, their faces illuminated by the glow of a laptop computer.

—Eric

but book ahead. To reserve a campsite or cabin, click on the park Web site at www.sepaq.com/en and navigate to Parc des Grands Jardins after linking to "Québec Parks." You'll discover all the park's campgrounds and cabins, plus information on summer and winter activities. Unless you decide to follow Highway 381 to Chicoutimi, backtrack 30 kilometers to Baie-Saint-Paul and turn left along the coast on Route 362 toward Les Éboulements.

The Charlevoix Coastal Drive

This is a fabulous drive, sometimes punctuated by exhilaratingly steep grades. The coastal views are extraordinary: lush hayfields, pastures dotted with grazing cattle, picturesque architecture, and the long strips of seigneurial farms slipping down, ribbon-like, to the blue waters of the St. Lawrence. It's headily picturesque; you'll want to drive slowly and putz along, exploring as you go.

As you approach **Les Éboulements,** which sits picturesquely on a rise of land on either side of the highway, watch for the **Seigneurial Mill of Les Éboulements** (formerly known as Moulin Banal) on the right (157 rue Principale, Les Éboulements; 418-635-2239; www.hcq-chq.org; open daily 10 a.m. to 5 p.m. June to Sept; adults $4, twelve and under free). An informative English pamphlet explains the history of the site, which has hardly changed from its construction in 1790 by seigneur Jean-François Tremblay. With its white clapboard exterior trimmed in jaunty red, it is lovely, nestled into the embankments of Rivière du Moulin (Mill River) in the woods beside the falls.

Enter inside to see the original mechanisms at work—with somewhat younger millers who still produce fresh buckwheat and wheat flour. Take a guided tour.

Just past the mill and not quite at the village of Les Éboulements itself, we turned off the highway to plunge down a 19 percent grade (test your brakes!) to the pretty coastal village of **Saint-Joseph-de-la-Rive.** Artists' studios abound, and you'll find **Économusée du papier (Economuseum of Paper)** (304 rue Félix-Antoine-Savard, Saint-Joseph-de-la-Rive; 418-635-2430; www.papeterriesaint gilles.com), where you can watch paper being made by hand using seventeenth-century techniques. Across from the quaint économusée is the **Exposition Maritime Museum** (305 rue de l'Église, Saint-Joseph-de-la-Rive; 418-635-1131; www.musee-maritime-charlevoix.com), where a giant wooden boat was under construction when we stopped at this old shipyard. Nearby the village church features a giant clam shell from Florida which serves as a baptismal font.

At the waterfront catch a free 15-minute ferry to **Île aux Coudres** (Hazelnut Island), a popular island with good B&Bs, nice beaches, and some museums.

Although not a museum, our top pick of attractions on-isle is picturesque *Les Moulins de Île aux Coudres* (36 chemin du Moulin, 418-438-2184; www .lesmoulinsiac.com). You cannot miss it: it's the only place where there's both a windmill and a watermill. Buy fresh bread here and watch the modern-day millers demonstrate the operation of the mills.

Near the village of Baleine you'll come to an area where peat (as in peat moss sold at horticultural nurseries) is vacuumed from the earth. Yes: it's an intriguing technology and industry—but one which forever alters a wetland habitat's rich biodiversity. This is sobering food for thought if you're a gardener.

The island is an extremely popular cycling destination where *les Québeçoises* enjoy the 24 km (16 mile) circuit of the island—as do we visitors. Rent a bike—singles, tandems or even quadricyles for a total of 8 people—from *Vélo-Coudres* (2926 chemin des Courdriers, 418-438-2118; www.charlevoix.qc .ca/velocoudres).

If you're wanting a B&B with a view of the mill, park your bikes (or car) at *Gîte au vent de l'Isle*, (39 chemin du Moulin; 418-438-2649; www.giteauvent delisle.com). Don't forget your binoculars: there's terrific birdwatching here.

Return to the mainland and drive back up the hill to rejoin Route 362 Est. The undulating countryside is stunning: it's one of the reasons everyone seems to sigh when they mention Charlevoix! With bluffs overlooking *la mer*—still actually the St. Lawrence River—combined with lush fields and tidy villages, well, it's gorgeous here and no matter how much time you have, we bet that like us, you will want to linger. Tip: come winter, this road is icy: be cautious. This road is termed *route du fleuve* (river route) and as you proceed, you drive into *Les Éboulements*.

Éboulements means "rock fall." In 1663 this region suffered a gigantic earthquake that caused a huge section of the hillside to slip into the St. Lawrence River. In fact, as you drive along this coast at low tide, you'll see large

WORTH SEEING IN QUÉBEC CITY ENVIRONS

Downhill and cross-country skiers shouldn't miss the slopes of:

Mont-Sainte-Anne
2000 blvd. Beau Pré,
Beaupré
(888) 827-4579 or (418) 827-4561;
www.mont-sainte-anne.com

Only 40 kilometers east of Québec City. Snow is plentiful in the winter and the view from the top of the mountain up and down the mighty St. Lawrence is magnificent. Summer activities include hiking, mountain biking, and paragliding.

Wanna be a Cowboy?

We both own horses so when we're playing tourist, often we like to ride. First, it's nice to get outside; second, we enjoy being with these big-hearted animals who—just like the dog-sled teams—so willingly work with people. Whether it's an hour's ride or a two-day excursion you're looking for, contact the **Centre Équestre Nature** (73 rue St-Jean-Baptiste; La Malbaie (Sainte-Agnès); 418-439-2076; www.quebec web.com/equitation/introang.html). Oh . . . and if you want, this sensible outfit can also book you a massage after your ride—if you register in advance, that is!

rocks that have rolled off the slopes. Today the farming community and village itself have taken painstaking care of the heritage buildings. You'll pass by many "photo opportunities," lots of artists studios, and, at 304 rue Principale, a display of charming miniature Québécois-style birdhouses and feeders (*mangeoires* in French). Made from wood and rocks, they are the handiwork of local craftsman Normand Simard.

Continue eastward, upriver toward **Saint-Irénée.** What unforgettable vistas greet you: this is one of our favorite scenic villages of Québec. You'll note many homes have stunning views over the St. Lawrence—and that it must be blustery, for most feature sheltered, glassed-in decks.

On your left, atop a hill, watch for a yellow and brown-trimmed B&B, **Gîte Manoir Hortensia** (850 chemin Les Bains, Saint-Irénée; 418-452-8180; www.manoirhortensia.com). Hosts Jacline and Pierre have fashioned a sun-filled lodging where some rooms have private balconies overlooking the St. Lawrence. It's a prime spot, and when we visited in early August, flowers were in full bloom and out front the little cherry tree was fruiting.

This stretch of coast is truly "B&B land." We'd advise you to arrive early, find a B&B that suits you, and then explore. Even in winter, with ice floes on the river, many B&Bs look cheerful and welcome visitors.

You start a long descent to Sainte Irénée. The promoter of the Québec-Charlevoix Railway, Rodolphe Forget, lived here in a superb mansion. Follow the signs in the village to the **Domaine de Forget** (5 rue Saint-Antoine, Saint-Irénée; 888-336-7438 or 418-452-3535; www.domaineforget.com). The mansion was bought in 1977 by a nonprofit company that has created a cultural center to promote the performing arts. Every summer, internships are offered here to musicians who come to study with international masters.

From mid-June through late August, you can attend what has become a renowned **International Festival** of classical music, although you may catch some jazz or even some dance, too. There is a concert hall which seats more than 600; on Sundays enjoy brunch on the outdoor terrace while you are serenaded by music.

Moreover, in the off-season at Domaine de Forget, student musicians' dorms are rented very reasonably: accommodating two persons, you can probably get a discount for longer stays.

Return to Route 362, turn east, and suddenly the road ascends, affording more great views of Saint-Irénée and its surrounding coves. The highway continues to traverse pretty farmland. Old homes, many with manicured lawns and ornamental pools, line the road. This is renowned tourist country, where the fresh salt breeze, magnificent forests, and river have conspired to attract visitors for well over 150 years.

Scoot past what was once U.S. President Howard Taft's favorite golf course, designed in 1925 by golf architect Herbert Strong. Then turn right to enter the **Fairmont Manoir Richelieu**. The hotel possesses a commanding view of the St. Lawrence. Next door to the Charlevoix Casino, the Manoir offers some very affordable packages, especially during winter. Try a romantic weekend of skiing followed by snuggling up near the Manoir's fireplace (181 rue Richelieu, La Malbaie; 866-540-4464 or 418-665-3703; www.fairmont.com/richelieu).

Nearby is the **Casino de Charlevoix** (183 rue Richelieu, La Malbaie; 418-665-5300 or 800-665-2274; www.casino-de-charlevoix.com). Although definitely not "our thing," this casino is decidedly the region's number-one attraction. If you're keen on gambling, you'll probably know that proper dress is *de rigueur*.

A bit farther along Route 362, find the village of **Malbaie.** It used to be called Murray Bay, after a former governor general of Canada, James Murray. Find the Tourist Information Center on your left and, to your right, the **Quai Casgrain,** a little park stretching out into the water—a good spot to stretch your legs, breathe in some salty air, and read historical plaques on the quay. You'll learn about the sandbanks here formed by deposits of the Rivière Mailloux, which have provided sand used in the construction of many buildings, including the Manoir Richelieu.

Kayaking La Mer

We've been talking about *la mer*—what locals call the St. Lawrence River here—for long enough. Want to paddle it with a guide and learn its ways, wildlife, and geology? Take a paddle with Sébastien Simard and gain a personal view of the ecology of this mighty river. Simard has a kayak school, but also guides through his sea-kayak company, **Katabatik** (595 rue Saint-Raphaël, La Malbaie; 418-665-2332; www.katabatik.ca).

Incidentally, if you want to go on an unforgettable rafting trip down one of the region's rivers such as the Plaisance, contact the folks at **Descente Rivière Malbaie** (316 rue Principale, Ste. Aimé-des-Lacs; www.descentemalbaie .com; 418-439-2265). And if you're exploring in wintertime, you can go on a three-hour, or up to three-day, dogsledding excursion with them. Where do you sleep? In cozy heated winterized tents (yes, you can be warm tenting in winter!) or a *refuge* (rustic lodge).

Back to the driving route . . . After crossing the bridge at the end of Malbaie the highway starts to rise. Very soon on your right, you'll see the shingled roofs of an old seigneurial home (marked private); and a few hundred meters farther, you'll find its match, on your left. This is the famous seigneury now owned by Francis H. Cabot, an American living in New York City. **Les jardins du Quatres Vents (Gardens of the Four Winds),** the largest private gardens in Canada, are at this home. They are open to the public by reservation only (418-434-2209; www.cepas.qc.ca) and only four times a year (four Saturdays in the summer—one in June, two in July, one in Aug). This is very popular, so call for tickets between Dec 1 and 15.

Next is the old resort town **Cap à l'Aigle** on the right, with its unusual 1872 Anglican church, **Saint Peter on the Rock,** overlooking the St. Lawrence. Farther on is a wonderful, bright yellow, pottery workshop and boutique, **Poterie de Port-au-Persil** (1001 Saint-Laurent, Saint-Siméon; 418-638-2349; www.poteriedeportaupersil.com), where you can sign up for pottery workshops. How lovely it would be to come here for a week of classes in these inspiring surroundings. We lingered as long as we could, delighted with imaginative glazes, forms, and colors we saw nowhere else.

Back on the coastal road, don't just rush past nearby **Saint-Siméon,** because its blond sand beach looks as though it will never end. To get there, follow the ferry sign in the village (the crossing goes to Rivière de Loups on the South Shore). There's a cluster of hotels, restaurants, snack bars—and a municipal campground costing around $18 a tent. The beach can be extremely hot (there's no shade, so be forewarned). There's a volleyball net and, next to the water, join all the children building sand castles. After sauntering about, absorbing the holiday atmosphere, we took Highway 170 leading northwest to Saguenay Fjord.

We could hardly wait to experience this world-renowned fjord, where beluga whales bask and where the cliffs are up to a thousand feet high. Unless you're going to return to this part of the world soon, instead of simply heading northwest on Highway 170, it's worth continuing for 35 kilometers instead on Route 138 to **Pointe Noire.** (You'll have to backtrack on Route 138 to Highway 170. There's no other route up the south shore of the

Charlevoix's Route des Saveurs (Flavor Trail)

Charlevoix is justifiably famous for its food. Get a copy of the *Guide de Route des Saveurs de Charlevoix/Charlevoix Flavour Trail Guide.* Then, ensure you're hungry—and enjoy following this delectable route! (Bilingual brochure is available from www.tourisme-charlevoix.com, 495 blvd. de Comporté, La Malbaie, QC G5A 3G3; 800-667-2276 or 418-665-4454.)

In spring of 2004 we visited the outstanding **Les Saveurs Oubliées** (350 rang Gode-froy [Route 362], Les Éboulements; 418-635-9888; www.saveursoubliees.com). It's still there wowing everyone who steps inside its cheery portal. This restaurant resembles a little bit of Paris—or should we say Brittany?—deep in the heart of Charlevoix. Enter the airy restaurant to dine on organically raised lamb. Be absolutely sure to sample some of their preserves: the name *saveurs oubliées* means "forgotten flavors," and refers to the old-fashioned recipes that French chef and proprietor Régis Hervé has collected while interviewing some of the region's elderly ladies who have been using time-honored recipes for generations in their homes. With the modern trend of both partners working, many such traditional recipes are being lost—all over the world, actually. Here at this restaurant you can taste and then purchase some real treasures, such as pine jelly made from local pine trees. It makes a refreshing, intriguing alternative to mint jelly!

Do you enjoy foie gras? This specialty is made through a technique called "gav-ving" where ducks are fattened using a cylinder that is put down their throats. Then, organically raised corn (in this case) is ground and forced directly into the ducks.

The livers become enlarged, fatty, and delectable. Despite how good the foie gras really is, we admit to being a bit squeamish about the technique. Nonetheless, millions of gourmandes would claim that the results justify the means. If you want to try this home-farm-raised product—or the duck leg confit, smoked duck breast, or other delicious items—go to **La Ferme Gourmande,** where you can purchase everything. (La Ferme Gourmande, 25 rang Sainte-Mathilde, La Malbaie [at Cap-à-l'Aigle], 418-665-6662; www.fumoircharlevoix.com.)

Another member of the Route des Saveurs is the **Restaurant le Saint-Pub** at 2 rue Racine (at the corner of Saint-Jean-Baptiste), Baie-Saint-Paul, (418-240-2332; www.microbrasserie.com). Enjoy the microbrewery beers made on the premises, as well as seasonal regional foods prepared and served with real panache.

Several establishments along the Route des Saveurs also offer accommodations. We stayed at **Auberge des Peupliers** (381 rue Saint-Raphaël, La Malbaie [at Cap-à-l'Aigle] 888-282-3743 or 418-665-4423; www.aubergedespeupliers.com). Chef Dominique Truchon prepares excellent meals with local produce including venison as well as pheasant, ostrich, and lamb. Be sure to stroll down to the St. Lawrence River after your dinner. For us, the canopy of stars in the inky sky was unimpeded by ambient light, making the night sky truly spectacular.

Saguenay.) Pointe Noire has an excellent (and free) boardwalk lookout and marine interpretation center, with a video in English. Bilingual staff set the mood for the Saguenay Fjord through a series of animations, offered during the summer season. While we were there, we stepped out of the information center to gaze at the confluence of the two rivers. Heads swiveled when Eric gasped, "There's a whale!" How thrilling it was to spy a minke whale in this rich estuarine channel.

Saguenay Fjord Tour

At Saint-Siméon, turn your back on the St. Lawrence and head inland. While we were there in early August *bluettes* (blueberries) were for sale everywhere. Delicious! The road passes outcrops of Canadian Shield, past beautiful Lac Deschênes (*deschênes* means "oak") and the village of Sagard, and then you drive right through the middle of a huge lumber mill. Almost immediately afterward, the valley opens up and you'll see dairy cattle grazing, with several old homesteads nestled along the road, making a welcome change from the poplar and mixed forest. On the left is the ***Reserve faunique de la rivière Petite Saguenay:*** the entire river is an ecological reserve managed by Sepaq (La Société d'Établissement de plein air du Québec; www.sepaq.com). Here the valley really opens up, and when we drove through it, giant round bales of hay wrapped in white plastic made the farms look as though they were growing marshmallows.

Turn right just before the village of Petit Saguenay if you want to find lodging at the ***Village-Vacances Petit-Saguenay*** (99 chemin St-Etienne, Petit-Saguenay; 418-272-3193; www.vvps.ca). Here you can camp or rent a cabin. It is on the Parc du Saguenay trail system, so there are good hiking opportunities to views of the fjord. The fjord has a sandy beach, and mountain bikes and kayaks are available for rent.

Back on Highway 170, the helpful Tourist Information Center can help you find accommodations. Also, you can find out all you'd ever want to know about the kayaking, hiking, biking, horseback riding, and fishing activities in summer or the winter dogsledding, snowmobiling, skiing, or snowshoeing. Pick up a detailed map of the fjord here. The ones with topographic contours and tidal information will be very useful if you plan to hike or kayak.

At ***Petit-Saguenay,*** the road crosses the salmon river of the same name. Boulder-strewn, it is reminiscent of Scottish rivers, or of the Cascapédia River in Québec's Gaspé region. Just after the bridge, a left-hand turn takes you along the river to the ***Club des Messieurs,*** a hunting and fishing camp. You can camp or rent cabins here at this designated salmon fishing river, where you can fish for Atlantic salmon and six other fish species. (For information on cabins, contact Club des Messieurs at 418-272-1169; www.petitsaguenay.com.)

We'd heard about a lovely viewpoint overlooking the fjord, so we turned right after the bridge at this village on what soon became a winding gravel road hugging the river. If you are tempted by the many designated fishing pools, remember that you must register to fish here. Suddenly we were there at a convenient parking lot, with a quay extending into the river and with a small picnic ground. Swimmers with a taste for chilly water jump in here.

We returned to Highway 170 to proceed up the fjord. As we drove, we reflected on the **Saguenay–St. Lawrence Marine Park**—the first park to be jointly created by the federal government of Canada and provincial government of Québec. It protects a 1,138-square-kilometer territory that's a combination of land and river. Several nonprofit organizations are coordinating efforts to educate people about protection of habitats and species and to develop sensitive, sustainable tourism. It's an exciting time. We met only a few naysayers who bemoaned the environmentalists, lack of new lumber mills, and increasing environmental regulations. For the most part, though, people recognize the need to manage our natural resources more responsibly.

Because of its many layers of lighter freshwater at the top and heavier salt water below, the Saguenay River and Fjord support astonishing and diverse life forms. The late oceanographer Jacques Yves Cousteau was the first to closely explore the marine biology here, in 1984. Four years later, a dive by teams of zoologists and biologists discovered the same aquatic life as in the Arctic Ocean, with several invertebrates found that were thought to be extinct.

Continue on Highway 170 to **L'Anse St. Jean.** Tourism promoters of today call it "a kingdom to discover"—and it's no small irony that the word "kingdom" is used! In our first edition (1999) we met "King Denys I," a local entrepreneur who played his role with great wit. These days, King Denys appears to have left his kingdom . . . but who knows; possibly he'll return any day, for the politics of Québec are ever-fascinating and ever-changing.

Watch for the sign and little parking lot marking the lookout to the town's covered bridge—*pont couvert* in French. You can walk up the hillside on a set of stairs nearby for your "photo op" of the 1929 **Pont du Fauberg.** Its likeness is one that not many of us have ever seen for a couple of reasons: it used to be the featured picture on Canada's $1,000 bill between 1954–92!

Return to the fork in the road and turn right to follow the road that wends about the cove to the Pointe au Boeuf. Watch out for the horses. You can ride horses throughout the many trails that cut through this pastoral region. To try it out, contact **Centre équestre des Plateaux** (34 chemin des Plateaux, L'Anse-Saint-Jean; 418-272-3231; www.cedp.ca). We were really impressed with the horseback riding trails that crisscrossed the road, winding their way through the woods. We passed by a group watering their mounts opposite one of the old farms. For now, continue past these old farms, including one that bears a plaque identifying it as the Ferme Nazaire Boudreault, built by Thomas Boulianne in 1844.

Continue up along the gravel road to a parking lot beneath an astonishing hydro tower, whose cables span the entire 1.6-kilometer breadth of the Saguenay. Phew! It's really a testament to human engineering skills and to the gigantic hydroelectric projects built by Hydro Québec in the northern hinterlands. There is a pretty hiking trail here, part of a network that can require up to a week for the traverse from Rivière Éternité to Tadoussac. As you drive you'll note many walking trails branching off on either side of the road. Get a good map at Rivière Éternité before you set off.

Rejoin the highway and, at the intersection, stop at the microbrewery right on the highway, ***Les Brasseurs de L'Anse*** (418-272-3234). There is a tour with tastes—including a delicious dark brew called Royale de l'Anse. You guessed it: It's the royal brew of the kingdom—fit for a king. We hear it's one of the most popular microbrewery beers in Montréal these days, and we can understand why.

Continue on to ***Rivière Éternité*** (Eternity River—what a romantic name). Turn off at the signs to the ***Parc du Saguenay,*** an abrupt right turn after the bridge. Almost immediately you'll be struck by the sight of dramatic, towering cliffs, surely a rock climber's dream. Continue along this curvy paved road to the end. Just as the ***Centre d'interprétation du Fjord du Saguenay (Saguenay Fjord Interpretation Center)*** comes into view, so does a parking lot on your left. Park here and walk down—but first, look up and check out the cliffs soaring above you. In late afternoon sunshine, they glow with a ruddy hue. At the park office, English signs welcome you and direct you to copies of an English-language audiotape.

You can rent kayaks from ***Québec Hors-Circuits*** from mid-June through mid-Oct: contact them at 418-544-5959; www.quebec-hors-circuits.com.

marineetiquette

Everyone wants to see whales. If you choose to progress northeast along the coast, up to Tadoussac and beyond, you'll be overwhelmed by the number of whale-watch tour operators. But can you imagine how disorienting it is for marine creatures like whales to hear the continual drumming underwater noise of these craft? Reputable whale-watching outfitters follow a code of ethical conduct. The Zodiacs rafts or cruisers, as well as kayaks and canoes, must not get too close to the whales. Be sensitive to this, and don't pressure your guides to go too close.

Long-distance hiking

Hiking the Saguennay Fjord is awesome. Sometimes difficult trails (check the route) reward with fabulous views of capes and bays. Want a long hike? Sentier des Caps is a three-day tour where you can stay in rustic refuges or campgrounds. For this and many other hikes, study up at **Parc national du Saguenay** (Rivière-Éternité; 418-272-1556, 877-272-5229; www.fjordsaguenay.com), where you'll click on tourism and outdoor adventure for a list of great hikes with good explanations of length and what you'll need to bring.

Guides will take you on a couple of hours' interpreted tour in the Saguenay National Park either by Zodiak or kayak. However, far more is available with this talented group: you can take 2 to 5 day sea kayaking excursions or 1 to 10 day canoe-camping trips.

August or September is usually the best time to hike to avoid the worst of the blackflies. But always come prepared with repellent, plus lots of gear for warmth. It is windy on the cliffs, and when we hiked and camped in August, we found that while the days were hot, the nights were quite cool.

Return to Highway 170. After 17 kilometers we turned right just before **Saint-Félix-d'Otis,** following the well-marked signs to the **Site de la Nouvelle France**. At this spot, the 1991 movie *The Black Robe* was filmed. The site was chosen by the filmmakers because the landscape resembles that of old Québec City. The cliffs across the fjord are like those of Lévis, and the peninsula to the west resembles Île d'Orléans. Because you'll have been to both the capital and the island, it will be fun to see if you agree. Today the site takes you back to Champlain's Nouvelle France: the set props are still there, depicting an Iroquois village, complete with actors who play the role of Iroquois of the time. Also on display is a replica of Champlain's home. The tours of the site take just over an hour (370, Vieux Chemin, Saint-Félix-d'Otis; 418-544-8027; www.sitenouvellefrance .com).

québectrivia

Jesuit priests were called "black robes" because of their flowing garments. The movie Black Robe tells a story of the Jesuits. You can see the movie set and animated depictions of Jesuit and native life at the Site de la Nouvelle France (Site of New France) near Saint-Félix-d'Otis.

Instead of returning to Highway 170, we remained on this back road, which quickly regained elevation. It teased us with glimpses of the Saguenay, now from a considerable height: quite a different perspective. Along the way you'll pass a highly recommended restaurant,

Auberge de la rivière Saguenay (9122 chemin de la Batture, La Baie; www
.aubergesaguenay.com; 418-697-0222 or 866-697-0222).

Soon we reconnected with the highway near ***La Baie des Ha! Ha!,*** which
was like a little English seaside town, with houses right on the road, overlooking the water. (The comical "ha! ha!" part of La Baie's name harkens back
to early explorers, when the deeply indented bay deceived them. They had
expected the bay to be another river. Evidently Mother Nature's trickery created some amusement for them.) The scene soon changes as you approach the
large aluminum plant, paper mill, and industrial sites of this busy port. It isn't
all industry though: La Baie also has the ***Passe migratoire de la Rivière-à-
Mars*** (salmon ladder), where you can watch salmon as they enter the river
(3232 chemin St-Louis; 418-697-5093). There is a nominal $3 fee to view the
spawning run of salmon jumping the ladders here ($7 for a family for the
season). People still refer to the Saguenay's waters here as la mer, or the sea,
largely because it's not only still tidal here but salty, too.

Our destination was only twenty
minutes farther, on the opposite side of
the Saguenay, at ***Saint-Fulgence,*** so we
proceeded from La Baie to Chicoutimi
on Route 170, turned onto Route 172
(Boulevard Saint-Paul), crossed the Pont
Dubuc Bridge, and immediately turned
right onto Route 172 Est (Boulevard
de Tadoussac). It was 8 kilometers
farther to the pretty lilac-pink sign to
La Maraîchère du Saguenay, our
B&B for the night (97 blvd. Tadoussac, Saint-Fulgence; 418-674-9384; www
.maraicheresaguenay.ca).

What an oasis of old-charm tranquility! We fell in love with it immediately. Owners Adèle Copeman and
Rodrigue Langevin have created a haven
out of a 140-year-old former house for
sawmill workers. Their home is a pretty,
shingled cottage tastefully decorated with antiques that Rodrigue has collected
over the years. But it is Adèle who has given these treasures a new life: her
tasteful, Victorian-inspired country touch is everywhere, and the mood she creates is one of understated Old World luxury. Also on the site is a cottage that
she designed and had built from found materials: all recycled.

learningfrench

Doing the research for this book
stretched my relatively limited
French. My vocabulary has been
pretty good for some time, but I've
always been shy to speak it. I hit a
real breakthrough while we stayed
at La Maraîchère du Saguenay. We
were chatting with our hosts and
some other guests from France
when I suddenly found myself
responding in French without
thinking about it in English first. We
both felt that a week in a place like
this would be a wonderful way to
polish our French and, who knows,
you might even meet us there
doing just that someday.

—Eric

And the food—superb! Breakfast was beautiful, served in antique dishes at the long kitchen table. Homey and honest, it gives the effect of another time, when folks could linger. All we can say is you simply must visit. Both your hosts speak English—Adèle with her Irish ancestry is the more fluent—and Rodrigue is so involved in local tourism initiatives that he'll fill your itinerary with lots and lots of must-see attractions.

We then turned our sights on *Chicoutimi.*

To get to Chicoutimi from Saint-Fulgence, follow Route 172 west and, immediately after crossing the Pont Dubuc (Dubuc Bridge), turn right onto Boulevard du Saguenay. You can't miss the sight of the flood damage: turn left at your first opportunity, onto Chemin Price, and cross the Chicoutimi River on Pont Price. Drive slowly and look right, up the hill toward the **Cathedral Saint-François Xavier.** To the right of it is the little white house that television coverage made famous when it somehow resisted the raging floodwaters surrounding it. We can all imagine the desperate plight of the village residents as they watched floodwaters surging through the top-story windows of their homes.

chicoutimi naturaldisaster

In July 1996, torrential rains saturated the earth and raised heights of rivers and reservoirs throughout the Saguennay. The Rivière Chicoutimi River turned into a raging torrent, with flow rates rising from 200 cubic metres to 1,200 cubic metres per second. On July 21st, the river turned into a hell on Earth, sweeping through the village of Chicoutimi where homes and businesses—and people—were swept away. A solitary, simple home—which became known as *la petite maison blanche* (little white house) in the midst of the flood became a symbol of defiant hope against all odds. More than a billion dollars were poured into the town to rehabilitate it.

Canadians from coast to coast responded to the 1996 crisis, giving aid generously. But real tribute should be made to the valor and hard work of the Chicoutimi people themselves for what they accomplished. They completely rebuilt their villages, roads, and bridges. To the outsider, both the infrastructure and the landscape appear to be completely restored, a remarkable feat after such devastation. Stop, take a photo of the way it looks today—and compare it to what you'll see next, at the museum inside the old pulp mill.

Drive up past the cathedral on Rue Taché. Turn right on Le Doré and park at *La Pulperie de Chicoutimi* (300 rue Dubuc, Chicoutimi; 418-698-3100; www.pulperie.com), an 1896 industrial complex that was the "world's finest and best" pulp and paper mill, according to an English journalist of the day. By 1910 it was the largest producer in Canada, and founder J. E. A. Dubuc is credited with starting the pulp and paper industry of the Saguenay.

The mill now it houses two attractions you shouldn't miss. One is film and photographs of the 1996 deluge that show the horrifying reality of the river carrying off people's homes, shattering their lives irreparably.

The second is the home of the late artist Arthur Villeneuve, a naïve-style artist whose house is preserved, in fully air-conditioned comfort, inside the old mill. On a brilliantly sunny, sultry day, it can be totally delightful to enter Villeneuve's cool yet vibrantly creative world.

Our next goal was Lac-Saint-Jean, so we connected with Route 170 through Jonquière toward Saint-Gédéon.

Lac-Saint-Jean

The route from Jonquière to Saint-Gédéon is, well, flat. After about 6 kilometers you'll cross the bridge over *Rivière des Sables.* Look left to see the dam shown in the video footage at Le Musée du Saguenay with water overflowing it during the 1996 flood. You can further appreciate the calamity of the deluge as you drive along here. After another 20 kilometers or so you arrive at Saint-Bruno and a T intersection with Highway 169. Follow the Route 170 signs to jog left, then right again, toward Roberval. As we passed by, golden barley rippled in the summer breeze in the fields. You'll catch glimpses of the lake as you approach Saint-Gédéon.

Lac-Saint-Jean is obviously a vacation destination: campgrounds and cottages hug the lakeshore. It is also blueberry country. The closer you get to Lac-Saint-Jean, the more blueberries and blueberry products you'll see. We bought chocolate-covered blueberries made by the Trappist monks in Mistassini. You'll also find blueberry liqueur and blueberry pies—as well as syrup and, in August, the delectable fruit itself. At wayside fruit and vegetable stands around the lake, we discovered all sorts of other local delicacies, including a rather odd potato candy filled with what turned out to be peanut butter.

We stopped for a picnic at *Métabetchouan,* meaning "meeting place" in the Montagnais language. It's easy to spot the sandy beach, *Le Rigolet:* On your right, watch for a left-hand turn that crosses the railway tracks. Here is yet another bike trail, soon to surround the entire lake. Good picnic facilities are here, and if you like beach relaxation and sports, this is the spot. It's free, too.

Our next stop, at *Desbiens,* was at the *Centre d'histoire et d'archéologie de la Métabetchouane (Métabetchouan Center of History and*

Archeology) (243 rue Hébert, Desbiens; 418-346-5341; www.chamans.com; open daily during summer, 10 a.m. to 5 p.m.; $7 adults, $3 children). You can ask the very helpful bilingual staff at the desk for the three-ring binder explaining the exhibits in English. Here, the early history of Lac-Saint-Jean comes alive, from the early Montagnais culture through to the years of the Hudson Bay Company fur trading post that was situated here then moved farther up the lake to Pointe-Bleue, now called by its Montagnais name, Mashteuiatsh. Beside the replica of the Hudson Bay post are laminated copies of an old letter written in English (since the Hudson Bay Company was British), detailing this move at Lake Saint John. The Montréal superintendent for Hudson Bay observed that since the natives came down from the hunting grounds to Pointe-Bleue, that site would make a more logical spot for the trading post.

coureursdebois ("runnersofthe woods")

In the 1600s, young men of Québec thrilled to the notion of adventure, excitement, and potential riches that the fur trade represented. Typically, they were based in Montréal and ventured deep into the interior, where they traded with the native peoples. The main fur trade years spanned from the mid-1600s to 1760.

Another intriguing exhibit is a cross-section of earth, mounted on the wall, that reveals past events, such as an exceptional flood that occurred sometime in the sixteenth or seventeenth century. Rather interesting, considering the deluge of 1996. In the museum's video room, you can watch tapes, with narration in French, depicting the construction of a pioneer bake oven, wool-making, and the making of a birch-bark canoe, among other things. There's also a good gift shop. Upon leaving, look right to the historic *poudrière* (powder house). You'll also find the memorial to the Jesuit Père Jean de Quen. In 1640 he was given authority over the territory from Tadoussac to Lac-Saint-Jean.

About 5 kilometers past Desbiens is a great lookout over the lake. Continue through **Chambord** and watch for the abrupt, albeit well-signed, left-hand turn to our destination, **Village Historique du Val Jalbert (Val Jalbert Heritage Village)** (95 rte. St. Georges, Chambord; www.valjalbert .com; 888-675-3132).

The Val Jalbert "ghost town" was a company town built by Damase Jalbert, a local merchant who founded the Ouiatchouan Pulp Company in 1901. The company built everything: roads, houses, a convent and school, post office, general store—as well as the mill with its generating station powered by a penstock from a dam atop *Ouiatchouan* Falls (Innu language for "river of clear waters"). In 1927 the mill shut down due to a sudden drop in demand for wood pulp and the town simply died. Folks drifted away, some unwilling to leave their homes but eventually forced to do so. By 1942 the bankrupt company's assets were transferred to the provincial government and the buildings, now abandoned, deteriorated.

Fortunately, in the 1970s some of the homes that had not completely collapsed under the snows of successive winters were restored. The village deserves a full day's exploration. In the summer months, students dressed in period clothes reenact those early days. In the convent a "nun" began lessons to the assembled crowd of tourist kids.

Although there is now a gondola lift, we had a lovely hike ascending the 785 steps to the top of 72 metre-high Ouiatchouan Falls (which is higher than Niagara Falls . . .). From this height, you can spy Chute Maligne (Maligne Waterfall) further upstream. However, from Ouiatchouan Falls, you get superb lookouts over the valley and Lac-Saint-Jean. We thoroughly enjoyed the views, perhaps in particular because we were completely alone after the town's gondola lift closed for the day. In a nutshell, this is the true benefit of staying overnight at Val Jalbert: you can wander about exploring the feel of this deserted spot on your own.

québec architecture

Old-style structures in Québec are typically steeply roofed, designed so that snow won't collect and collapse or damage the dwelling. Such roofs are often up to one-third of the elevation of the building and often are punctuated by quaint dormers. The roofline ends at the eaves with a bell-cast curve, which gives the pitch a picturesque finish. A characteristic feature of these traditional structures is the casement window with as many as twelve panes.

As night fell, the stars emerged and the falls were illuminated. The former generating station at the base of the chutes is now a dining room where you eat overlooking the restored interior of the power plant. Who knows . . . perhaps, at *la crepuscule* (twilight), you'll see the ghost of Ovide Tardif, who died after being caught in the drive belts of the mill.

For sure, stay overnight in the former one-company town if possible. Different kinds of accommodations can be booked, with the main hotel being in the now modernized old general store. (Nowadays, unlike when we first visited in 1999, it boasts air conditioning, televisions and showers!) Because the hotel was full, we stayed in a renovated worker's home directly opposite the general store. Our two-bedroom unit had a living room, dining room, and full kitchen, so you can stay awhile and cook some or all of your own meals if you wish.

We recommend using this ghost town as a base as we did. Experience it, then venture farther afield to explore more of Lac-Saint-Jean. Follow Highway 169 Ouest to learn about the local Amerindian lifestyle and history at nearby *Mashteuiatsh (Pointe Bleue)*. Visit the *Musée amérindien (Amerindian Museum)* (1787 rue Amishk, Mashteuiatsh; www.museeilnu.ca; 888-875-4842 or 418-275-4842; open mid-May through mid-Oct daily, 9 a.m. to 6 p.m., and shortened hours the rest of the year; $10 adults, $8.50 seniors, $6 students, $28 family). The museum depicts the lifestyle of the Pekuakamiulnutsh people (Montagnais from the Lac-Saint-Jean region). Exhibits include stone knives, old photographs, and videos. There's also a museum boutique. The Hudson Bay trading post moved here from Desbiens. You can learn more about how the fur trade influenced the early economy of this region and purchase some original Montagnais creations at the *Maison René Robertson Fourrures* (1619 rue Ouiatchouan, Mashteuiatsh; www.fourruresrobertson.com; 418-275-0795), an artisans' studio.

To return to Québec City, you could continue on Route 169 to circumnavigate the lake or return through Métabetchouan to Hébertville. After about 75 kilometers on Route 169 South, you'll join Highway 175 to take you through *Parc Jacques Cartier.* The park is within the *Réserve faunique des Laurentides* (wildlife preserve), with magnificent views of the Jacques Cartier River valley. Only thirty minutes from Québec City, this popular weekend destination has a wide range of activities as well as semi-equipped and wild camping. The visitor center, 9 kilometers off Highway 175, has maps and information as well as exhibits describing the park and its natural habitat (www.sepaq.com/rf/lau; 800-665-6527 or 418-848-2422; operating hours vary by season).

Winter of 2009 saw me back mushing in Québec's wilds yet again. This time, I explored Jacques Cartier Park with a team of huskies from *Aventures Nord-Bec Stoneham* (www.traineaux-chiens.com). My team swept along the forested trails and, as we sped out into open fields, I felt as though I was flying. For me, a large part of the appeal is that dogsledding is a traditional means of exploration. And because I love and enjoy working with animals very much, I find it particularly moving to do a sport with a healthy, athletic team of animals who surely are having as much fun as I am! Don't want to mush? For $3 you can simply tour this well-kept kennel where the dogs are very friendly.

Since writing our fourth edition, the family who operates Aventures Nord-Bec Stoneham have built a small complex of yurts (round tents which, in this case, are open year-round like cottages) to rent. As well, there is a gift shop, plus a restaurant which serves hearty fare including Amerindian foods. Although these special meals must be reserved in advance, it's worth it so you can taste such delicacies as moose stew served with the "three sisters" of beans, corn, and squash.

If you decide to trek west from Lac-Saint-Jean toward Lake Superior, consider taking Highway 167 from Saint-Félicien to Chibougameau and on to Val-d'Or on Highway 113. From there you can continue west through Val d'Or, Rouyn-Noranda and Kirkland Lake in Ontario to connect with Highway 11 to take you to Lake Superior. It isn't much shorter than the more heavily traveled southern route, but it does offer an interesting alternative. Stop at the information center in Saint-Félicien for current road conditions and services: there are long stretches of wilderness along this route. (See the Outaouais section for the Abitibi-Témiscaming drive.)

Northeast of Québec City: Brrr . . . the Ice Hotel

Okay, now we're taking you in a completely opposite direction: immediately west of Québec City. Head out of the capital on Route 40 Ouest (west), then turn right (north) on route 367 Nord. In twenty minutes you've left the walled capital of New France behind you and are driving past forests and lakes. What a difference!

Watch for signs to *Station écotouristique Duchesnay* (140 Montée de l'Auberge, Sainte-Catherine de la-Jacques-Cartier, Québec; 877-511-5885 or 418-875-2122; www.sepaq.com/ct/duc). Formerly a forestry station where students learned the tricks of the logging trade, today it's a provincial park operated by Sepaq. Miles of hiking, horseback riding, or cross-country skiing or snowshoe trails are available, and from Jan through the end of Mar it's home to the *Ice Hotel* (75 Montée de l'Auberge, Pavillon Ukiuk, Sainte-Catherine-de-la-Jacques-Cartier, Québec; 877-505-0423 or 418-875-4522; www.icehotel-canada.com). We had a great time here in winter, snowshoeing in the mixed hardwood forest—and Eric experienced mushing his first team of sled dogs across frozen Lac Saint-Joseph.

The park boasts 14 comfortable lakeside cabins, complete with screened porches and wood stoves. Ours had a big kitchen and an even larger common room/living room, while our bedroom was cozy country-chic. The 1920s-era log buildings once housing dormitories and classrooms have been beautifully transformed into little boutique-like auberges full of inviting bedrooms for couples or families.

A central building houses both a cafeteria and dining room, where the food is inexpensive, delicious, and, perhaps best of all, tastes homemade. What's available? We enjoyed a salad and poached salmon, while families with kids devoured hot dogs and fries. So there's a good selection for most tastes. Plus, a little anteroom next to the front door shows videos for kids, a most welcome relief for parents who want to linger over their meal after their children have finished theirs.

Another inn has been built since our first of three visits. **Auberge Duchesnay** has beautiful rooms overlooking the lake. And whereas the Ice Hotel is only open from Jan to Apr (yes: it melts!), the *auberge* and all the other lodgings are open year-round. As well, some Ice Hotel packages allow you to retreat to the Auberge for the night, should you wish.

But what of the Ice Hotel, you ask? This incredible "oversized igloo" comes complete with an "ice bar" where you sip vodka from ice "cube" glasses, ice sculptures, and, of course, bedrooms. Yes, you can sleep in your own room, on an ice block. "Gee, do I hafta pay for that," you ask? Well, yes—but we assure you, you won't freeze.

Everyone is given a little talk before spending the night in the Ice Hotel. After all, most people are a wee bit concerned. "What if I have to get up in the middle of the night to go to the bathroom? What do I wear so that I won't get cold? What if . . . ?"

Yes, yes. We had exactly the same questions. So it was amusing for us to gather with other hardy, if not bashful, visitors who wanted to try out the Ice Hotel and get the skinny on what to do to keep warm. Everyone is given an arctic sleeping bag with a freshly dry-cleaned liner bag. (Tips: Wear fresh, dry, wool or wool-blend socks; thermal underwear; a *toque*—that's pronounced tuke to rhyme with "duke." It's a very common Canadian term for a wool or polar fleece snugly fitting hat which will prevent you from losing all that heat via your head! Also to keep warm think layers, layers.) Don't despair: If you have to get up in the middle of the night, there is a bathroom in the central core of the hotel.

But what about the bed—and the rooms? The bedrooms really are made of snow and ice. Each has its own theme. We've stayed there three times—yes, you may say we're bears for punishment but winter really is our favorite season! The theme in our last room (themes change annually and there are sculpture/design competitions) was *La Vague* (The Wave), so the walls showed a wavelike motif. Our queen-size bed was carved of ice: inset into it was a foam mattress upon which were thrown several caribou hides. This is where we rolled out the thermal sleeping bag, and you'll be pleasantly surprised by how comfy it all is.

Go to the Ice Hotel. It's a unique experience in North America. And do hang around at Station écotouristique Duchesnay, where you can spend your next night in more usual accommodations and enjoy skiing, dogsledding, or even a winter horseback ride.

Places to Stay in Québec City Environs

BAIE-SAINT-PAUL

La Grande Maison,
160 rue Saint-Jean-Baptiste,
G3Z 1N3;
(418) 435-5575
www.grandemaison.com

Auberge la Maison Otis,
23 rue Saint-Jean-Baptiste,
G3Z 1M2;
(418) 435-2255 or
(800) 267-2254
www.maisonotis.com
A former bank, now renovated completely—select from old-style rooms with bunk beds or modern, larger rooms.

Auberge La Muse,
39 rue Saint-Jean-Baptiste,
G3Z 1M3;
(800) 841-6839 or
(418) 435-6839
www.lamuse.com
Touted as Charlevoix's first eco-bistro, this auberge avoids any trans-fats in their cooking, and we say a hearty Bravo! Note: La Muse is on the *"route des Saveurs de Charlevoix,"* the driving route that connects inns and restaurants featuring regional products. To find out more about other establishments on this fine-dining route, contact the Table Agro-Touristique de Charlevoix,
6 rue Saint-Jean-Baptiste;
www.routedesaveurs.com
(418) 435-3673.

Auberge de Jeunesse Le Balcon vert,
22 Côte du Balcon Vert,
G3Z 3B6;
(418) 435-5587
www.balconvert.com
International hostel where an inexpensive campsite tent space ($23) or cabins (sleeping four; from $53) can be thoroughly enjoyed from mid-May through mid-Oct.

POINTE-AU-PIC

La Romance Inn,
415 chemin des Falaises,
La Malbaie G5A 2V4;
(418) 665-4865
www.aubergelaromance
.com.

Places to Eat in Québec City Environs

L'ANSE-SAINT-JEAN

La Maringoinfre,
212 rue Saint-Jean-Baptiste,
G0V 1J0;
(418) 272-2385

LA BAIE

Auberge des 21,
621 rue Mars,
G7B 4N1;
(800) 363-7298 or
(418) 697-2121
www.aubergedes21.com

BAIE-SAINT-PAUL

Le Saint-Pub—Microbrasserie Charlevoix,
2 rue Racine (corner of Saint-Jean-Baptiste),
G3Z 2P8;
(418) 240-2332
www.microbrasserie.com
A microbrewery pub (*microbrasserie*), this place serves up great beer and good regional cuisine.

Smoked meat is a specialty. Tours of the brewery are also available.

CHICOUTIMI

La Bougresse,
260 rue Riverin,
G7H 4R4;
(418) 543-3178

ÎLE AUX COUDRES

Auberge La Coudrière
2891 chemin des
Coudriers,
G0A 2A0;
(418) 438-2838
www.aubergelacoudriere
.com

LA MALBAIE

Vices Versa
216 rue Saint-Etienne,
G5A 1T2;
(418) 665-6869
www.vicesversa.com
Husband and wife team
Danielle Guay and Éric
Bertrand dreamt of owning
their own restaurant . . .and
here it is. They like cooking
different things—he likes
butter and bacon; she likes
emulsions and pastries.
So . . . each has their own
stove. Abandon yourself to
their talents!

SAINT-ANNE-DE-BEAUPRÉ

Auberge la Camarine,
10947 blvd. Saint-Anne,
G0A 1E0;
(418) 827-5703
www.camarine.com

MONTRÉAL AND ITS NORTHERN PLAYGROUNDS →

Welcome to cultural diversity here in the island city of Montréal. The 3.8 million plus inhabitants of today's metropolis hail from eighty or so different ethnic peoples, a fact that lends this city an exhilarating, cosmopolitan flair. There's the Greek section of town along Avenue du Parc. Haitians tend to live in Montréal-Nord, Portuguese near rue St. Urbain, Jamaicans in Griffintown, Jewish communities in Outrement and Côte des Neiges. Throughout the city, immigrants from all over the world are settling in, making this land of opportunity their home.

Even the original coat of arms of the city, designed by the first mayor, Jacques Viger in 1883, honors early Europeans who carved their niche in the land. The four insignia are the Irish clover, Scottish thistle, English rose, and French *fleur-de-lis* (lily). Lying on a log on top of them all is the Canadian beaver, uniting all groups.

In Montréal you can "time-travel" back to the 1500s to catch a glimpse of what life was like back then. French explorer Jacques Cartier sailed up the St. Lawrence River on his second trip to the New Land in 1535. Stopping on the island, he climbed **Mont Royal,** proclaiming its name for the King

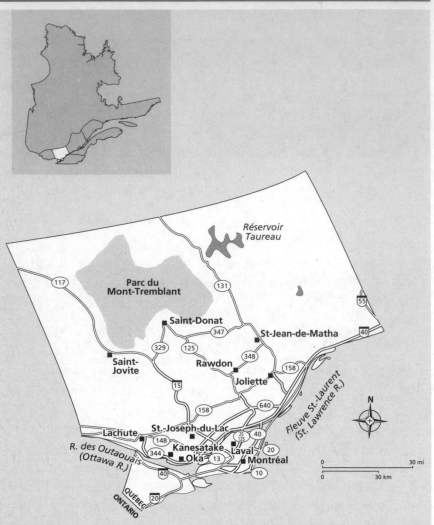

of France. But on his 1556 map of Cartier's discoveries, Italian cartographer Giovanni Battista Ramusio unwittingly gave the site its modern name, writing "Mont Real" on the island. It's hard to imagine now, but when Cartier explored Mont Royal, he found an Iroquois village of 1,500 inhabitants, nestled against the protection of the mountain—a village that had evidently disappeared by the time Champlain first arrived in 1603.

How can you locate this past? By exploring the cobbled streets of Old Montréal. For instance, down in the crypt of Chapelle-Nôtre-Dame-de-Bonsecours in the *Vieux Port* (Old Port) sector of the city, you can glimpse life in 1642, when Montréal was founded as the French religious colony known as Ville Marie. Across from the Chapelle's gilt Virgin is today's circa 1725 Pierre du Calvet B&B, named after the merchant who resided there. Calvet once offered lodging to Benjamin Franklin—which brings us to a story of the bubbling fervor of those times.

One can almost hear the impassioned words as these two men met. Surely they talked long into the night: you can imagine them springing up from their chairs, perhaps shaking their fists, and decrying the British overlords. During these times of the twin nation's growth, American colonists strained at the British leash while, after the 1759 British Conquest of New France (see Québec City section), the seeds of rebellion were stirring here in Montréal.

But the British were wise. Although General Wolfe won the decisive battle on the Plains of Abraham in Québec City in 1759, they knew that the French people's first loyalty was to the Catholic Church. To secure their victory "on the streets," out of respect (and of course as part of wise, strategic governance) Governor James Murray permitted the French to continue their Roman Catholic faith, law, and language. And as we all know, both French- and

AUTHORS' FAVORITES FOR MONTRÉAL AND ENVIRONS

Chapelle-Nôtre-Dame-de-Bonsecours

Le Petit Train du Nord bicycle trail

Maré Jean Talon (market)

McCord Museum of Canadian History

Musée régional d'Argenteuil

Olympic Stadium site with Biodome, Insectarium, and Botanical Gardens

Parc du Mont-Tremblant

Pierre du Calvet Gîte

English-speaking Québecers continue to dance the dance of negotiation, compromise, and respect.

On the streets of this city, you'll discover that most Montréalers are bilingual. Although French predominates (Montréal is the second-largest French-speaking city in the world) the reality is that this old port city is a vibrant mosaic of world culture.

Of course, no city stands still, and Montréal is no exception. Recently completed renovations to the **Quartier internationale** (International Quarter) include seating and lighting, as well as access to the Underground City's network of pedestrian walkways. Right downtown at Square Victoria the old meets the new. The Métro station is famous for its original, authentic Parisian Art Nouveau "grille," or metal work. It makes a fine architectural contrast to the modern architecture of the constantly growing city.

The St. Lawrence lowlands with their old seigneurial farms stretching in narrow swathes north from the broad river lie outside the city. Bountiful produce such as delectable strawberries in June are there for the picking. As you drive north you'll find fields of flowers in Laval, then undulating green hills dotted with black-and-white Holstein dairy cows. Suddenly the land steeply rises, and you will cycle or drive through the ancient Laurentian Mountains, once taller than the western Rockies.

This is the playground of Montréalers. Auto routes stream people north to a cluster of luxury resorts offering bicycle paths, spas, lakes, rivers, and golf courses in summertime; dogsledding, snowshoeing, skiing—and more "spaahing" in winter: Grey Rocks and Mont Tremblant. Famous names—and for good reason, for this is spectacular country. Still farther north lies the stunning natural beauty of Mont Tremblant Park, where you can spot a moose from the car or dip your canoe into a lake and paddle off into the sunset.

But not so fast . . . Montréal and Laval are islands—and in the St. Lawrence River there are many islands, accessible by car, ferry, or bike. Famous for its birds, **Parc des Iles de Boucherville** is only a few moment's drive from Montréal *Est* (east).

Truly, Montréal and its environs are a wonderful playground. Shall we explore?

Montréal

We'll start our explorations in the heart of *Vieux* (Old) Montréal. Find Rue Bonsecours and drive down to the **Chapelle-Nôtre-Dame-de-Bonsecours** (400 rue Saint-Paul Est; 514-282-8670). You can't miss it because it is at the end of Rue Bonsecours at Saint-Paul Est. A gilt Virgin above the front door welcomes worshippers. Look up to see the steeple; this is our eventual destination, as not one but two levels of lookouts offer outstanding perspectives of the old port (*vieux port*) of Montréal.

For now, step inside the cool interior of this 1771 chapel. Modified in 1890, it stands on the site of the original chapel of 1657, when Saint Marguerite-Bourgeoys founded the congregation of Nôtre-Dame. When we visited the chapel, our guide told us it had just reopened after a two-year restoration of the nave's circa-1888 frescoes, discovered only in 1996. During a short work project, workers had disturbed the stretched canvas ceiling of the nave. The canvas ripped, exposing the hitherto hidden frescoes. Today your upward gaze will be rewarded by paintings that extend themes depicted in the stained-glass windows. This chapel is particularly famous for its ex-votos, or offerings of thanks. Suspended from the ceiling of the nave are wooden boats carved by sailors who gave them in thanks for their safe passage on stormy seas. English Mass is on Sat.

Enter the attached **Musée de Marguerite-Bourgeoys** (400 rue St Paul Est, Vieux-Montréal; 514-282-8670; www.marguerite-bourgeoys.com; $8 adults, $5 seniors/children, $16 family; closed mid-Jan to end of Feb; times vary). Climb the stairs to the two steeple lookouts, which we think give you the

The Mother of Montréal

Sainte Marguerite-Bourgeoys came to New France in the early 1630s and became founder of the congregation of Nôtre-Dame. Realizing that women were needed to create families—and French settlers—in *Nouvelle France* (New France), in 1653 the French king sent boatloads of young women as wives for the men of the colony. Known as *filles de roi* (daughters of the king)—some as young as twelve—Marguerite-Bourgeoys understood they needed careful guarding. She took them under her wing, giving them safe haven, offering them both religious education and household management skills such as sewing and cooking.

She also rallied the community, inspiring them to build Montréal's first stone chapel in 1655. As well, she sheparded a hitherto-unheard-of community of uncloistered women to become the Congregation of Notre Dame—with official approval from the Catholic Church in 1700.

The doll collection in the Musée de Marguerite-Bourgeoys depicts her life and times. When you exit the main doorway of the chapel, look left to see the marble plaque to her memory, with the obvious addition of the word "Saint"—a canonization bestowed upon her in 1982. Because of her dedication to Montréal's poor and sick, and to *les filles de roi*, Marguerite-Bourgeoys is considered the Mother of Montréal. She died in 1770, at almost eighty years old. What a life!

best perspective of Montréal. Look south to the harbor and time-travel back to 1535, when Cartier sailed upriver. Find *Île Notre-Dame*, the artificial island Mayor Drapeau had built from twenty-eight million tons of fill. This island was designed for Expo '67. Not only was this a World's Fair, but it was also the celebration of Canada's centennial anniversary of Confederation. Today the French pavilion houses a casino.

Look north to spy Mont Royal. To the northeast find the white 190-meter "neck" of the 1976 *Olympic Stadium*, often referred to as Drapeau's Folly because its Kevlar roof still leaks. To date, the always-controversial stadium, designed by Parisian architect Roger Taillibert, has cost Montréalers more than $1 billion. Extending below to the west and east are the cobbled streets of Old Montréal. Look west, immediately below you, to see the grand dome of *Maré Bonsecours* (Bonsecours Market). Opened in 1849, its grand Classical Revival style sports columns imported from England. It has served the city well: For more than one hundred years it was the marketplace of the city, where everything from cheese and honey through fish and fowl were sold. Its imposing walls also housed the city hall for a while. Today it is home to a cluster of boutiques and restaurants showcasing Québécois art, design, and cuisine.

Before descending, notice how the stone buildings of Old Montréal all have raised gable ends, a required fire-retardant feature in stone homes of the eighteenth century in the city. Below you is a prime example: the 1726 *Pierre du Calvet*, an exceptional gîte with an enclosed, parrot-filled courtyard (405 rue Bonsecours, Vieux-Montréal; 866-544-1725 or 514-282-1725; www.pierre ducalvet.ca). Now walk down, down, down to the chapel's crypt to view an exhibit of artifacts dug from the old walls of the city. The original wooden palisade walls have been discovered, and the dig still continues. A maquette in the crypt depicts what archaeologists are revealing even today. Catch an *archaeological tour* if you can (limited to groups of eight).

Musical Interlude

Don't miss the *Musée du Château Ramezay* (280 rue Notre Dame Est, Vieux Montréal; 514-861-3708; www.chateauramezay.qc.ca). This former governor's residence, built in 1705, is not only a superb museum but also offers a newly restored heritage garden. On the last Sun of the month, for the price of admission to the museum, enjoy two classical concerts at 1:30 and 3 p.m., held in ornate Salle de Nantes. Your eyes will lap up the exquisitely carved wood paneling dating from 1725. Not original to the house, the paneling was installed in the château during Expo '67.

Return outside to Rue St. Paul Est at Rue Bonsecours. Turn left on Rue du Maré Bonsecours to visit the harbor and perhaps have a picnic on the grass at **Parc du Bassin Bonsecours** (no fees, just a pretty, grassed park beside the river). As you cross Rue de la Commune, look right. Beside the broad boardwalk you'll spy gaily decorated **horse-drawn calêches,** which give tours of old Montréal. In winter, bearskin rugs and the lively tales of the drivers conspire to keep you warm. Then, too, the frozen surface of the Bassin Bonsecours is shoveled clear of snow so that you can join Montréalers skating. In Feb Montréal's **Winter Carnival** is held here; in summer the Bassin comes alive with paddleboats.

Take the time to stroll in the parks along this restored heritage waterfront. You'll notice several piers, or quays, jutting into the harbor. On **Clock-Tower Pier** (de l'Horlage), climb the steps of the tower to take in the view of the islands in the channel of the St. Lawrence River and decide which ferry you'll take to explore them. Descend and walk along the waterfront, with Bassin Bonsecours on your right, to Jacques-Cartier Pier (where ferries dock). Reflect on how this waterfront must have looked in the 1600s, with wooden ships harbored at wooden piers. Imagine the snorts of horses and the bustle of people and wagons as goods were taken on and off the boats.

claudejutra

Born in Montréal in 1930, Claude Jutra was one of the province's most accomplished and beloved filmmakers. His 1971 movie Mon Oncle Antoine, set in a little Québec town on Christmas Eve, portrays the journey of a youth to manhood. Tragically, this leader of Canadian filmmaking disappeared in Nov 1986, only to be found drowned five months later in the St. Lawrence River at Cap-Santé.

Connect with **King Edward Pier** and visit the **Montréal Science Centre,** a huge science and technology center that also houses an IMAX theatre. We had great fun at the Immersion cinema, where members of the entire audience sit at their own computer consoles, in a group activity, trying to save the life of an astronaut (333 La Commune West, Montréal; 514-496-4724 or 877-496-4724; www.montrealsciencecentre.com).

Cross to Rue de la Commune, to find **Place Royale,** the birthplace of Montréal in 1642. Here find the **Pointe à Callière, Montréal Museum of Archaeology and History** (350 place Royale; 514-872-9150; www.pac museum.qc.ca). You'll discover the entire history of Montréal, from its early years as a native settlement to European discovery and settlement. Six centuries are depicted using the latest technologies.

Press on, heading north to Rue Saint-Paul Ouest (West). We enjoy rambling about here, exploring such finds as the wonderful **Auberge les Passants du Sans Soucy** (171 rue Saint-Paul, Montréal; 514-842-2634; www

TOP TIPS FOR MONTRÉAL

Tourist Info Centre:
is at 174 rue Notre Dame Est
www.tourisme-montreal.org

Museums Pass:
WOW! How cool is this? For $45
you can purchase a 3-day pass to
thirty-four city museums (or $50 to
include unlimited bus and métro); www
.montrealmuseums.org or purchase
the pass at major hotels, museums or
tourist information centers.

U.S. Consulate Office in Montréal:
(514) 398-9695

Public Transportation:
(514) 288-6287

Ferry for pedestrians and cyclists:
from Old Port to Parc des Iles, Ile
Charron, or to Bellerive in East Montréal.
(514) 281-8000
www.navettesmaritimes.com

.lesanssoucy.com). At this small boutique hotel, owners Daniel Soucy and Michael Banks will regale you with stories of the city. The breakfast, served in an airy room with a crackling fire, is filling and delectable. Close to everything and moderately priced, this inn is a treasure.

Nearby find **Galerie Parchemine**, home of the **Économusée de l'encadrement** (economuseum of framing), where you'll learn everything about the history of framing pictures (40 Saint-Paul Ouest; 514-845-3368).

Around the corner from the Auberge les Passants du Sans Soucy, you'll find a second restaurant with fine dining that the two proprietors have opened: **Bonaparte's Auberge et Restaurant** (447 rue Saint-François-Xavier, Montréal; 514-844-1448; www.bonaparte.com). We can personally vouch for the superb cuisine and service at this former bank, and our tour of the inn's thirty rooms revealed that two rooms have balconies overlooking the private gardens behind Notre Dame Cathedral.

Why not complete your exploration of Vieux Montréal by going to the city's oldest English-language playhouse, the **Centaur Theatre**? Located just a couple of doors north of Bonaparte's, it has shown plays and served as a cultural bastion to the city's Anglophone community since 1973.

But, hey, after the theater you're ready to taste some of Montréal's famous nightlife, no? Check out the lively (okay . . . boisterous) night scene at **Aux Deux Pierrots** (104 rue Saint-Paul Ouest; 514-861-1270; www.lespierrots .com). Either listen or sing along with the rest of the amiable, relaxed crowd belting out "Québec" and other pop songs.

Exploring Old Montréal can be a tad depressing, as there are tons of junky souvenir shops. Just ignore them and have fun—for example, by quaffing one of Québec's deservedly renowned microbrewery beers at one of **Place Jacques Cartier's** restaurants. (Try Unibroue's La Fin du Monde—the End of the World—but beware, it's 9 percent alcohol.) Trendy cafes spill out onto the broad expanse of this once open-air marketplace in a lively, jovial atmosphere. Artists, craftspeople, street actors, and jugglers entertain you in summertime, as will the sound of a multitude of languages floating on the evening air. More than anyplace else in Old Montréal, the spirit of convivial laissez-faire and joie de vivre is infectious here.

At the head of Place Jacques Cartier find the **Colonne Nelson (Nelson Column),** which symbolizes British merchants' desire to publicly express their loyalty to the Crown in 1809. This tribute to Nelson is one of two such columns in the world. The other is in London's Trafalgar Square.

Although the city of Montréal is itself on an island, it includes a number of other interesting islands. At the lower end of Place Jacques Cartier, cross the Rue de la Commune and find the **Navettes Maritimes ferry** terminus on **Jacques Cartier Quay.** (Ferries operate May through Oct; call 514-281 8000). Admission tickets to the Biosphere include free round-trip passage and bicycle transport aboard the frequent ferry to **Île Sainte Hélène.**

The **Biosphere,** housed in one of the few remaining exposition buildings of Expo '67, is a geodesic dome designed as the U.S. pavilion by American Buckminster Fuller ($12 adults, $8 seniors/students, under seventeen free; 25 percent discount for green transportation users; June 1 to Oct 31, 10 a.m. to 6 p.m. daily; Nov 1 to May 31, Tues to Sun 10 a.m. to 6 p.m.; closed Mon; 514-283-5000; www.biosphere.ec.gc .ca). Enter to explore the habitats of the St. Lawrence River and Great Lakes regions as well as to visit an interpretive center that explains sustainable use of water resources.

eco-friendlybixi

Bixi, an acronym of "bicycle" and "taxi", is a public bike rental network that is gaining international popularity. Montréal Bixi was inaugurated in 2009, giving city explorers access to 3,000 bikes located at 300 stations throughout downtown. An online map (www.bixi.com/home) gives users real-time availability at each pickup spot.

Montréal was the first Canadian city to join the Bixi movement, joining London (England), Paris, Stockholm, Barcelona and others.

What's the goal? Reduce our car dependency, aka carbon emissions by making bicycle access easy and convenient. So go Bixi and go green!

Ghosts of the City

You can bet Montréal's old port harbors ghosts from the past, whether they be the spirits of the young *filles-de-roi*, explorers, *coureurs-de-bois*, or famous politicians. Discover the haunts during an **Old Montréal Ghost Trail** (Old Port of Montréal, Place d'Armes; 514-868-0303; www.fantommontreal.com), and you can become part of one of Montréal's most infamous murder trials. For information on other guided tours in Montréal, visit www.montrealtours.net.

In daytime, cross to *Île Notre-Dame*, an island created in a mere ten months from fill excavated during construction of the Métro. Unless your visit coincides with the exciting Grand Prix Formula One racing event in mid-June, you can enjoy the peace and beauty of the *Jardin des Floralies*, a twenty-six-hectare expanse of gardens from the 1980 Floralies Internationales. If the weather is suitable, visit the plage (the beach)—*Plage de Île Notre-Dame.* It makes a fascinating counterpoint to the Biosphere's theme of sustainable use of water resources, as the water you swim in is filtered naturally by an assortment of plants such as bulrushes.

Just north of the Biosphere, you'll find the *Fort de Île Sainte Hélène*, which was built in 1825 after the American and British War of 1812 from red stone quarried from the island. Inside is the newly refurbished *Musée David M. Stewart* (514-861-6701; May to mid-Oct, daily 10 a.m. to 6 p.m.; Oct to Apr, 10 a.m. to 5 p.m. daily except Tues; $8 adults). It houses a collection of seventeenth- and eighteenth-century maps and firearms, among other objects, all collected by this Scottish Montréal industrialist.

Even if you don't like rides, you shouldn't miss another legacy of the 1967 World Exhibition, at the north end of Île Sainte Hélène: *La Ronde.* This is Québec's largest amusement park, with thirty-four rides, lots of games, and, during June and the first half of July, the incomparable *International Fireworks Competition.* Consider walking back to the city across the *Jacques Cartier Bridge*, from whose pedestrian walkways you get a breathtaking view of this island city, particularly at night. Tip: cross on the west side for the best view of the city. Your bonus, of course, is that it's free and you're enjoying an unforgettable stroll in the fresh air.

Former Mayor Drapeau's other significant legacy is *Le Métro* (the underground). Convenient, inexpensive, and safe, its subway stops are identified by circular signs with a white arrow on a blue background. There's a whole "underground happening" here: buskers play, and some stops have extensive underground markets. Maps are easy to follow, and, as in London, Tokyo, and

TOP ANNUAL EVENTS IN THE MONTRÉAL ENVIRONS

Montréal is the city of festivals. Find complete listings at www.montreal.com, but here's a sample of new or more unusual festivals.

FEBRUARY

Festival Montréal en Lumière (888-477-9955 or 514-288-9955; www.montrealenlumiere.com) impressed us with its outside art installations that creatively mixed light, sound, and color against the backdrop of snow. Films are projected on building facades. Dress very warmly: *toques* (woolen hats), serious winter boots, and mittens are *de rigueur!*

MARCH

Who says Québec is unicultural and French-only? The city has one of the largest **St. Patrick's Day parades** in the world, where the streets come alive and green. Join the fun! (www.montrealirishparade.com)

JUNE

In early June check out **MUTEK** (www.mutek.org) where digital creativity in sound, music and audio-visual art is celebrated.

Another wild-side festival is **Infringement!** (www.infringementfestival.com), a direct descendent of Edinburgh, Scotland's 1947 Fringe festival (which sparked the development of the international Fringe festivals). Infringement!, however, was started in 2004 to boycott "corporate oppression" and create what organizers say "put the fringe back into the hands of the artists and the community."

Attend Montréal **First People's Festival** (514-278-4040; www.nativelynx.qc.ca).

Explore the **World of Beer (Le Mondial de la Bière) Festival** (514-722-9640; festivalmondialbiere.qc.ca).

Music Festival Nuits d'Afrique (African Nights) (514-499-9239; www.festivalnuitsdafrique.com).

JULY

Just for Laughs Festival (2101 St.-Laurent Blvd., Montréal H2X 2T5; 514-845-2322 or 888-244-3155; www.hahaha.com) in Montréal's festive Latin Quarter brings eleven days of more than 2,000 French and English comedy routines.

SEPTEMBER

Celebrate ethereal light after twilight at the at the Jardin Botanique's (Botanical Gardens') **Magic of Lanterns Festival** (www2.ville.montreal.qc.ca/jardin/propos/lanternes.htm; continues through end Oct; 514-872-1400).

NOVEMBER

Retreat from chilly weather: attend **CINEMANIA** film festival (French films are sub-titled in English) http://cinemaniafilmfestival.com.

Locavore lifestyle: eat fresh!

Québec has a thriving gastronomy born from farm-fresh regional foods. Enter the locavore movements where consumers focus on eating only locally or regionally produced foods grown within 100 km of wherever you're at. How to support local produce? Visit markets such as the really local (read: off the beaten track) *Maré Jean Talon* (www.Mare-jean-talon.com) where stalls display everything from honey to lavender to preserves—to regional wines. These wines as well as regional specialties are sold in a separate building outside the main market complex—a market within a market. Called *Le Maré des Saveurs* (Market of Flavors; 280 Place du Maré du Nord, 514-271-3811; www.lemaredesssaveurs.com), it helpfully and attractively showcases the region's foods. Artisinal wines are also here, sold at a special SAQ (provincial liquor) store called *La Maison des Vins et des Boissons artisanales du Québec.* Small samples are available for free.

The three other main farmers' markets in Montréal are: the upscale *Atwater* (absolutely fabulous cheeses here), *Maisonneuve,* and *de Lachine.* (Check www.mares publics-mtl.com for details, seasonal produce, market locations and special events.) Go, sample, buy breakfast or lunch on-site at Moroccan, Indian or other restaurant stalls—or buy the fixings for your private picnic. Either way, "it's a yum!"

Mexico City, the network of routes are color-coded. For instance, if you decide not to walk across the Jacques Cartier Bridge, enter the very well-marked *Île Sainte Hélène* Métro station and return to the city.

You mustn't leave Montréal without hopping on the Métro and exploring what is known as the *Underground City*—the largest underground pedestrian network in the world. More than two thousand shops, over forty theaters and cinemas, and services thrive in six different zones, all beneath the city's streets. To get a taste of it, we recommend that you descend beneath the train station at *Place d'Armes* to enjoy the market flavor there. The underground city has grown to incorporate the Quartier international. Certainly, inclement weather—or winter's chill—is no excuse. By hook or by crook, Montréalers want you to explore all of their city, both above and below ground!

A key Métro stop is *Viau,* being central to the *Biodome* (Montréal Biodome, 4777 Pierre-de-Coubertin Ave.; www.ville.montreal.qc.ca/biodome; 514-868-3000), *Insectarium*, and *Botanical Gardens* (Jardin Botanique). These interrelated attractions are located at a shared, expansive site with a free shuttle bus to take you from the station to each of these attractions, and if you're tired of walking, there's a free train that drives around the Botanical Gardens, once you pay the admission, that's a lifeline for parents with kids—or even for couples like us who've been "walking forever." We feel so inspired in these gardens. Here you can learn all you want to know about planning your garden, whether from the point of view of color, fragrance, or medicinal qualities of plants.

One exhibit at the Jardin Botanique is the *First Nations' Garden,* celebrating the Great Treaty of Montréal signed at Point à Callière on August 4, 1701. The focus of the gardens is the relationship between Amerindian cultures and plants (Jardin Botanique, 4101 rue Sherbrooke Est, Montréal; 514-872-1400; www2.ville .montreal.qc.ca/jardin/). Feb through Mar, the garden's greenhouses flutter with color during the *Butterflies Go Free* event, when tropical butterflies are released during a five-week event held in conjunction with the nearby Insectarium.

The *Pie IX* stop, close to the *Olympic Stadium,* is a major landmark and tourist draw. But if you want to check out a section of town that Montréalers love, walk south on Boulevard Pie IX 3 blocks to Rue Ontario. Turn left to find the lesser-known *Maré Maisonneuve* (market) in the area of town called Hochelaga Maisonneuve. Hochelaga was the name of the Iroquois village Cartier visited on the island of Montréal in Oct 1535. Populated in the 1870s by mostly French-speaking laborers for nearby factories, this once-industrial sector is now mainly residential. When it was officially incorporated in 1883, bustling Maisonneuve was comparable to the city of Pittsburgh.

In front of the Beaux Arts 1914 market building is an eye-catching fountain. Sculptor Alfred Laliberté's composition includes some puckish-looking

dragonbeard candy

Whaaat? Yes, we're not kidding, this really is the name of a sugary delight, made in Montréal's Chinatown by Johnny Chin, "right on the street." Watch him fashion this concoction of cornstarch, chocolate, sesame seeds, and other delectables, spring through autumn, at 52B Rue de la Gauchetière Ouest.

Canuck Humor

Stephen Leacock was one of Canada's great, award-winning humor writers. Today the annual Leacock Award commemorates his name throughout our country while recognizing published humorists. But not many folks—even Canadians—realize that he spent more than thirty-five years teaching economics here at Montréal's McGill University.

madonnaof thebathtub

Roadside Madonnas are a Québec feature. Dressed in blue robes and often with hands outstretched, the religious figurine is mounted in a little garden or roadside shrine. Local wags often call such a figurine "the Madonna of the bathtub," since shrines resemble (and often actually are) upended, old-fashioned bathtubs.

boys grasping market animals, such as a calf and a turkey. But the real pièce de résistance is the lifelike bronze statue called La Fermière (the Farmer's Wife). Her swinging skirt makes her look as though she's about to stride off the pedestal. Facing her, cross to the market building on the right to find the deli *Première Moisson,* where you can buy healthy breads and a variety of pâtés and patisseries (www.premiere moisson.com). All are exceptional, including the coarser pâtés called *rillettes*, most of which are made from game meats such as deer, rabbit, or bison.

Want a free swim after lounging in the market square? Walk down Morgan Street (opposite the fountain) to 1875 Morgan, the *Piscine Morgan,* a pool that was once one of the city's public baths (514-872-6657; afternoons Tues to Fri). The front of the building is decorated with another of sculptor Alfred Laliberté's lifelike bronzes.

Our final tip for exploring Montréal is to visit the outstanding *McCord Museum of Canadian History* (corner of Sherbrooke and Victoria, McGill Métro stop). Here secrets of the city are revealed in the delightful permanent exhibit. It introduces you to the city's social history and has an excellent display on winter. There's also a rare photo of working-class Montréal, which contrasts neatly with other displays of fancy balls and the good life.

The McCord houses a superb Amerindian collection and the outstanding William Notman collection of 700,000 photographs of Canada, which the photographer took in the late 1800s. We think this museum's a gem; don't leave town without visiting (690 rue Sherbrooke Ouest; 514-398-7100; McGill Métro or bus 24; www.mccord-museum.qc.ca; open Tues through Fri 10 a.m. to 6 p.m., weekends 10 a.m. to 5 p.m., Mon in the summer 10 a.m. to 5 p.m. adults $13, seniors $10, students $7, children six to twelve $5, under six free, family rate $26; note that admission is free on the first Sat of each month).

As you leave Montréal, drive north to the mountain *Parc du Mont-Royal,* designed by American Frederick Law Olmsted, creator of New York City's Central Park. The summer walking paths are good cross-country trails after the snow flies. From its belvédères (lookouts), look down over the city. As a nice counterpoint to the beginning of your trip, look east to the Old Port and the Chapelle-Nôtre-Dame-de-Bonsecours.

But not so fast! Before we point you north, we must add that outdoorsy types should head south over the Pont-tunnel L.-H.-Lafontaine (from Montréal east via Highways 25 and 138) to ***Parc des Iles de Boucherville,*** famous for its birds. Here you can bike or walk, feeling as though you were miles away from Montréal.

North of Montréal

Now we'll start our exploration of the environs to the north of the city. From the park follow Côte-des-Nciges north to Rue Jean-Talon. At this five-way intersection, turn into the park on Boulevard Laird into the town of Mount Royal—where English-language signs suddenly become evident in a neighborhood of gracious elms and stately homes. Find Highway 15 Nord near where Boulevard Laird meets the Autoroute Métropolitaine.

Laval

The best way to get to the island of Laval is to travel north via Highway 15. Formerly known as Île Jesus because it was granted to the Jesuits in 1636, the island was the cottage country of wealthy Montréalers from 1880 to 1914.

Today it is home to a flourishing horticultural industry, and you can drive along pretty backcountry roads (mostly paved) that lead from one fragrant spot to another. A brochure, La Route des Fleurs, is available at tourist centers and in commercial establishments along the way. Most spots are close to the town of Sainte Dorothée, touted as the flower capital of Québec, and for good reason.

From Highway 15, turn west onto Autoroute Laval which soon becomes Avenue des Bois. At the T intersection, turn left at Rue Principale and watch for the sign to ***Fleurineau Boutique et Serres*** (1270 rue Principale, Sainte-Dorothée; 450-689-1349; Mon through Fri 9 a.m. to 6 p.m., Sat 9 a.m. to 5 p.m., Sun 10 a.m. to 5 p.m.).

In 1994 Louis and Martin Marineau started their business, Fleurineau, so as to grow, dry, and

kingofthenorth: curéantoinelabelle

Curé Antoine Labelle was born in Laval's Sainte-Rose village in 1833. A giant of a man—180 cm (6 ft) and 300 lbs, he was ordained as a Roman Catholic priest in 1856. He moved to the Laurentians and, dismayed by the exodus of Québécois to work in mills in the New England states, he did his best to encourage settlement of the Laurentians. Labelle is credited for persuading 5,000 or so to settle Québec's Laurentians—hence the title "King of the North."

WORTH SEEING IN MONTRÉAL

Cirque du Soleil
is one of Québec's major attractions.
Its 50-meter blue-and-white big top
(grand chapiteau) is only visible on Quai
Jacques Cartier (Old Port of Montréal)
in spring. The rest of the year, this
internationally renowned troupe, known
for its astonishing acts, travels. Since its
creation in 1984, Cirque du Soleil has
played to sellout crowds
worldwide.
(514) 722-2324 or (800) 678-2119;
www.cirquedusoleil.com
for performance information.

**Fur Trade at Lachine National Historic
Site**
1255 blvd. Saint-Joseph,
Lachine;
(514) 637-7433;
www.pc.gc.ca;
$3.90 adults, $3.40 seniors, $1.90
children, under six free, $9.80 family.
Open daily from mid-May to mid-Oct,
9:30 a.m. to 12:30 p.m. and 1 to 5:00
p.m.; closed Dec through Mar. This
interpreted site depicts the mainstay of

economic life in Nouvelle France: the fur
trade. The Lachine Canal was critical
to this trade, and it was here that the
Hudson Bay Company established its
main offices. The company's warehouse
was built in 1830. Excellent for kids.

**Musée des Beaux-Arts de Montréal
(Museum of Fine Arts)**
1379 and 1380 rue Sherbrooke Ouest;
(514) 285-2000;
www.mmfa.qc.ca;
A world-class museum; the permanent
exhibits are free. Call to find out what
the temporary exhibit is when you visit.
Adults $15; students $7.50; half price
on Wed 5:30 to 9 p.m. Open 11 a.m. to
5 p.m., Wed until 9 p.m.

Mont Royal Cemetery
is a huge Protestant cemetery that will
give you insight into who was who of
old and new Montréal. The famous
governess popularized in The King
and I, Anna Leonowens, is buried
here, as are many Molsons of brewing
fame. Found on Voie Camillon Houde,

arrange dried flowers. At first, they simply thought of growing statice for the local market in Sainte Dorothée, but their business literally blossomed, and now they ship all over the province and into the United States and Ontario. As well, there is a boutique selling everything flower garden related, from vases to cut and artificial flowers, to garden paraphernalia.

However, the Marineau family also grow their own fruits and vegetables at their fifty-acre operation: strawberries, raspberries, corn, tomatoes and more. Language tip: the French word for "farm" is *ferme*; but note that if picking is finished at a fruit farm, a sign with *fermé* (closed) will appear. Note the tricky accent on the last letter; this is your clue that *la ferme est fermé* (the farm is closed)!

Close by find **Paradis des orchidées** (1280 Montée Champagne, Sainte Dorothée; www.leparadisdesorchidees.com; 450-689-2244), which is open to it is situated near Montréal's largest cemetery, the **Cimitiére Notre-Dame-des-Neiges**, final resting place for over a million souls.

Farther along the road is the **Oratoire Saint-Joseph** (3800 chemin Queen Mary; 514-733-8211; www.saint-joseph .org; open daily 7 a.m. to 8:30 p.m.; donation requested—no actual fee). Over two million pilgrims traverse the 300 stairs annually, sometimes on their knees.

Nôtre Dame Basilica

110 rue Nôtre Dame Ouest; (514) 842-2925; www.basiliquenddm.org can't be overlooked. It's ever so picturesque, with the always-present horse-drawn calêches waiting outside. Built between 1824 and 1829, its magnificent Gothic Revival architecture and Casavant organ will surely inspire admiration, regardless of your faith.

Just for Laughs Museum

You gotta love a museum of laughter, don't you? This is a must-see. Started in 1998, this gem highlights the evolution of comedy, with events for the entire family.

2111 blvd. St.-Laurent; (514) 845-2322; www.hahaha.com for prices and performances; reservations are recommended.

World Trade Centre Montréal

747 Sq. Victoria, at the Métro station of that name. This complex is part of the new Quartier internationale that's worth exploring. Find sections of the Berlin Wall here, plus the old Ruelle des Fortifications. The Centre is aptly named: On the northwest edge of the Old Port Sector, there are many examples of fine architecture, including the gorgeous Hôtel Intercontinental—one of the city's prestigious hotels.

visitors daily from 9 a.m. to 5 p.m.; free. We couldn't believe our eyes when we entered the greenhouse. As far as the eye could see were wall-to-wall flowering orchids. And it does seem preposterous that such an exotic-looking flower has little or no fragrance.

From there, rejoin Autoroute Laval to Highway 15 North to the Boulevard Sainte-Rose exit east. From there, rejoin Autoroute Laval to Highway 15 North to the Boulevard Saint-Rose exit east, which connects to Boulevard des Mille Îles Est. The road hugs the north shore of the island and before long you'll see the *Fromagerie du Vieux-Saint-François* (4740 blvd. des Milles-Îles; www .fromagerieduvieuxstfrancois.com; 450-666-6810; Tues and Wed 10 a.m. to 6 p.m., Thurs and Fri 10 a.m. to 8 p.m., Sat and Sun 10 a.m. to 5 p.m.; closed Mon; reservation needed for a guided tour). This is a great spot to see how yogurt and goat's milk (*chêvre*) cheese are made.

LAVAL FESTIVALS

Just because Laval is Québec's smallest tourism region doesn't mean it doesn't celebrate, big-time. Here are our fave festivals on-island.

APRIL

It's always good to support youth's creative ventures and in spring, 400+ young people come to compete in the *Festival des orchestres de jeunes du Québec* (www.orchestres.qc.ca). Every year international orchestras, conductors and special artists join in.

MAY

The beautiful flower region of Laval is *Le vieux quartier de Sainte-Dorothée* (Old quarter of Saint Dorothée). So it's no wonder the annual Symposium des

artistes sur la *Route des Fleurs (Flower Route Artists Festival* (450-978-5959) is located in the village square. Check dates but usually first weekend in May.

AUGUST

In mid-August for two days in Sainte-Rose village, the festival *Un chemin de roses, La Semaine des Artisans de Laval* (The Way of the Rose: Artisans of Laval; www.semainedesartisansdelaval .org) celebrates 150+ artisans of the area—for an entire week. Producers of *produits du terroir* (products of the earth) are on-hand to introduce you to their delicious wines and artisinal foods. Enjoy!

Maintaining an agricultural tour theme is easy on this pastoral isle. To do a loop back onto Route 15, rather than retracing your steps to Sainte-Rose, head to 4305 rang du Haut-Saint-François, to the apple orchardist (*verger en français*) at **Verger N. Bolduc et fille** (450-664-7378). With well over 1,000 trees in thirteen different varieties, this is a pretty spot to learn about apples or buy apple products to accompany the cheese you just bought! Picnic areas are available on the site, or you may wish to wait for our next destination—a pretty park west of Sainte-Rose.

To get there, continue southwest on Rang du Haut-Saint-François, head west (ouest) on Route 440 and north on Route 15 Nord. Exit at Boulevard Sainte-Rose and go west on this road. You'll soon reach 345 blvd. Sainte-Rose (450-622-1020), the **Parc de la rivière des Mille-Îles (Thousand Islands Park),** which is a northerly bayou, a special wetlands ecosystem (open daily mid-May to early Sept; weekends Sept to mid-Oct; hours vary; check Web site for winter opening times. Paddle boats as well as *rabaskas* can be rented here and it makes a great contrast to Montréal's hustle-bustle if you get out on the water here. The *rabaska* is a large canoe inspired by First Nations peoples, so it's a little piece of history well worth trying. In winter or summer, there's lots to do here, from a canoe or kayak exploration of the pretty islands to skating and skiing.

You'll surely see mallard and black ducks and great blue herons and possibly spy beaver, muskrat, bullfrogs, and leopard frogs. If you require information in English, don't be shy—English brochures and help are available. Bring binoculars and camera for wildlife watching.

There are boat launches, picnic areas, and hiking trails here, too, though no camping. If you use Highway 15 north of Montréal, you can be here in just twenty minutes. So you could stay in your Montréal lodgings and come for the day. The closest camping and RV facilities are at *Parc du Mont-Laval* (7675 blvd. Saint Martin Ouest, Sainte-Dorothée, Laval; www.parcmontlaval .ca; 450 689-1150; from $34).

beammeup, scotty!

Who knew *Star Trek's* Captain Kirk is a Montrealer? Born there in 1931, William Shatner was trained as a Shakespearian actor who performed at Ontario's Stratford Festival of Canada. He "became" Captain Kirk between 1966–69 and, from 1979–91 played Kirk in the first six *Star Trek* films. Never a Has Been (although that's the name of his 2004 album!), Shatner breeds American Saddlebred horses, is an author, musician—and always-controversial speaker who frequently appears on late-night talk-shows.

From Thousand Islands Park, head west on Boulevard Sainte Rose until you reach the junction with Route 148. Turn right (north) and cross the Rivière des Mille Îles on the Pont Arthur Sauvé to *Saint Eustache.* During the last days of the 1837 rebellion, hotly pursued by the British, the patriots fled to *L'Église du Saint Eustache* church, where bullet holes are still visible in the walls. In late August you can catch the beginning of the Descente des Mille Îles—a 20-kilometer descent of the river by canoes, including rabaskas, which ends in Parc des Milles-Îles.

Now we'll press on toward Oka via a diversion to a winery and orchard area. Turn left onto Highway 640 at St. Eustache. Watch for exit 2 north (nord), and turn off here. Your destination, *La Roche des Brises,* is on this exit road—rue Principale. Drive north approximately 15 kilometers through the pretty village of *St.-Joseph-du-Lac,* where apple orchards throng the charming protected village.

At 2006 rue Principale find *La Roche des Brises,* a gold award–winning winery (*vignoble*), where their Mariebriand wine (named for the proprietors' children, Marie and Brian) is sold. Stretch your legs and take in the gorgeous views by taking the guided tour (reservations are necessary) of the vineyard where more than 45,000 vines soak up the sunshine. Finish by enjoying a wine-tasting (2007 rue Principale, 450-472-2722). Dine at the on-site *Restaurant La Roche des Brises* (2006 rue Principale, St.-Joseph-du-Lac; 450-472-3477; www.rochedesbrises.com).

sainterose

The *vielle village* (old village) was founded in 1740 and by the 1860s it had become a tourist Mecca for wealthy Montrealers.

This gentle valley is well known for its orchards, and everywhere there are *vergers* (orchards) and *cidreries* (cidermakers). Choose from many superb places at which to visit, taste, and marvel.

Continue north from *La Roche des Brises* (whose romantic name means "Breezy Rock," by the way). Go north on Montée Robillard, then west (left) at Rang de la Fresnière to 10291 rang de la Fresnière to visit **Intermiel,** the world of bees (*miel* is "honey" in French). Get a free tour (English is spoken well here) and marvel at the sliding bee wall. Purchase—or at least sample—mead (honey wine), bee propolis, honey, and many other products created by busy bees that dwell here in more than 2,000 hives. Intermiel is open seven days a week, 9 a.m. to 6 p.m. (450-258-2713 or 800-265-6435; www.intermiel.com).

Now continue to **Oka,** home of wonderful cheese, as well as the site of a First Nations' reserve and the ferry embarkation point to Hudson, Québec. To get there, continue past Intermiel, west on Rang de la Fresnière to Point aux Anglais. Turn south (left) onto Highway 244 Sud (South) to Oka. Or return via rue Principale to exit 2 and drive west (turning right) on Highway 344 Ouest (West). This latter option allows you to see (and perhaps stretch your legs, bike, picnic, or camp at) **Parc d'Oka** (Recreational services du Parc d'Oka, 2020 chemin Oka; www.sepaq.com/pq/oka/; 450-479-8365). You could spend several nights camping here. There are more than 800 camping spots, many miles of walking trails, an observation tower, picnic grounds, sandy beaches, and lovely paved cycling trails. You can ask for reductions in the normal fees if you are camping Mon through Thurs, excluding Saint-Jean-Baptiste Day (June 24) and Canada Day (July 1).

As you swing north beyond Oka, the countryside that hugs the Outaouais (Ottawa) River is incredibly pastoral. You'll pass lots of tiny little huts parked on the river's edge. These are ice-fishing huts, and in winter they will look jaunty, dotting the surface of the river while fishermen sit inside, hunched over the hole cut in the river and warmed by a little stove.

Now we enter Argenteuil County, a 1682 *seigneury* (estate) named for a region of France. It is also a good spot to see the evolution of the Canadian seigneurial (or feudal lord) system. Look toward the river to see some homes on the water's edge. These are at the sites of the original houses. At first, seigneurial lots were wider and extended far back from the riverbank, as long swaths of fifty to one hundred acres. However, as the children of the original settlers came along, land was severed to increasingly thin strips extending inland. It was important for houses to hug the riverfront, as waterways provided the only means of transportation. Then, as roads were cut parallel to the river, houses "migrated" to border them, for roads superseded river travel in the mid- to late 1800s.

Soon you arrive at *Saint André Est,* the site of Canada's first paper mill (1804) and birthplace of Canada's third—and first Canadian-born—prime minister, Sir John Joseph Abbott. He wasn't exactly enthusiastic about becoming prime minister, ruefully commenting that he was a likely candidate "because I am not particularly obnoxious to anybody."

Continue along Highway 344 for a few kilometers to the solid-looking Georgian-style stone building, now the *Musée régional d'Argenteuil* (44 rte. de Long Sault, St-André-d'Argenteuil; www.museearg.com; 450-537-3861). The museum is located in the historic village of *Carillon,* where the old portage around the Carillon Rapids on the Ottawa River began. The Carillon area was but one small stretch of a mighty series of rapids on the Ottawa called *Long Sault Rapids.* In order for boats carrying settlers and goods to bypass them—the last great stretch of rapids between Ottawa and Montréal—a canal and locks were built. Between 1816 and 1843, the 22-kilometer Carillon-to-Grenville Canal was constructed, led by Captain Henry du Vernet, civil engineer of the British Royal Staff Corps. Around 1834 he designed the barracks—which are today's museum.

The barracks played their role in the Rebellion of Lower Canada in 1837. A total of 126 women and children were

nativeblockade

In the hot summer of 1990, members of the Mohawk community at Oka staged a seventy-seven-day blockade of the highway after the Oka Golf Club tried to expand its grounds. In so doing, it infringed on an ancient burial ground. What was perceived as an out-and-out affront to native rights and territory sparked a heated, lengthy standoff.

Eventually the provincial government called in the federal government and Canadian armed forces. The Oka standoff remains a reminder that strong passions can be easily inflamed by insensitivity.

sheltered from the attacks of the patriots here. It is now owned and operated by Parks Canada. Because this is a federal government department, the extensive exhibits are bilingual. In the museum gift shop, there are many books that explain this region's rich history. There are also antiques for sale here: we purchased a rare "Canadiana" pressed-glass drinking vessel in the shop in 2006.

This not-to-be-missed museum contains not only fascinating reminders of military history and canal-building but also one of Québec's finest regional costume collections. Why? Bilingual, keen historian, curator, and museum guide Jean Claude de Guire told us that this part of Argenteuil was one of the first to be settled by Loyalists and, later, wealthy Scots, who helped construct the Carillon Canal. Irish, too, came here to work on the canal. After its completion, they lingered on, and their wealth permitted them to accumulate fashionable clothing, household items, and fine furniture, much of which was eventually donated to this museum.

Jean Claude also created an art room, where you'll discover paintings and sculptures owned by residents of the region. Find the statuettes by sculptor Lionel Fosbary, the artist who made the sculpture of Canada's first prime minister, Sir John A. Macdonald. (That sculpture is on Ottawa's Parliament Hill.) Ask him about the statue of Adam Dollard des Ormeaux. A particularly good time to visit this museum is during *Les journées de la Culture (Culture Days)* in Sept. Telephone for specific dates and times of this Québec-wide celebration of the arts.

After exploring the museum, don't miss touring Carillon, home to many particularly fine heritage residences. Also visit the most powerful generating station on the Ottawa River, the *Carillon Dam and Generating Station.* Hydro Québec gives free seventy-five minute tours here mid-May through Aug (800-365-5229; www.hydroquebec.com). In the park adjacent to the station is a monument to the 1660 Battle of Long Sault. Adam Dollard des Ormeaux and sixteen other Frenchmen died here, ambushed by Iroquois. Here, too, is a lock that allows 19-meter-long boats to navigate the Ottawa River.

An Outdoor Paradise

We'll now head into another exciting region. Start by backtracking to Saint André Est and follow Highway 327 north to *Lachute.* Since the early 1950s, the village has been renowned for its flea and antique markets—as well as a horse auction. Tuesday is the best day to take in the full-throttle sight of miles of booths, though the market is also open on Sundays (26 rue Principale, Lachute; Tuesday market open throughout the year from 8 a.m. to 6 p.m.; smaller market open Sunday from mid-Apr to mid-Sept; www.lachutefarmers market.com; 450-562-2939). There's an indoor antique mall and also a farmer's market on-site, too, as well as restaurants.

Ready for some exhilaration? Just beyond Lachute find *Nouveau Monde River Expeditions* (25 chemin Rourke, Grenville-sur-la-Rouge; 800-361-5033 or 819-242-2168; www.newworld.ca), and thrill to some whitewater rafting.

If you are short on time, consider turning east on Highway 158 to Saint-Jérôme and then north onto the broad autoroute that whisks Montréalers north to Mont Tremblant. However, a more interesting route north is on the lesser-used Highway 327. This gives an intriguing glimpse into history as you drive through towns reflecting early British settlement patterns: Brownsburg, Dales-ville, Pine Hill, Lakeview, Arundel—all the way north to *Saint-Jovite.* There's a good tourism center here (48 chemin Brébeuf, Mont Tremblant; 819-425-3300), with brochures and seasonal information on *Parc du Mont-Tremblant,* our destination.

If you're up for a taste of luxury, venture north from Saint-Jovite to *Mont Tremblant Village.* Although this development is undeniably (and extremely) commercial, you may want to drop in just to say you've seen it or to take advantage of its world-class resort facilities.

The village is home to fabulous hotels like Fairmont's *Château Mont Tremblant* (3045 chemin de la Chapelle, Mont Tremblant; 866-540-4415 or 819-681-7000; www.fairmont.com/tremblant/). A four-star hotel right on the mountain, its interior decor features Québécois folk legends, some of which you'll recognize from the microbrewery beer labels you've looked at while downing a brew. Even if you don't stay here, step inside the foyer to both see and read these legends. Hungry? Fairmont presents its signature buffet here, featuring regional specialties. Just ensure you're hungry because the bounty is scrumptious: everything is beautifully displayed and delicious.

You can also rent a fully equipped apartment in one of the mountain condominiums from *Les Suites Tremblant* (866-253-0093; www.lessuitestremblant

North to James Bay

For something really off the beaten path, consider continuing from Saint-Jovite to the *James Bay hydroelectric power projects* on La Grande River, which flows into James Bay. This is about as far north as you can go by road in Québec and it's a long drive: 1,400 kilometers and twenty-two hours from Montréal. The road is paved all the way, although you should be prepared for rough patches and be on the alert for animals and trucks.

If you (and your vehicle) are up for the drive, continue on Highway 117 from Saint-Jovite for 250 kilometers through La Vérendrye Park to Lac Simon. Turn west on Highway 117 to Val-d'Or, then north on Highway 111 to Amos. From Amos, Highway 109 takes you north to Radisson. You can visit the immense Robert-Bourassa Dam, with its generating station carved 140 meters into the Canadian Shield rock. Farther west, you can also visit the La Grande-1 generating station at Chisasibi near where the La Grande River meets James Bay. (Free tours at 8 a.m. daily except Tues from mid-June through Aug, or on request. For information and reservations forty-eight hours ahead of time, call 800-291-8486; www.hydroquebec.com.)

.com). If you stay here, ask about any special add-ons like Jacuzzis. Mind you . . . ours didn't work, and we discovered it was because the owner who rented the unit turns it off. Fair enough, but don't be charged for a luxury item you cannot use even if you want to do so! Also, in summer, guests also have the use of a private beach at a nearby lake, but you may not be told about it (we were not, and only found out about it later). So ask what is included—and enjoy what you are paying for.

Mont Tremblant Village has lesser-known attractions to offer. If mountain biking is your thing, find out about the astonishing route that hurtles you down the mountain; it's not for the uninitiated. If backcountry skiing appeals, try the increasingly popular "glade skiing" routes on the back side of the mountain, where you glide through snow-clad evergreens (breathtaking!). If you just like great views, go up in the gondola to take in the spectacular topography of the region. Once you've gained the elevation, you don't need to descend immediately; there are excellent hiking trails—again, don't forget your binoculars. Of course, if you want to go downhill skiing, this is the place.

Prior to leaving Mont Tremblant, don't even think of missing **Le Scandinave,** the prettiest, most unique spa we've ever had the pleasure to visit (4280 Montée Ryan, Mont-Tremblant; 819-425-5524; www.scandinave.com).

A group of post-and-beam cedar buildings, some of which cascade down the embankment of *Rivière le Diable* (Devil River) and are elegantly connected by stone steps, introduces you to various stages of sheer indulgence. One building houses a Finnish sauna, another a Norwegian steam bath, while outdoor Jacuzzis and even pools of ice-cold water fed by waterfalls complete your hot-cold immersion program. We went in winter, and while we relaxed our ski muscles in the outside hot tub, curious white-tailed deer approached, peering at us through swirls of mist. Finally, the *pièce de résistance* is to jump into a small black hole, cut into the Diable River for your ultimate body shock! And, yes, we did it and in a word? Brrrisk: that was one chilly splash! Try it and, just like us, dash upstairs and jump back into the hot tub!

Continue on by returning to Saint-Jovite and heading southeast to **Saint-Faustin** on Highway 117. Now turn north to Lac Supérieur toward gorgeous, wild **Parc du Mont-Tremblant.** Lac Supérieur is a pretty little village. Watch carefully, and after 3 kilometers you'll see a left turn to Mont Tremblant Park. On your right after the turnoff is a picturesque fieldstone bed-and-breakfast, called **La Marie Champagne** (654 chemin Lac Supérieur; 819-688-3780; www.mariechampagne.ca). With its powder-blue tin roof, in traditional bell-shaped Québécois style, it makes a pretty show in the meadows.

After 20 kilometers you enter the gates to Parc du Mont-Tremblant. Now drive a loop that takes you through two of the southernmost sectors of the

Cycler's Paradise

The 200-kilometer bicycle route called *Le Petit Train du Nord* extends north from Saint-Jérôme through Mont Tremblant to Mont Laurier. Avid cyclists will simply not want to miss this wonderful route. If you do cycle along Le Petit Train, you'll arrive at enchanting little villages such as L'Annonciation (northwest of Mont Tremblant). We recommend you check out the old railway station, which is a Tourist Information Center and local art gallery. This town has several delightful restaurants along the main street, and locals say all the businesses are benefiting from the cyclists in summer and the snowmobilers in winter. We particularly liked the local cheeses and light lunch at *La Cigale* (157 rue Principale, L'Annonciation; 819-275-3731), where old photos of the town are hung on the walls.

park and out to Saint-Donat, a drive of less than 100 kilometers. As you go, you pass many hiking trails, waterfalls, and campgrounds. This park is a treasure. From remote lakes that offer superb wilderness canoeing to little walks just off the roadway, it offers tremendous natural beauty to every level of nature enthusiast. Keep your eyes peeled for wildlife. White-tailed deer are common, as are raccoons, beavers, muskrats, red squirrels, and porcupines. Bears are around but less visible.

In the *Sector de Diable (Devil's Sector),* there's a *sentier* (trail) called *Le sentier du Toit-des-Laurentides* (Roof of the Laurentians Trail), whose trailhead is at the bridge called *Pont de la Sablonnière,* a couple of kilometers inside the park gate. A 15-kilometer round-trip hike, it takes six to seven hours and reaches an elevation of 935 meters. It leads to Mont Tremblant and, get this, you can descend the mountain by the gondola lift and explore Mont Tremblant Village this way. If you attempt this, be sure to find out how to deploy your vehicle. You may be able to stay overnight at Mont Tremblant Village, take the gondola back up the mountain, and return to your car the following day. Investigate by calling the park office at 819-688-2281.

If that trail sounds like too much, drive on. At *Lac Monroe* there are lots of activities, including swimming, mountain biking, hiking, and boating. Lac Monroe also provides access for the disabled to swimming, and there is quite a selection of campsites, both serviced and not. For those of you who are driving on but want to quickly see some natural scenery, try the easy 800-meter walk to *Les Chutes du Diable (Devil's Waterfall).* Your reward comes as soon as you hear the rush of water, surely one of the most soothing sounds on earth.

None of the signs or park information pamphlets are in English, but everyone we spoke to was able to deal with our questions. All campsites should be reserved in summer's peak seasons in Parc du Mont-Tremblant (819-688-2281 from mid-May through mid-Oct for reservations).

Stay on the main road and before long the Saint-Donat park gates appear. This loop through the park took us one hour and twenty minutes, which included the walk to Les Chutes du Diable. The road now becomes Highway 125; in ten minutes you arrive at **Saint-Donat,** where flags from all over the world lined the street when we passed through. This prosperous-looking town is thriving thanks to recreational tourism. (For information on Saint-Donat's lodgings and attractions, check with the tourism office at 536 rue Principale; 888-783-6628; www.saint-donat.ca); it's also a good alternate number for information on Parc du Mont-Tremblant.) Traveling in winter? You can rent snowmobiles at **Sport and Marine M.V. Inc.** (1108 rue Principale; 819-424-3433). There is an amazing network of trails in the park.

At Saint-Donat, **Lac Archambault** (819-424-2833) has a wonderful sandy beach, which is great for kids. You can also take a boat tour with **Les Belles Croisières du lac Archambault** aboard the Evelyne (May through Oct; call the Manoir des Laurentides, 290 rue Principale; 819-424-1710).

Our destination now is **Saint-Côme.** We're heading east again, to avoid the main route south to Montréal. It is 14 kilometers to **Notre-Dame-de-la-Merci.** Here are beautiful glimpses of the **Ouareau Forest** and a suspension bridge over the river that you can explore (for information call 819-424-1865).

Pass Highway 329 Sud to Montréal and, after approximately ten minutes, watch for the church at Notre-Dame-de-la-Merci. Turn left; it is then 28 kilometers to Saint-Côme. After about 8 kilometers watch for a signed right-hand turn to Saint-Côme. Almost immediately there's a sheer rock

Montréal's Indie Bibliophelia

You know what we mean: independent bookshops vie for their lives beside megachains. Hooray for Montrealers who not only love their books but also love to support independent thinking—and bookstores. Go to cash-only **The Word Bookstore** which 'features' a rotary phone behind the desk—so no, you won't be surprised there's no Web site! (469 rue Milton; 514-845-5640). Are you a polyglot (linguist)? Head to **Librairie Michel Fortin** which not only sells books but also games, CDs, DVDs covering the 240 or so world languages (3714 rue St. Denis; 514-849-5719; librairie michelfortin.com). Join literary talks, find good selection of Québec authors at **Olivieri Librairie-Bistro**—and yes, after shopping or chatting after the lecture, nosh at the on-site bistro (5219 Cote-des-Neiges; 514-739-3639; www.librairieolivieri.com).

cliff on your left. Take care on this winding road. Although spectacularly picturesque, it has soft shoulders and goes from paved to gravel surface a few times. Drive on, past the turnoff to Parc Chute à Bull, toward *Sainte-Émelie-de-l'Énergie.*

At the *Town Hall* (241 rue Coutu, Sainte-Émelie-de-l'Énergie; 450-886-3823), you'll find a rare collection of old photographs on the history of the village, which was nearly destroyed by fire in 1924. Note the surnames: although many are French, other nationalities are represented through names like Bernhardt and Johnson. Nearby, opposite the park, find the blushing hot-pink *Auberge d'Emilie,* (331, rue Principale, Sainte-Émélie-de-l'Énergie; 450 886-3311; www.emelie.qc.ca). This is an inn, spa and restaurant. It has six suites, plus what they call a *gîte familial*, with its own kitchen and dining area. Whether or not you're a couple or a family, such separate accommodations can make a welcome alternative to camping or hotel rooms.

Want to go on a hike leading to seven spectacular waterfalls? Head north on Highway 131 (also called *Route des Sept-Chutes*—Seven Waterfall's Route) towards Saint-Michel-des-Saints. Turn right at Rang 4 (Rural Route 4) where you'll find a parking lot. Along the *Matawinie Trail* (explore www.matawinie.org) you can hike to view seven waterfalls that cascade into the watershed of the *Rivière Noire* (Black River). Let the trails, lakes, and waterfalls draw you into simply spectacular nature here. One *chute* (falls), *Voile de la Mariée* (Bridal Veil Falls) is 60 metres high—and simply stunning. You can pick and choose from several *sentiers* (trails). *Sentier Mont Barrière*, for instance, introduces you to several different ecosystems as you climb 150 metres, where you overlook the village you just visited, Sainte-Émélie-de-l'Énergie, as well as Lac Rémi.

Joliette is one of Montréal's "playground" destinations northeast of the metropolis. But there are some notable aspects to this town. First of all, during winter, you can skate for more than 4 kilometers on the Assomption River.

joliette

Joliette is one of Montréal's "playground" destinations northeast of the metropolis. But there are some notable aspects to this town. First of all, during winter, you can skate for more than 4 kilometers on the Assomption River. Joliette is well known for its early-July through early-August classical music festival called *Festival International de Lanaudière* (1500 blvd. Base-de-Roc, Joliette; 450-759-7636; www.lanaudiere.org). Also of special note is the *Musée d'art de Joliette,* which houses a superb collection of Québec art (145 rue du Père Wilfrid-Corbeil, Joliette; 450-756-0311; www.musee joliette.org; open in summer Tues through Sun noon to 5 p.m.; $8 adults, $6 seniors, $5 students, $4 children six to twelve).

Joliette is well known for its early-July through early-Aug classical music festival called **_Festival International de Lanaudière_** (1500 blvd. Base).

Accommodations are pretty easy to find around here but beware: because it is so close to Montréal, places fill up for events, so book ahead. **_L'Auberge du Vieux-Moulin_** (www.auberge-lanaudiere.com) is a country inn on the banks of the Rivière Noire. Not only does it have rooms and cottages, but also, two tipis, as well as a spa where you can book a soothing massage after hiking (or camping . . .). Chef Yves Marcoux is also the owner—his wife also works here so this auberge represents a family's dream.

astronaut!

Montréal-born Julie Payette is a Canadian Space Agency astronaut—the second female in the country's team (Roberta Bondar is the other). During Payette's most recent mission in 2009, she brought _Montréal Canadien's_ hockey hero Maurice "Rocket" Richard's autographed hockey sweater into space . . . successfully launching the Rocket during "the Habs'" 100th anniversary!

Return to Sainte-Émelie-de-l'Énergie and follow Highway 131 (Sud) South for 16 kilometers to **_Saint-Jean-de-Matha._** This is the hometown of Louis Cyr, known as the world's strongest man. His life and times are honored at the **_Musée-halte Louis Cyr_** (185 rue Laurent; 450-886-1666), directly behind the town hall. There's parking here as well as a tiny, beautiful garden complete with a gazebo where you can sit and admire the statue commemorating the competitive Cyr.

Go on to **_Rawdon._** Continue south on Highway 131 for Highway 348 toward Sainte-Mélanie, where you'll drive through a broad, open valley. The long, low, gray barn-like sheds are on poultry farms—this region is known for its turkeys. Past Sainte-Mélanie you'll note how the topography has dramatically altered, from the rugged Mont Tremblant Park to undulating farmland—until the land soon becomes almost flat: this is one of Québec's great agricultural regions. Lush pastures of prosperous dairy farms complete with lovely old farmhouses—some with Second Empire–style Mansard roofs—and tidy flower and vegetable gardens now predominate.

At time of writing this fifth edition, our favorite B&B was changing management and being altered (**_Le Gîte du Catalpa;_** 3730 rue Queen; 450-834-5253)—so although we recommend you check it out, we unfortunately cannot vouch for it right now. The catalpa tree (also called "tree of heaven") for which the B&B is named is covered with beautiful white and pink blossoms resembling horse-chestnut flowers, in mid-June.

Rawdon is intriguing because of its multi-racial mix. It was settled by the English in the early 1800s—along with French, Irish and Scots—and until the mid-1900s the village was primarily English-speaking. In the 1930s, Germans arrived and post-WWII, Russians, Polish, Hungarians and Czechoslovakians moved here. Instead of seeing only the predictably immense Roman Catholic church, there are also Anglican, United, and other denomination churches here.

Another unusual aspect to Rawdon is it's the site of the *Festival Country de Rawdon,* held annually on the last weekend of July (www.festivalcountry.com/rawdon/). If you enjoy down-home country music, put it on your itinerary.

Before leaving town, visit newly updated *Parc des Chutes Dorwin (Dorwin Falls Park)* (off Route 337; 450-834-2596; www.rawdon.ca; $5 adults, $3 youth, children free for access to the falls, beach and park; May through Oct open daily 9 a.m. to 7 p.m.). The rivière Ouareau descends through a chasm here, and the falls take their name from the family who owned the property. However, they could have been called *Chutes de Sorcerer Nipissingue.*

Why? A legend spins a story about an Algonquin First Nations sorcerer who fell in love with a maiden, Hiawhitha. She became a Christian and, as daughter of the chief, she was able to choose her husband. No surprise as such legends go: she didn't want Nipissingue and instead chose the noble Arondack as her partner. Fast forward through the predictable tale of woe: her husband was almost killed in a war staged by the vengeful Nipissingue. While healing Arondack's injuries, Hiawhitha went to a cliff to gather wild sarsaparilla, a

Strongest Man in the World

Imagine the scene on Dec 10, 1881: More than 10,000 spectators gasped in awe as strongman Louis Cyr dramatically held back a team of four straining workhorses with his bare hands. The stunning feat was only one of many, for he was truly a legend in his own time. A farm boy from Saint-Cyprien, Québec, Louis' strength enabled him to push a railway engine up an incline, lift a platform holding eighteen men whose combined weight was 4,300 pounds, and lift 588 pounds off the ground with one finger. Cyr impressed the world. Before his death at forty-nine in 1912, he thrilled spectators throughout the United States, England, and Europe, earning his title the "Canadian Samson."

medicinal herb. Meanwhile, Nippissingue spied her and, in a fit of rage, pushed her over the edge—whereupon her white robes created the frothy waterfall we see today.

To forever torment Nippissingue, the Great God Manitou turned the sorcerer into stone and when you ascend Dorwin Falls to a lookout, you'll spy the sorcerer's face, gazing upon the falls' beauty. (Unbelievably, our guide here told us that sometimes locals actually jump for sport from these cliffs, into the boiling waters. *Please don't try this!*) Instead, enjoy the site's 2.5 kilometers of trails that are part of a 35 hectare ecological reserve, home to thirty or so woodland species of trees and plants.

For an unforgettable dining experience, go to **Au Parfum de la Nature** (6703 chemin Pontbriand; www.parfumnature.qc.ca; 450-834-4547 or 877-834-4547; open Tues through Fri 5:30 to 10:30 p.m., Sat and Sun 11 a.m. to 10 p.m. by reservation for groups of four to thirty persons; closed Mon). This is an intimate concept, where you actually have your meal in chef Bruno Gagné's home, set in a wooded glade. You must book ahead at least two weeks in advance for large groups; a "few" days for two to four people. Bruno will discuss the menu with you—he features local produce and

lowercanadais today'squébec

Canada's Constitution Act of 1791 established Lower Canada (now Québec) and Upper Canada (Ontario). Québec City was the capital of Lower Canada and is now capital of the province.

game such as bison, pheasant, and guinea hen—and he buys the ingredients from the local farmers' market. He doesn't have a liquor license, but as in many other Québec restaurants, you can *apportez votre vin*—bring your own wine. Consult with Bruno to see what he would recommend, and ask about our Québec wines.

Now drive toward Montréal on Highway 337 Sud. You pass many flea markets and market gardens en route through this flat, agriculturally rich countryside. The road becomes Autoroute 25. Pass the exit to Mascouche and watch now for exit 22 east for **Terrebonne.** Terrebonne is a cultural center on **L'Île des Moulins (Island of Mills).** It is a "village," or collection of nineteenth-century buildings, such as the 1846 flour mill, 1850 seigneurial office, and an 1803 bakery. Wander its streets, and relive pre-industrial French Canadian life (for information call 450-471-0619; www.ile-des-moulins.qc.ca).

Return to Highway 25 Sud and scoot back to Montréal.

Places to Stay in Montréal

McGill University
550 Sherbrooke Ouest,
West Tower, Suite 490,
H3A 1B9;
(514) 398-5200
www.mcgill.ca/residences/
summer
Residence rooms can be
rented; some have great
views over Mont Royal and
have kitchenettes, refrigera-
tors, etc.

Hôtel Auberge
Universel Montréal
5000 Sherbrooke Est,
H1V 1A1;
(800) 567-0223 or
(514) 253-3365
www.auberge-universel
.com
Near Olympic Stadium at
Viau Métro, cinemas, and
malls (good for kids!).

Montréal Oasis B&B
3000 chemin de Breslay,
H3Y 2G7;
(514) 935-2312
www.bbcanada.com/694
.html

Mont Tremblant Village
1000 chemin de Voyageurs
Mont-Tremblant,
J8E 1T1;
(888) 738-1777
www.tremblant.ca
Arrange unusual but
fabulous accommodations,
such as a condo on the
mountainside.

Le Petit Prince
1384 Overdale,
H3G 1V3;
(514) 938-2277
www.montrealbandb.com
1876 house in the heart of
downtown at Lucien-L'Allier
metro station, Wi-Fi and
decorated with local artists'
works.

Hôtel Gault
449 rue Sainte-Hélène,
Old Montréal;
(514) 904-1616 or
(866) 904-1616
www.hotelgault.com
An old bank converted
to a very trendy boutique
hotel. Fantastic staff; highly
unusual bedroom decor;
art and architecture library
in foyer; superb breakfast
(included in price of room)
or fresh baked goods, fruit,
and hot food. Stay here!

Le Centre Sharaton
Montréal Hotel
1201 Blvd Rene-Levesque
Ouest (West)
H0B 2L7;
(514) 878-2000
www.starwoodhotels.com
Why is the Sheraton off-
the-beaten-path? Ask
them about their popular
literary event called "Books
and Breakfast," a reading
series. Who knows? You
may hear Canadian writers
such as Jane Urquhart or
Margaret Atwood read from
their latest works while you
enjoy your breakfast.

OUTSIDE MONTRÉAL

Les Menus-Plaisirs, Restaurant-Auberge
244 blvd. Sainte-Rose
Sainte-Rose, Laval,
Québec;
(450) 625-0976
www.lesmenusplaisirs.ca
Why not choose to dine
at this comfortable inn?
This restaurant/auberge
is a delicious spot and as
bonus, it is also part of
the "Passeport des chefs"
(Passport of Chefs). This
allows you to partake of
a "gastronomic rally" here
and in four other restau-
rants in Old Sainte-Rose
Village (see Web site and
contact to organize).

Places to Eat in Montréal

Schwartz' Montréal Hebrow Delicatessen
3895 blvd. Saint-Laurent;
(514) 842-4813
Serves absolutely the best
smoked meat. You don't
go for the decor; you do go
for excellent food.

The Main
3864 blvd. Saint Laurent;
(514) 843-8126
The meat is marinated and
smoked on the premises.

Titanic
445 rue Saint-Pierre
Old Montréal;
(514) 849-0894
www.titanic-mtl.ca
Open five days a week,
8 a.m. to 430 p.m. Mon
through Fri. A popular little
"underground" bistro.

Want to wine, dine, and
dance at what is arguably
this city's most famous dining room? The internationally renowned
Beaver Club
900 blvd. René-Lévesque
Ouest, located in the
Queen Elizabeth Hotel,
(514) 861-3511,
will set you back big bucks,
but your meal will be unforgettable. On Sat evening
there is live music and
dancing.

Want something a tad
more affordable in a lively
bistro setting?
L'Express
3927 rue Saint-Denis;
(514) 845-5333
We enjoyed a café au lait
and crème brûlée. Mmm.

Binerie Mont-Royal
367 ave. Mont-Royal Est;
(514) 285-9078
serves *fèves au lard* (baked
beans), otherwise called
"binnes."

Chez Clo
3199 rue Ontario Est;
(514) 522-5348
daily 6 a.m. to 3 p.m.
is a typical Montréal
neighborhood restaurant
with loyal local clientele;

inexpensive and large servings; try the *tourtière,* a
ground meat specialty.

Globe
3455 blvd. Saint Laurent;
(514) 284-3823
www.restaurantglobe.com
Simply outstanding fare in
a trendy restaurant—try the
lamb salad!

For an inexpensive Greek
meal, try the delicious
chicken souvlakis at
Arahova
just east of avenue du Parc.
256 Saint-Viateur Ouest,
(514) 274-7828
www.arahova.com.

Montréal is famous for its
bagels, so you mustn't
miss heading to
Wilensky's
4 Fairmount Ouest at St.
Urbain;
(514) 271-0247
The eight-or-so-seat "soda"
counter harks from the
1930s. Honest. Go, eat, be
merry.

To satisfy your craving for
America's favorite dog,
head to the
Montréal Pool Room
1200 Saint-Laurent (south
of rue Sainte-Catherine),
(514) 396-0460
where you have to stand
to eat.

Pied du Cochon
536 rue Duluth Est;
(514) 281-1114
www.restaurantaupied
decochon.ca
is simply packed and
no wonder—downright

fabulous food featuring
many kinds of "heart-attack
waiting-to-happen" poutine
as the Québécois say! Very
loud. Very friendly. A Montréal experience: go!

OUTSIDE MONTRÉAL

Le Saint-Augin
15196 rue de Saint-Augin
Saint Augin (Mirabel)
J7N 1X2;
(450) 475-8290
A fabulously cozy res-
taurant in a frame house
on the main street of this
village northwest of Saint-
Joseph-du-Lac. Do not
miss this most superb
establishment with its fresh
regional cuisine served by
informed, welcoming staff.

Masala Mantram
3424, boul Cartier Ouest
(corner Chomedey),
Laval, Québec
H7V 1K2;
(450) 688-6866
This independent family
restaurant serves authen-
tic (read: excellent) Indian
food: try the baltis, butter
chicken.

THE EASTERN TOWNSHIPS →

The **Eastern Townships** lie south of the St. Lawrence River between Montréal and Québec City. We'll explore this region using Montréal as the starting point, heading east through a historic area of Québec known as Montérégie before plunging into the environs known as L'Éstrie, or the Eastern Townships.

The Richelieu River flows north from Lake Champlain through the heart of Montérégie. This was a historic water route, its strategic importance underscored by a series of forts such as Fort Chambly, built by the French in 1665 to protect the city of Montréal from their fierce enemies, the Iroquois. Farther south, star-shaped Fort Lennox was originally French; it, too, fell to the British and, briefly, to the Americans.

This region strongly reflects the passions of patriotism throughout the centuries. After the Americans declared independence in 1776, hundreds of immigrants streamed north to settle in a country still governed by Britain. These were the United Empire Loyalists, and during your explorations of this area, you'll see many houses and buildings reflecting colonial American architecture. As we drive some of the scenic back roads, we'll hug the American border south and east of Frelighsburg.

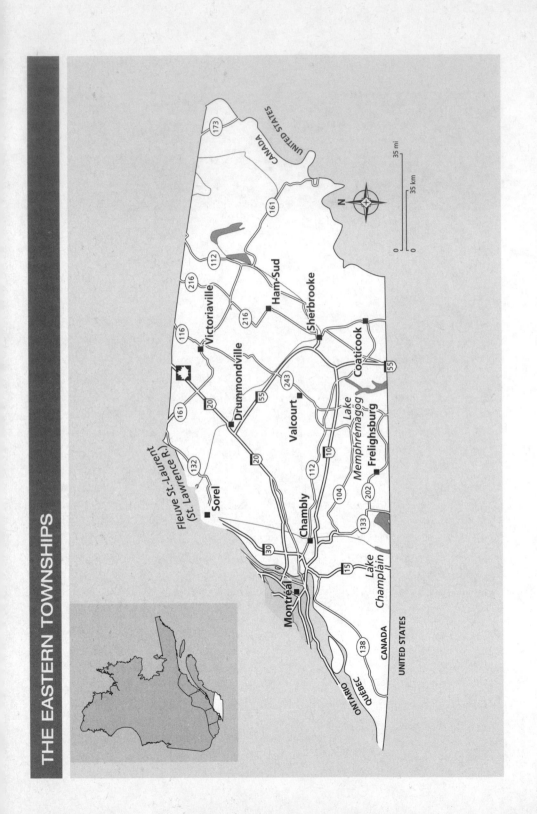

THE EASTERN TOWNSHIPS

In the 1800s another influx of immigrants came to the New Land. After Northern Ireland became part of the United Kingdom, many Irish families crossed the Atlantic to settle here. Twenty years later, another Irish "invasion" occurred—but this time the potato famine spurred their departure from home.

In 1837 French patriotism flared in rebellion against British rule. The *Maison nationale des patriotes (Museum of the Patriots)* in Saint-Denis honors the memory of French Canadian freedom fighters.

Incidentally, Saint-Denis is the only place where the patriots enjoyed victory in battle. They were routed in another Eastern Townships village named Saint-Charles-sur-Richelieu. As you explore the Richelieu Valley in particular, you tread in the footsteps of rebellion!

abenakilegacy ofnames

Québec's Eastern Townships were the home of First Nations' called **Abenakis,** who allied themselves with the French during the time of European contact and trade. Thanks to the Abenaki, whose ancestral homes lay in present-day New England, you'll discover names such as Megantic, Coaticook, Missisquoi, and Lakes Memphremagog and Magog.

By the 1860s many French Canadians lived in this region because so many of them worked in the lumber, agricultural, and railway industries. As the demographics shifted, with a greater proportion of French-speaking inhabitants toward the end of the nineteenth century, the region started to become known as L'Éstrie, or the *Cantons-de-l'Est,* the Eastern Townships.

Traveling through this region today is delightful. An increasingly easy rapport between national and ethnic mixes is discernible here. People of

AUTHORS' FAVORITES IN THE EASTERN TOWNSHIPS

Abbey Saint-Benoît-du-lac

Capelton Mine in North Hatley

Cidrerie du Verger Gaston

Cidrerie artisanale Michel Jodoin

Fort Chambly

Fort Lennox

J. Armand Bombardier Museum in Valcourt

Mansonville Museum

Missisquoi Museum in Stanbridge East

Parc de la Gorge de Coaticook

American, French, and British ancestry rub shoulders amicably. And as you discover the pastoral beauty of this area, it is easy to understand why settlers would flock here, for this is a rich agricultural land. Orchards full of blossoms that turn to crisp, tangy apples in fall, ripe for the picking, will surely beckon you. Grand, historic lakes and rivers offer themselves for recreation.

In *Montérégie* strange cone-like "mountains" erupt from the otherwise flat valley floor. These mountains are Cretaceous igneous plugs that forced their way into fissures in the limestone that forms the valley floor. When the softer sedimentary limestone eroded, the harder igneous rock remained exposed. At 416 meters, Mont-Saint-Hilaire is the highest of these remarkable formations. Once part of the Gault Estate, a large part of it was designated as a bird sanctuary in 1952 and six years later was bequeathed to McGill University of Montréal (less than an hour away). In 1978 it became an international biosphere reserve. Montérégie Tourism can be reached at 2001 boul. De Rome, Brossard, J4W 3K5; (866) 469-0069 or (450) 466-4666; www.tourisme-montergie.qc.ca.

As you can see, it's a diverse region, so let's not waste any more time. We'll start out from Montréal right now.

The Richelieu River Environs

In Montréal get on Highway 20 Est and drive to *Mont-Saint-Hilaire,* about 24 kilometers, then turn south on Highway 133 toward Otterburn Park. This area is known as the Montérégie region of Québec.

Whether it is winter or summer, *Centre de conservation de la nature du Mont Saint Hilaire (Nature Conservation Center)* beckons with a network of 24 kilometers of hiking or skiing trails on this, the first UNESCO Biosphere Reserve in Canada, created in 1978. The mountain offers outstanding examples of the vegetation that once covered 90 percent of western Québec but which is now reduced to 17 percent. Biologists have recorded 187 species of birds nesting in the mixed deciduous/coniferous woods, so bring along your binoculars. (The center is at 422 chemin des Moulins, Mont-Saint-Hilaire; 450-467-1755; www.centrenature.qc.ca; $5 adults, $4 seniors, $2 children six to seventeen; open year-round from 8 a.m. until an hour before sundown.)

Proceed now down the Chemin des Patriotes on the east side of the Richelieu River. We're going to satisfy our passion for sensational Belgian chocolate now. Are you with us? Once in *Otterburn Park,* turn left on Rue Prince Albert, then left again to find *La Cabosse d'Or Chocolaterie* (973 chemin Ozias Leduc, Otterburn Park J3G 4S6; 450-464-6937; www.lacabossedor .com). Before indulging, try the mini-golf course celebrating and explaining the history of chocolate. The Belgian proprietor of this chocolaterie, Martine

Crowin, told us that four times a year she imports five-ton blocks of Belgian chocolate. We can tell you that the chocolate milkshakes are richly and darkly outstanding.

From here proceed north along Chemin Ozias Leduc (named for one of Québec's famous artists, 1864–1955) and turn right onto Chemin de la Montagne, which hugs the base of the mountain. We're en route to **Cidrerie du Verger Gaston** (1074 chemin de la Montagne, Mont-Sainte-Hilare; 450-464-3455; www.vergergaston.ca). With claims of being a working certified organic orchard and cider-making operation, products here are both fresh-tasting and delicious. Tip: By May 23 the orchards are usually in blossom, making this a fabulous, fragrant destination for biking in particular.

This establishment has an excellent apple and cider interpretation centre, where you can see old-time as well as modern tools, as well as techniques explained. Don't leave without tasting the cider. There's sparkling juice; a dry, light cider that is 7.4 percent alcohol; and also a *pommeau,* which is a sweeter, heavier aperitif with 17 percent alcohol content. Buy now and drink later, after you've finished driving. Try some of the other delicious apple products, too. We loved the cider mustard, the apple syrup (divine on pancakes), and apple jelly.

Now that you're full of chocolate and apple delights, continue along the Chemin de la Montagne. You now enter the Rougemont area, noted for its apple orchards. In 1913 the co-op started, and by 1926 there were twenty-seven orchards here. Today this region of Québec is known as the province's main apple-producing area: 50 percent of annual apple production and 55 percent of the producers are here. You'll note that many, like the Cidrerie du Verger Gaston, are organic. Others, termed *écologique,* do use some chemicals. We traveled these roads in June, when we could just see baby apples starting to plump up. We can only imagine the sight and fragrance here in this gentle valley when trees are blossoming. It's hard to say whether a trip would be best in spring or during autumn's harvest.

daytripupthe richelieuriver

Explore the northern section of the Richelieu River to where it joins the St. Lawrence at Sorel by following Highways 133 and 233 along its banks. Be sure to stop at *Maison nationale des patriotes* in Saint-Denis (610 chemin des Patriotes; 450-787-3623; www.mndp.qc .ca). This village is the site of the only victory enjoyed by the patriots in the Rebellion of 1837. It is a place of pilgrimage for those who want to learn about the nationalist movement in Québec. Closed Mon; check the Web site for variable hours (and note that November is Patriot Month).

You'll turn right briefly on Highway 227 and then make almost an immediate left onto Rue Rougemont. The terrible ice storm of January 1998 was extremely severe here, leaving people without electricity for five to six weeks. You can imagine how devastating 6 inches of ice buildup on the trees was. All around as we drove here even several years later, the shattered remains of once-lovely forests and ornamental trees were a sad sight. Because they are pruned to be weight-bearing, many of the orchards were relatively unscathed, however.

Continue to *Rougemont,* named after Sir Étienne Rougemont, who left La Rochelle in France in 1665 on the ship *Justice* to fight the Iroquois here. As you enter this village, you will note many signs of the English, Irish, and Scottish settlers. As in Otterburn Park, many of the street names are English, and St. Thomas Anglican Church dates back to 1840.

Find the tourist information center (Tourisme Montérégie; 11 chemin Marieville; 866-969-2309). Helpful staff here had trouble with English but, with

Ice Apple Wine?

Although you may be familiar with award-winning ice wine made from grapes, have you heard of ice apple wine or ice cider *(cidre, en français)*? We prefer it to the ice wine made from grapes, because the apples give this dessert wine a delightful hint of tartness. Here in Québec's Richelieu Valley, the climate offers perfect conditions for growing apples—and for keeping them on the tree until well after the first frosts. Pickers come and pick the frozen apples, which are then crushed, the golden juice captured, fermented, et *voilà*, bottled and sold.

In winter of 2004 we sampled ice apple wine products from two cidreries that we strongly recommend you visit. *Clos Saint-Denis* is located on the Chemin des Patriotes, and the president and owner Guy Tardif lives in a French Canadian style heritage home built in the early 1700s directly across from the orchard (Clos Saint-Denis, 1150 chemin des Patriotes, Saint-Denis-sur-Richelieu; 450-787-3766; www .clos-saint-denis.qc.ca). Open all year for visits, tastings and on-site purchases, but call to make a reservation between mid-Oct and mid-Apr.

The second cidrerie we visited was *La Face Cachée de la Pomme* ("the hidden face of apples") located south of Montréal, in Hemmingford, Québec. Billed as "a taste of Québec's winter . . . and warmth," one of this cidrerie's delicious ice apple wines is appropriately called *Neige* (snow), the other is *Frimas*. Both are worthy of your interest. François Pouliot, the extremely engaging proprietor, informed us that ice cider is "a creation unique to the soil of Québec." Visit La Face Cachée de la Pomme at 617 Rte. 202, Hemmingford; www.appleicewine.com, (450) 247-2899.

We highly recommend you visit these cidreries, chat with the hospitable proprietors, and book a tour and tasting. Remember if you are driving, at 11 percent alcohol, the wine is potent!

persistence and goodwill, lots of information was obtained. Ask for pamphlets in English, including the *Richelieu Valley Tourist Guide*. Cider is not the only product grown and produced here in the Richelieu Valley: the staff will be happy to give you details about the 132-kilometer *route des vins* (wine route), too. In fact, there are thirty wineries to visit in the Montérégie and Eastern Townships regions. Discover them all by visiting the Web site (with map) at www.vignerons-du-quebec.com.

Outside the center is a small **demonstration orchard** with a walking circuit where old varieties of apples are being grown. Apples were first brought to Québec in 1617 by Louis Hébert, and the first orchards of any size were managed by monks on Mont Royal in 1650. Some of the old apple varieties are delightful. See if you can find Honey Gold, Lubsk Queen (from Russia), and the Ladi, or Lady, named because its taste was supposedly "just as lovely as the kiss of a beautiful woman."

For something completely different, turn left onto Chemin Petite Caroline to find the *atelier,* or studio, of the intriguing artist **Claude Gagnon** (245 chemin Petite Caroline, Rougemont; 450-469-1148; www.laclaude.com). Her studio is unmistakable: it's the only brilliant purple barn you'll find on the road. Step inside to discover this amazing woman's allegories, peopled by characters she knows and themes that are universal, such as war and love. This atelier must not be missed. Claude herself will probably be there and is delightfully chatty. Her self-portrait hangs on the central chimney, dressed for renovation work and clutching a chain saw.

As an interesting contrast to Cidrerie du Verger Gaston described earlier, continue along Chemin Petite Caroline to **Cidrerie artisanale Michel Jodoin** (1130 Petite Caroline, Rougemont; 450-469-2676; www.cidrerie-michel-jodoin .qc.ca), where the cider is aged in the old style, in oak casks. We enjoyed a superb tour of the welcoming coolness of the aging cave before sampling the delicious ciders.

Then proceed on this road, doing an abrupt turn at its end to return to Route 112 on Chemin Grande Caroline. For yet another apple product—albeit less appealing to taste—we recommend a stop at **Verger Pierre Gingras,** which makes cider vinegar (1132 Grande Caroline, Rougemont; 450-469-4954; www.cidervinegar.com).

Press on to **Chambly.** To get to this gorgeous historic town, head west on Highway 112 through Marieville and Richelieu. Cross the bridge at the opening of the river to the Bassin de Chambly (Chambly Basin), which forms a picturesque lake.

Our destination is **Fort Chambly** (2 rue de Richelieu, Chambly; 450-658-1585; www.pc.gc.ca/fortchambly; open daily from 10 a.m. mid-May through

TOP ANNUAL EVENTS IN THE EASTERN TOWNSHIPS

FEBRUARY

Grand Prix Ski-doo of Valcourt
(450) 532-3443
www.grandprixvalcourt.com
is three days of vigorous international snowmobile competitions "with best drivers in the world" plus rock concerts. Largest snowmobile festival in Canada.

MAY

Festival des harmonies du Québec
in Sherbrooke; hosts thousands of Canadian musicians of all ages. Contests, training courses, many shows (819) 823-7229
www.festivaldesharmonies.com

La Fête de chocolate de Bromont (Chocolate Festival)
for chocoholics! Sculptures, music from countries where cocoa is produced, international gastronomics. Yum!
(450) 534-4078
www.chocolat.ca.tc

JUNE

The Warwick Cheese Festival
is where you can sample fabulous cheeses *fait au Québec!* Cheese-makers from Les Îles-de la-Madeleine through to the center of the province tempt you. Many culinary—and sports—events (819) 358-4470
www.festivaldesfromages.qc.ca

JULY

Bromont's International Equestrian Competition
(450) 534-0787
www.internationalbromont.org
includes international equestrian World Cup competitions: fabulous horse-jumping events (end of July/beginning Aug: check site for dates)

AUGUST

Potton Multicultural Festival
Mansonville
(450) 292-3313
celebrates the twenty different cultural groups comprising the region's residents.

Cookshire Agricultural Fair
(819) 875-5776
www.townshipsheritage.com
is one of the oldest fairs in Québec (1845) with animal judging, horse pulls.

SEPTEMBER

The Big Brome Fair
(450) 242-3976
www.bromefair.com
Since the 1840s one of the biggest gatherings of agricultural competitions from horses and dairy cattle to sheep and goats . . . to craftspeople, truck pulls and more.

Brome Lake Duck Festival
(450) 242-2870 or (877) 242-2870
www.cclacbrome.com
All things duck—tastings, cooking demos at this gourmet festival in Knowlton.

The Magog-Orford Grape Harvest (Fête des Vendanges);
(877) 847-2022
www.fetedesvendanges.com
is a celebration of Québec wine and cuisine.

NOVEMBER

Patriots' Day in Saint-Denis
(450) 787-3623
www.mndp.qc.ca
commemorates the 1837–38 patriot's rebellion.

early Sept, Wed to Sun Apr to mid-May and mid-Sept through late Oct; $5.65 adult, $4.90 senior, $2.90 youth, $14.20 family). Operated by the federal Parks Canada, this historic site is bilingually interpreted. Fluent interpretive staff are on hand to assist with any questions; otherwise, it's a self-guided tour you'll enjoy here. Don't miss Fort Chambly, and do ask for the English video. You can discover all sorts of things about American and Canadian politics and about the patriot and separatist movements in this province. Whatever the settlers' backgrounds, they were passionate about their roots. Today, we reap the harvest of such sentiments—just as we reap our delicious Québec apples.

Although first constructed of wood by Jacques de Chambly of France in 1665, the fort was rebuilt in stone by the French (1709 to 1711) to protect themselves from the British army's cannon artillery. The fort succumbed to British attack on Sept 1, 1760; in the American invasion of 1775 it fell into U.S. hands, but they lost it again to the British the following year. During the War of 1812, the British increased their fortifications here, but by 1870 they closed the fort. A local resident, Joseph-Octave Dion, recognized its historical significance and, after getting federal funding to restore its walls, actually lived inside the fort until he died in 1916. A remarkable historian, he was the fort's first curator.

Is all this history revving up a thirst? Head to the **Unibroue Brewery** (80 des Carrières, Chambly; 450-658-7658; www.unibroue.com). Arrange a tour and you'll not be disappointed. This young brewery is making quite a mark in Québec and further afield with its selection of natural beers such as *Fin du Monde* ("end of the world"). Watch out: these brews are more potent than American beer! Their bottle labels are dramatic, inspired by Québec history and folk tales. You'll recognize an old painting of Fort Chambly on the label of their Blanche de Chambly beer.

You must be ready to sit down and enjoy a French Canadian meal. We heartily recommend dining at **Fourquet Fourchette,** a restaurant and beer interpretation center (1887 ave. Bourgogne, Chambly; 450-447-6370; www.fourquet-fourchette.com). The food is superb. All main dishes are prepared with beer and presented by servers dressed in old-fashioned costumes. Outside is a patio overlooking a garden with hops and herbs used in beer brewing. Beyond the patio is the Richelieu Basin,

breweries

Unibroue is by no means the sole beer maker in Québec. In 1782 Englishman John Molson came to Montréal and founded a family of brewers and bankers. He established his first brewery at St. Mary's Current in the harbor of Montréal. Molson also introduced steam navigation to the St. Lawrence in 1809. Eventually his steamers plied the Ottawa and St. Lawrence Rivers, as well as the Great Lakes.

and in the near distance you'll spy Fort Chambly. Try some of the fresh, ripe cheeses made from raw milk—real local specialties. We also enjoyed heart of bulrush, and we're convinced you will, too.

Fourquet Fourchette also has a pub: the *Chasse-Gallerie Taverne* takes its name from a Québécois legend which is depicted on the label of Maudite, a strong amber-red ale made by Unibroue microbrewery. Dine here for a relaxed, convivial atmosphere and great food.

Drive south on Highway 223, where you will see sections of the *Chambly Canal* as you drive along the west bank of the Richelieu. Built between 1831 and 1843 by more than 500 workmen, the canal was constructed to improve trade between Lower Canada and the New England states. Until 1910, barges plied the waters, heading south with Canadian lumber and agricultural products and returning from the States with coal. But by that year, road and rail transportation gained supremacy, and by the 1970s recreational boating took over.

This 19-kilometer canal extends from Chambly to *Saint-Jean-sur-Richelieu.* This southernmost entry to the canal sports a Victorian charm. Cafes, such as *Le Manneken-Pis* (320 rue Champlain; 450-348-3254), directly opposite the locks, invite a patio pick-me-up. A good, paved *bike path,* which follows the old towpath used by horses when they pulled the barges, is almost flat, so it's a great spot for kids or those who simply want a leisurely tour. Note the "islands" defining the canal channel, which attest to the amount of soil and fill those 500 men dug with their pickaxes and shovels. You can park your car at the northern end of the canal, at *Parc des Ateliers* (1840 Bourgogne Ave., Chambly); however, there is a fee of $4 or so for your vehicle.

Stay south on Highway 223 to the town of Saint-Paul-de-l'Île-aux-Noix, named for the annuity tenant Pierre Jourdanet had to pay his seigneur: a bag of walnuts. Our destination here is *Fort Lennox* (at 1 Sixty-first Ave.; 450-291-5700; www.pc.gc.ca/fortlennox), a star-shaped British island fort and one of the four defense posts on the Richelieu. The first fort here was built by the French, who lost it during the siege of Saint-Paul-de-l'Ile-aux-Noix in 1760. During the American occupation of 1775, American general Shulyer used it as his base of operations for his attack on Montréal. A year later the Americans retreated, and the fort became the most southerly defended spot on the Richelieu. The British refortified it and, between 1819 and 1823, did so again. It was at this time they named it Fort Lennox after the Duke of Richmond, Charles Lennox, who died in 1819 after a rabid fox bit him. The British feared an American invasion from Lake Champlain and so decided to construct shipyards here, too, but after many years of peace, they closed the fort in 1834. Concurrent to this was the opening of the Chambly Canal.

Note the huge marinas on a big turnaround cut directly northwest of the fort. People boat upriver from New York, navigating the Hudson River, Lake Champlain, and finally the Richelieu River, following in the footsteps of such settlers as Philemon Wright, the American who founded the Québec town of Gatineau.

Continue south on Highway 223, passing flat fields full of strawberry farms where you can pick your own in season (mid- to late June). Stop at the **Blockhouse** at Lacolle, built in 1781 and approximately 8 kilometers south of Fort Lennox. It's the only surviving original blockhouse in Québec and houses a particularly excellent hands-on collection of artifacts that will get adults and kids thinking about our military past. Look for the musket-ball holes in the blockhouse wall.

A bit farther south, turn left onto Route 202 toward Noyan. As you cross over the Richelieu River, look down on the tops of trees in the woods devastated by the 1998 ice storm. The resort town of **Venise-en-Québec** is situated on the north end of Lake Champlain, with many campgrounds and wall-to-wall RVs. Some beach campgrounds, like the **Domaine Florent** (272 ave. 23 Est; 450-244-5607; www.domaineflorent.com) have wheelchair access, a pool, and washers and dryers for clothes.

Loyalist Country

During the course of the revolution between the British and their American colonists (1775–83), thousands of Loyalists avoided persecution or worse by fleeing north to the Canadian colonies, settling primarily along the southern borders of Southern Ontario, the Gaspé region, and Eastern Townships. In 1789 Lord Dorchester, the governor-in-chief of British North America, proclaimed that those who had crossed into Canada during the war should be called United Empire Loyalists (UELs) to honor their support of the Crown. This area, close to the current U.S.-Canadian border, is home to many descendants of UEL settlers, living in little tidy towns like Frelighsburg and Stanbridge East.

Genealogical Research

Loyalists traveled north from America to settle in the Canadas in 1795 and later. Loyal to the British Crown, these immigrants to what is now the Eastern Townships prospered. Today many English- and French-speaking North Americans want to search their Loyalist family trees. The Web site at www.uelac.org provides helpful information and excellent links.

To get there, continue east along Highway 202 through Pike River and Bedford to **Stanbridge East.** En route you drive through flat farmland filled with corn and poultry barns. Note all the names with Belgian, Swiss, Polish, and Dutch origins on the mailboxes, and the street in Bedford called Rue Dutch. About 5 kilometers east of Bedford, watch for signs to Stanbridge East; you'll turn left (north) to jog up to this town with its beautiful Gothic church.

In Stanbridge East, be sure to visit **Musée Missisquoi (Missisquoi Museum)** (2 River St., Stanbridge East; 450-248-3153; www.museemissisquoi .ca; open 10 a.m. to 5 p.m. daily from late May to early Oct; adults $5, seniors $4, children $1). This is a real treasure with three different buildings. The Cornell Mill is an 1830 brick structure housing the main collection as well as an exhibit that is changed annually. Up the street is the old-time country store operated by the Hodge family for seventy-seven years—still jammed full of original merchandise. Still farther up Main Street is the Annex, where interesting old farm machinery has found a home. Museum staff are English-speaking and extraordinarily helpful. Stay for a picnic and find the old cannon in the mill's park that was hauled out of the Richelieu River. Note that the Missisquoi Historical Society is old for Canada: It was founded in 1898 and is often approached by genealogists searching for family records.

Go southeast to Frelighsburg on Highway 237, which continues to the U.S. border. Frelighsburg was named for a Dutch doctor, Dr. Abram Freligh, who used to live in Albany, New York. Stop in **Frelighsburg's General Store:** We defy you to find better maple syrup pies. How we managed to stop at only one tart each remains a mystery. Wander behind the store to eat yours on the bank of the stream. Look left here to spy the old mill built in 1839 by one of Dr. Abram Freligh's sons, now a private home. Beyond the village, hiking trails to nearby Pinnacle Mountain will reward you with good views over the undulating farmland. Beyond to the south, you can see the Green Mountains of

---

blue-thumb gardeners?

We've all heard the old saw that successful gardeners have a green thumb. But do water gardeners have a blue thumb, we wonder?

Who knows—but at **Les jardins d'eau de la vallée (Water Gardens of the Valley)** in Stanbridge East, you'll walk flower-strewn trails alongside pools where aquatic plants amaze you. Canada's only such watery garden is located in Dunham at 140 Rte. 202 (450-248-7008; www .afleurdeau.qc.ca/jardins/; open daily June through Aug 9 a.m. to 5 p.m., Sept and Oct 10 a.m. to 4 p.m.; $8 adults, $5 youth, $3 kids, $20 family). We've been inspired to try water lilies . . . what will you attempt?

Vermont's Appalachians, including Mounts Sutton and Mansfield. This area is well known for its local artisans' work and has an art festival called ***Festiv'art*** on Labor Day weekend (first weekend in Sept; www.festivart.org).

Just south of the village, turn southeast toward Abercorn on the Richford Road, surely one of the most beautiful country roads you could ever find. Stop at the sleepy **border station** on *Chemin de la frontière* (Frontier Road), where the lone customs officer on duty seemed to welcome our brief visit and chat. Ahead of you is the United States, but turn left here and slowly drive along this lovely border road. Off in the distance, you'll see our peaceful, shared border cut through the wood-clad hills. Especially because of all the wars and skirmishes in our shared past, it's a good time to reflect on our peacefully shared present.

You eventually connect with Highway 139 Nord to Abercorn, getting splendid views to the south of the Appalachian's Green Mountains as you go. At Abercorn, turn east again onto the well-named Chemin Scenic for the 11 kilometers or so to **Glen Sutton.** The road becomes even prettier—if that's possible—following the broad Rivière Missisquoi on your right. At Glen Sutton you pass the inviting ***Auberge Glen Sutton*** (1338 de la Vallée-Missisquoi; 450-538-2000). You can eat here, rest up, and head off, invigorated.

Continue to tiny ***Dunkin,*** settled in 1798 by Colonel Hendrick Ruiter, who came here from New York as a UEL. He was granted 2,400 acres of land and, with the help of his large family, set to clearing the bush and building the first grist- and sawmill.

Proceed on Route 243 toward Mansonville in Potton township, just a few miles from the Vermont border. Colonel Ruiter sold this part of his land to John Lewis and Joseph Chandler, who built a sawmill here, then sold it to Robert Manson in 1811.

stay in a treehouse?

Why not sleep "al fresco"—like a bird in a tree—after kayaking under a full moon or a herbal workshop? You can at Glen Sutton's *Au Diable Vert,* a 200-acre property with a 100-year-old mountain lodge, camping, wood-heated cabins and . . . treehouse cabins. Au Diable Vert means Green Devil (www.au diablevert.qc.ca).

We've been traveling on beautiful side roads through old hamlets. ***Mansonville*** is completely different as it caters to the Mont Owl's Head ski area just west of Lake Memphrémagog. Find the ***Mansonville Museum,*** operated by the *Association du patrimoine de Potton* (Potton Heritage Association) in the 1850 ***Reilly House.*** A multifunctional abode, it houses a local museum, tearoom, and Internet café (302 rue Principale, Mansonville; 450-292-3109; www.maisonreillyhouse.org; open daily 9 a.m. to 4 p.m.). Brochures on historical facts about this region are available here, and staff members are bilingual. If you are interested in biking and hiking, stop here first to get brochures like Cyclo-Route Potton, about a well-interpreted 28-kilometer bike route.

At the Mansonville Museum you'll find all sorts of intriguing if not perplexing items, including a supposedly ancient, fanciful lion's head (we thought it looked more like a dragon's head) that was reputedly found in the area. Tall tales as well as intriguing archaeological finds and postulations reside here, and they're fun.

Now continue up Rue Principale and, opposite the Catholic church, find the circa 1910 *round barn.* Folklore dictates that such barns were circular so that the devil couldn't hide in the corners. Round barns were first introduced in North America by the Shakers, who built one in 1865 in Hancock, Massachusetts. Shakers considered circles the perfect form. Moreover, four-cornered structures were also supposed to sap energy from living beings, either man or beast. Hence, round barns were considered less stressful.

Proceed up Highway 243 Nord to South Bolton. The road still hugs the Missisquoi River. On your right look for Sugar Loaf Mountain, so named because settlers bought slices of sugar cut from a pressed "sugarloaf." Its astonishing shape and dramatic elevation make it a famous landmark of this area, lying on the west bank of Lac Memphrémagog.

This region was known for its five copper mines, a railway, cheese factory, and bobbin mills, the last of which closed in 1995. But don't for a minute think it has the look of a stolid, dilapidated major industrial region. *South Bolton* is very pretty. Once known as Rexford's Corner, the village is distinguished by many lovely buildings, including the 1832 schoolhouse. *Bolton Centre,* 5 kilometers north, was settled by Loyalists, and both the 1866 United and 1875 St. Patrick's Anglican churches are beautiful. Stop and wander around on foot.

Take Highway 243 Nord from Bolton Centre toward Eastman. As you drive, you'll see the Western side of *Mont Orford,* one of the major ski centers in this region. Cross the autoroute into Eastman, then turn right on Highway 112. Watch for a left turn onto Chemin Georges-Bonalie, which goes north to Highway 220, where you turn left (west) to Bonsecours.

Once Active Russian Community

Just beyond Mansonville (between Knowlton Landing and Vale Perkins) is the community of *Voroktha,* where you'll discover a Russian Orthodox church and monastery. Cyrillic characters adorn the gravestones in the cemetery.

White Indians?

The Mansonville Museum is really thought-provoking. Look for the brochure written by Gérard Leduc called *Arkeo Potton: The Fingerprints of a Lost Culture in the Eastern Townships*. Leduc claims that petroglyphs (writing on stone), stone cairns with quartz rocks placed at their summit, and many other archaeological finds prove there was a permanent, not nomadic, native culture here. More than this, Leduc conjectures that this group was a caucasoid (white and European-based) group. "What happened to these White Indians?" Leduc asks. He postulates: "Native Americans have themselves reportedly told early European settlers that the stone builders were white people and that they had been exterminated by Red Indians."

Leduc claims that in the woods and meadows surrounding Mansonville, there are several ancient sites built, among other things, to celebrate the solstice. To inquire about how to see the sites that are on private property, contact the Tourist Office of Mansonville (450-292-3313).

At Bonsecours turn right on Rue de l'Église to drive 6 kilometers to **Mine Cristal Kébec** (Québec Crystal Mines and the Crystal Sanctuary) (430 rang 11, Bonsecours; 450-535-6550; www.minecristal.com). Continue on this gravel road past Lawrenceville until the T intersection with Rang (Rural Route) 11, where you turn right and follow blue signs to these "new age" mines, supposedly the only ones in Canada that produce top-quality quartz crystal. In the gift shop you can purchase crystals and read about the mines' discovery in 1959 by farmer Gerard Adam, who was curious about the sparkling stones in his fields. Today's operation was started by Gaudry Normand in 1989. His brochure says, "Our hope is that, by freeing the crystals from the dark underground, the ancient knowledge of quartz energy may be brought to light." Many believe that crystals transform and focus energies. For $10 you can take a ninety-minute tour, but call first to confirm timing as it fluctuates seasonally. While there, don't miss Normand's "crystal vessel symphony," which is like an auditory massage: he creates a beautiful sound while "playing" twenty large crystal bowls.

Let's proceed now to a different type of power. We're headed to **Valcourt.** Drive east on Rang 11 to reconnect with Highway 243 Nord, then watch for Rang 4, which is a signed left-hand turn to Valcourt. Follow the blue signs there, where winter and sport are celebrated at the museum that honors the inventor of the snowmobile. This is the **J. Armand Bombardier Museum** (1001 J. A. Bombardier Ave., Valcourt; 450-532-5300; www.museebombardier .com; adults $7, student and senior $5, family $15; open daily 10 a.m. to 5 p.m. May through early-Sept, closed Mon from Sept through Apr).

Visit an Abbey

At Bolton East, take a side trip on Chemin Bolton-Est toward Austin, then follow the signs southeast to the **Abbey Saint-Benoît-du-lac,** operated by Benedictine monks. There is a daily Eucharist where you can hear a Gregorian chant at 11 a.m. as well as evening Vespers starting at 5 p.m., except for Thurs, when it starts at 7 p.m. The abbey itself is a collection of different architectural styles. Parts were built by the internationally celebrated French Benedictine architect Dom Paul Bellot (1876–1944). Situated near Lake Memphrémagog on its west bank, the abbey commands a splendid view and is a noted landmark. Its gift shop not only sells recordings of the chants but also the cheese and cider made here by the monks. It's open Mon to Sat from 9 to 10:45 a.m. and 11:50 a.m. to 4:30 p.m.; closed Sun.

Want to stay in this most peaceful of surroundings? You can. There's a men's guesthouse retreat on site, and women can stay nearby at a home operated by nuns. Room and board is $50 per person. Men must reserve by calling (819) 843-4080; women must call (819) 843-2340; see full details at www.st-benoit-du-lac.com.

This high-tech museum tells of Joseph Armand Bombardier, a Valcourt boy who doggedly pursued his dream of creating a machine that could give ease and comfort to travel during the long Canadian winter. The museum chronicles the development of the original dangerous, but exciting, machines. They had open propellers in the rear, no brakes, and couldn't back up: yikes! Bombardier technology is also credited with the Montréal Métro subway cars and the trains for the Chunnel linking France with England. Attached to the museum is this gentle family man's original workshop, a white- and red-trimmed garage that quaintly defines the man himself. The guides are passionate in their admiration and love of this man, who died in 1964. And no truck is given to any "greenie," or environmentalist, who might murmur that the machines are bad for the environment. After all, Bombardier is the employer of this region, and when environmental issues raised their "ugly" heads, production plummeted and the townsfolk were unimpressed.

Because snowmobiling is banned in most of Europe, many tourists come to Québec for this winter sport. The Eastern Townships have a network of more than 2,000 kilometers of snowmobile trails. For snowmobile rentals, contact **Centre de la motoneige enr.** (9060 de la Montagne, Valcourt; 450-532-2262; www.centredelamotoneige.com). Want to find out about Québec's entire network of trails and procure a free map? Also, remember that snowmobile passes must be purchased in Québec, and there are various prices. Trails are monitored. Contact the **Québec Federation of Snowmobiling Clubs** (4545 ave. Pierre-de-Coubertin, P.O. Box 1000, Station M, Montréal H1V 3R2; 514-252-3076; www.fcmq.qc.ca).

Drive east from Valcourt, passing the gigantic Bombardier plant, to rejoin Highway 243. Turn north toward **Melbourne** for about 20 kilometers to visit two museums. One covers the history of the area; the second has exhibits on the history, geology, and use of slate.

The first historical museum, ***Musée de la Société d'histoire du comté de Richmond,*** is located at 1296 Rte. (Highway) 243, Melbourne (819-826-1332). Endearing to us is the historical society's notice that "cyclists are welcome." The museum is open late June through mid-Aug, Wed to Sun 2 to 6 p.m.

Leave the historical museum, and as you drive, you'll notice not only roofs of slate but also slate outcrops at the road-side. To get to the slate museum, pass Highway 55 to Drummondville, drive to the end of Highway 243, and turn left at Rivière Saint-François onto Chemin de la Rivière. Turn left again on Rue Belmont to find the 1853 church, home of the ***Centre d'interprétation de l'ardoise***

woolydiversion

Head north from Melbourne on Highway 243 Nord (north) to Ulverton, a former English village, whose elegant Heritage architecture is well preserved. Of special note is the re-created woolen mill, which operated between 1850 and 1945 (210 Porter Rd., Ulverton; 819-826-3157; www.moulin.ca). Tours, 5-kilometer walking path, and picnic sites are included.

(Slate Study Center) (5 rue Belmont, Melbourne; 819-826-3313; www.centre ardoise.ca; adults $6, students $4, family $14; open daily 11 a.m. to 5 p.m. July and Aug, Sundays only in June and Sept; rest of year by appointment only). The roof of this redbrick church is slate and at the rear is an example of how roofs are constructed of these slate "shingles."

Watch for more slate outcrops as you proceed northeast via Highway 116 Est through dairy farms and cornfields to Danville, where the Victorian architecture is simply breathtaking. Old homes are obviously cherished here. You'll find gaily painted Queen Anne–style houses with whimsical massing and turrets. Of the four Protestant churches, one has been converted into a restaurant that serves regional cuisine. ***Le Temps des Cerises*** is a restored clapboard church. Here you can get delectable Danville lamb as well as caribou (79 rue du Carmel, Danville; 800-839-2818; www.cerises.com).

Head approximately 9 kilometers north to ***Kingsey Falls*** and ***Parc Marie-Victorin*** (385 boul. Marie-Victorin, Kingsey Falls; 819-363-2528; www .parcmarievictorin.com). Named for a famous botanist, the twenty-two-acre park beside Rivière Nicolet has bird and medicinal plant gardens. If you are a gardener, it's an interesting place to go to get ideas on landscaping and plants.

WORTH SEEING IN THE EASTERN TOWNSHIPS

For information about activities in this region, contact
Tourisme Cantons-de-l'Est
20 rue Don Bosco Sud,
Sherbrooke
J1L 1W4;
(800) 355-5755 or (819) 820-2020
www.easterntownships.org
There are many special-interest pamphlets, such as the superb Cycling the Eastern Townships. In fact, cyclists should check out Québec's "green route" of networked bike paths at www.routeverte.com.

Randonnées J. Robidas
32 chemin McFarland,
North Hatley;
(819) 563-0166 or (888) 677-8767
www.randonneesjrobidas.qc.ca

Offers lessons and day trips on horseback and winter sleigh rides in the countryside. This outfitter will take you by horse-drawn buggy on guided tours of North Hatley. Enjoy exploring with your horse and have fun hearing about the region's history!

Musée de Golf du Québec (Club de golf les Cèdres)
669 Coupland St.,
Granby;
(450) 372-0167
www.golflescedres.com
has interactive games to test your knowledge and skill, as well as exhibits detailing the history of golf.

Kingsey Falls was founded in 1886 and named for a village in Oxford County, England. Early on, the first settlers built a flour- and sawmill on the banks of the Nicolet River, taking advantage of the waterfalls. Later, a paper mill was built, and today Kingsey Falls is home to its descendant, *Les Industries Cascade Inc.,* the largest paper recycling center in Canada. (In fact, the garden benches at Parc Marie-Victorin are composed of recycled materials.) Find Cascade Inc. beside the gardens. Admission to it is part of the gardens tour, and a convenient walkway over the Nicolet River takes you to the plant. Also ask at the gardens for information about the 19-kilometer canoe ride down the Nicolet. Admission to the Parc Marie-Victorin, Cascade Inc., the canoe ride, and an evening supper-theater put on by *Théâtre des Grands Chênes* (Theater of the Great Oaks) varies depending on the package you buy and the season; refer to the Web site for details.

Now drive north on Highway 116 through Warwick to *Victoriaville.*

québectrivia

Frederick Simpson Coburn (1871–1960), a famous Canadian portrait painter, was born in Upper Melbourne. The town gets its name from two towns in England—Derbyshire and Hampshire—which also gave their names to Melbourne, Australia.

Notice how many names here are very English. Although one francophone resident of Danville insisted they were of aboriginal derivation, all are British. Don't miss visiting the exceptional ***Économusée de cuir (Leather Museum)*** (857 blvd. des Bois-Francs Sud, Arthabaska, a suburb of Victoriaville; 819-357-3138). Inside you will find an assortment of intriguing displays, including samples of hide from creatures as odd as a frog. The craftspeople inside will explain the difference between real alligator (or ostrich) hide and stamped imitations, and you'll also see cuir haché—reconstituted leather made of pieces of hide bonded together. Descend to the basement workshop where you can see the craftspeople at work. Free, and very intriguing.

Before leaving the Arthabaska sector of Victoriaville, stop at the Canadian National Historic Site ***Musée Laurier*** (16 rue Laurier Ouest, Victoriaville; 819-357-8655; www.museelaurier.com). The home was built in 1876 for Sir Wilfrid Laurier, Canada's eighth prime minister, for the then-princely sum of $3,000. The Victorian mansion is suitably impressive, being graciously set back from the street. Born in 1896 in Saint-Lin, Québec, Laurier is renowned for promoting reconciliation and partnership between the English and French.

Sir Wilfrid and his wife were unable to have children—but maintained a welcoming rapport if not friendship with neighbourhood children along with their nephews and nieces. Therefore, a very special touch at Musée Laurier is the adjacent building of ***Grange Fleury*** (Fleury Barn) which is operated as a children's theatre during summer. Kids are encouraged to participate, and sometimes puppet shows are featured (check Web site for details).

Now proceed southeast on Highway 161 through gentle hills and rich dairy land along the Nicolet River.

At the junction with Highway 216 Sud, turn right toward Saint-Adrien. Situated on top of a hill, the lofty spires of the village's white clapboard church survey the rolling countryside. Watch for Highway 257 Est and drive southeast

Bois Francs

Meaning "hardwood forest," Bois Francs is a region of Québec north of Asbestos, and boasts the greatest number of sugar maple trees in the province. In Oct enjoy the colorful leaves while driving (or cycling) one of several themed drives created in 2008. *La route de l'érable* (Maple Route; www.laroutedelerable.ca) is centered in Plessisville; *La Route Celtique* (Celtic Route; www.larouteceltique.org) is centered in Inverness and celebrates Irish settlers; *La Routes-des-Fromages-et-Trouvailles-gourmandes* (Cheese and Gourmand Discoveries circuit) centred in Warwick; and the *Routes des Antiquaires* (Antique circuit; www.lesantiquaires.ca).

Fly Fishing

Calling all trout fishermen! If this is your sport, and if you have your own equipment, then we have a spot for you. Turn right (south) on Highway 161 into **Notre-Dame-de-Lourdes-de-Ham,** where you can arrange to fish for brown trout in two sectors of the Nicolet River. The 11-kilometer length of river is open for fishing and has pools and rapids for fly and spinfishing. You need to purchase a right of access ($25 to $35) at the Reception Center (44 rue Principale, Notre-Dame-de-Ham; 819-344-5844 in fishing season; www.pourvoirie-bois-francs.qc.ca). The center is open during fishing season (Apr 25 through Oct 5).

Only thirty-five persons are allowed on the river each day. You must reserve a date, purchase a right of access, get a Québec provincial fishing license, and you must return to the Reception Center to register your catch. Fishing is on foot (no boats). Camping is available but it is completely rustic.

to **Saint-Joseph-de-Ham-Sud.** Turn right to proceed to **Mont Ham,** which rises to 713 meters, just north of the next village, Saint-Camille. Mont Ham is one of the highest mountains in the region. It has a 16-kilometer network of hiking trails, one of which affords a great view of the surrounding countryside from the summit. It's seasonally open, so first call the **Mont Ham reception center** (103 rte. 257 Ouest, Ham-Sud; 819-828-3608; www.montham.qc.ca;). It's a good spot for families because interactive exhibits as well as games and a picnic area keep kids engaged.

québectrivia

Je me souviens (I remember). In 1883 this phrase was carved into the provincial coat of arms on the houses of parliament in Québec City. These days, you'll see it on Québec license plates: in 1978 it replaced the previous slogan, *la belle province.* Redolant with meaning, it reminds Québecers to remember and take pride in their heritage of glories, misfortunes— and rich culture as a people. As well, it can serve as a separatist slogan where the spirit of *les patriotes* and nationalist pride are celebrated—and never allowed to be forgotten.

Continue southwest on Route 216 to **Saint-Camille,** one of the Eastern Township's oldest francophone villages, founded in 1848. The hills around the Sainte-Antoine Chapel rise to 400 meters, so you can easily see nearby Mont Ham. In Saint-Camille find **Le P'tit Bonheur de Saint Camille,** a rural community interpretation center (162 Miquelon St.; check www.ptitbonheur.org; 819-828-2664 to see what exhibitions are on. Open daily, but Sat by reservation only). The center was created to honour Québec folk singer, poet, playwright and political activist Félix Leclerc.

Follow Highway 216 southwest into **Sherbrooke,** a city with a population of about 148,000, and the pretty regional capital of the Eastern Townships. Orient yourself to Sherbrooke by visiting the ***Centre d'interprétation de l'histoire de Sherbrooke,*** which has bilingual audiotape tours of history for walking and driving (275 Dufferin St., Sherbrooke; 819-821-5406). If you reserve ahead, you can get a guided tour, but the English tape is useful for self-guided walking or driving explorations. Also, the center's computerized archive is open to the public. Otherwise, contact ***Tourisme Sherbrooke*** (785 rue King Ouest, Sherbrooke J1H 1R8; 800-561-8331; www.tourismesherbrooke.com).

You'll see lots of bicyclists in Sherbrooke. The 50-kilometer cycle loop called ***Les Grandes Fourches*** (contact Tourisme Sherbrooke at 800-561-8331; www.tourismesherbrooke.com) is a must if you are a cyclist. It takes you around Lake Massawippi, to North Hatley, along rivers, and to the old Capelton copper mine, where shafts extend more than a mile underground. Do a mine tour; there are stands to secure your bike. The bike route also goes over one of Québec's classic covered bridges. These bridges were covered to preserve the wood from rot. Or so they say. They're also known as kissing bridges, for their seclusion allowed unchaperoned lovers to steal a kiss. This cycling path is the very best way to check out this area's rich heritage.

Les Patriotes

Les patriotes was the name given after 1826 to people in the popular movement of mostly French-speaking merchants and liberal professionals who rebelled against British rule. The rebellions of 1837 and 1838 resulted in the torching of *patriotes'* homes, hangings, and imprisonment. Their demands for the right to self-government were rejected by Britain but laid the foundation for today's call for separation from Canada.

In May of 2003, former Québec premier Bernard Landry (then the leader of the separatist Parti Québécois) tried to change the name of the May 24 holiday from Victoria Day to *la Journée des Patriotes* (Patriot's Day)—despite the Rebellion having taken place in Nov. He wasn't successful: roughly 50 or so celebrants turned out that year in Montréal, waving *les patriotes'* flag of white, red and green. Landry's plan was a bust: Québecers sniffed, typically being contrary, preferring to keep the memory of Britain's queen alive. Victoria Day—or la fête de la Reine (Queen's Day)—it remains.

But not so fast . . . in the early 1980s, Victoria Day's name was altered to *la Fête de Dollard de Ormeaux* (Dollard de Ormeaux Day). This chap defended Montréal from an Iroquois invasion in 1660.

So, what's in a name? With Québec bureaucrats continually changing names of streets (*boulevard Dorchester* in Montréal became *boulevard René Lévesque*) and villages (*Quyon* to *Pontiac*) . . . revisionism is alive and well—and heritage becomes obscured.

A Foot in Two Countries

The *Haskell Free Library and Opera House* straddles the Canada-U.S. border. One-half of the library is in Rock Island, Québec, while the other is in Derby Line, Vermont. Why? It was built in 1904 by a wealthy benefactor, who wanted both communities to benefit. Both in the library and upstairs opera house, a diagonal line shows the border, and while listening to music, the audience sits in the United States watching actors on stage in Québec!

Whether you venture there by bike or by car, North Hatley is an intriguing diversion. It is a well-known artistic enclave (check out noted English-language *Piggery Theatre,* once part of a farm; 819-842-2431 or www.piggery.com for what's playing). Find this village on Route 108 Sud, on the north shore of Lac Massawippi.

Continue south to *Lennoxville* via Highway 143. Because it is home to the Neo-Gothic–style *Bishop's University,* this city is the English language educational and cultural center of the Eastern Townships. St. Mark's Chapel, part of Bishop's, was built in 1855 and is a beautiful replica of thirteenth-century Gothic architecture.

An interesting section of Lennoxville is where Highway 143 becomes *Queen Street.* There are lots of colorful flower markets, all open-air and joyful looking. Around 240 Queen St. find antiques row, which gives you some shopping opportunities. Along this road you'll find a student area with inexpensive places to eat. *Sebby's* offers all-you-can-eat meals (83 rue Queen; www.sebbys .com; 819-569-9755); *Café Cordelia* has trendy espresso and cappuccino (111 rue Queen; 819-569-4646). Just before crossing the Rivière Massawippi, you'll see Les Grandes Fourches biking trail.

Beyond the bridge on Highway 143, Highway 147 veers to the left. Stay on Highway 143 for a few kilometers, then turn right onto Highway 108, to find the old *Capelton Mine* (800 Rte. 108, North Hatley; 819-346-9545; www.mines capelton.com). This is the oldest mine in Canada, and visitors can try their hand at mining copper with a pick and shovel. Call or refer to their Web site for seasonal openings and admission fee packages. The property contains 650 acres and offers good hiking, biking and, in winter, dogsledding and skiing. Directly opposite the mine is the covered bridge, originally built in 1842. The ice storm of January 1998 badly damaged the bridge, but it has been restored.

Return the short distance to Highway 143 and turn right (west), and you'll soon see a sign to Waterville. Turn left (south), following the Waterville signs as you jog for a block on Highway 143. The road changes to Chemin de Compton to take you through Waterville and out along the gentle slopes of the west bank of the Coaticook River. Watch for the sign directing you east across the valley to **Compton.** As you cross the river, you'll see the remains of another covered bridge. Compton is the former home of one of Canada's prime ministers, Louis St. Laurent. Stop at the **Louis S. St. Laurent National Historic Site** (6790 rte. Louis-S.-St-Laurent, Compton; 819-835-5448 or 888-773-8888; www.pc .gc.ca/st-laurent). Stop in at **J.B.M. St. Laurent's General Store**—originally Louis St. Laurent's father's store—which is part of the site and displays merchandise of the sort sold in the early 1890s. Compton also has a "heritage circuit" to trace a century of history of local mills, buildings, and bridges.

moopower

Of all Canadian provinces and territories, Québec is the largest dairy producer. 2006 figures reported more than 7,000 dairy farms producing 38 percent of Canada's milk production (www.lait.org)

Farther south on Highway 147, you'll reach Coaticook, a name derived from the First Nations' word *Koatikeku,* meaning "river of the land of pines." The region is known as Québec's main milk producing region: more than 300 of the region's 600 farms are dairy producers. Two annual fairs held in the village celebrate the agri-food industry: in Mar since 2004, the **Vins et Fromages Agropur** has featured regional wines and cheeses; and since 1997, end of July and early Aug's **Festival du Lait** (Milk Festival) has celebrated the dairy industry (819-849-6010, ext. 249).

International Dark Sky Reserve

Is your interest piqued with peaks? A new driving route in 2009—*La Route des Sommets* (the Summit Tour)—has a good Web site with route maps for driving, cycling and hiking (www.routedessommets.com). But don't miss the *International Dark Sky Reserve* (Réserve internationale de ciel étoilé du Mont-Mégantic).

The reserve is dedicated to interpreting and preserving darkness during the night. Sounds counterintuitive? Not really: it's impossible to see the stars in the midst of a city . . . This reserve reminds us of the importance of reducing light pollution so that astronomical features can be observed. As well, many animals (migrating birds, for instance) depend upon darkness and stars for navigation.

Explore the reserve and discover both the ASTROLab and Mount Megantic Observatory (astrolab-parc-national-mont-megantic.org) devoted to making the science of the stars (astronomy) accessible to the public. Take tours of the facility and participate in the *Astronomy Festival,* which occurs throughout summer on Sat nights (June until Sept—check details on Web site).

Stop for a picnic and explore ***Parc de la Gorge de Coaticook*** (135 Michaud St., Coaticook; 819-849-2331; www.gorgedecoaticook.qc.ca). The gorge, more than 50 meters deep, is not only spectacular in itself but also features the longest suspended footbridge in the world at 169 meters. (The current bridge was built after floods in 1998 destroyed the original 1887 wonder.) In the park you'll find the reproduction of a round barn, as well as an 1887 covered bridge.

Don't miss ***Beaulne Museum*** (96 rue de l'Union, Coaticook; 819-849-6560; www.museebeaulne.qc.ca; open Tues to Sun, 10 a.m. to 5 p.m. mid-May to mid-Sept and 1 to 4 p.m. rest of year; $5 adults, $4 seniors, $2.50 students, $10 family). A wonderful collection of costumes and antique textiles is housed in a whimsical wood and fieldstone Victorian Queen Anne–style home, complete with turrets and a broad, sturdy veranda entryway. The collector made his fortune by designing and patenting a railway-car jack. Perhaps appropriately, the museum is nestled among old trees just below the railroad.

Head west now on Highway 141. After about 8 kilometers, you reach ***Barnston,*** a small rural village renowned for its still-operational round dairy barn. To see it, drive through the village. The barn is on the north side of the road on the outskirts of town. Avoid turning around on this fairly narrow road by taking the next right turn, then right again, to reconnect with Highway 141. Turn left (northwest).

Now drive through more dairy country to ***Ayer's Cliff,*** situated on the banks of Lac Massawippi, a popular fishing lake where fisher folk come to catch salmon, pike, bass and yellow perch. And yes, there are fishing tournaments here. Moroever, this large lake—voted as one of the province's ten most beautiful—is on the migratory flight path. Every spring and autumn, thousands of Canada and Snow Geese rest here before moving to their seasonal territory. Recreational boaters love it here: there is both a good public beach as well as boat launch.

There are many reasons to linger: spectacular sunsets over the lake, hiking trails ascending nearby Mont Pinacle, a farmers' market on summer Saturday mornings, and one of the best (and longest-running) agricultural fairs come August (www.ayerscliff.ca; 819-838-5006).

turntocliffs?

What is in a name? Makes you wonder sometimes, and the story of how Ayer's Cliff got its name is amusing. It was first called Langmaid's Flat for a New Hampshire UEL. Then, in 1799 Thomas Ayer arrived—perhaps staying in Langmaid's hotel while building a railway line. After the line's completion, the town became Ayer's Flats. But we gather that "Flats" didn't sound sexy enough. In 1904 townsfolk adopted the more compelling name, "Ayer's Cliff."

Continue on Highway 141 to Magog, a major recreational resort on the northern tip of *Lac Memphrémagog*. Not surprisingly, neighboring *Parc du Mont Orford* is another major draw for recreationalists. Its two mountains, Orford and Baldface, are 853 and 600 meters high, respectively. In winter, downhill skiers thrill to a vertical drop of more than 540 meters on 61-plus kilometers at Mont Orford trails. You can rent equipment here, and if you don't want to commit for a full day, you can buy a ski pass in 2- to 3½-hour blocks. In other words, if you feel like trying it out, there's no excuse not to. For information about skiing and snowboarding, or about hiking in summer, contact *Ski Mont Orford* (4380 chemin du Parc, Orford; 866-673-6731, 819-843-6548; www.orford.com). There's even day care for kids. If exercise isn't particularly your thing, simply take the gondola to the summit of Mont Orford for a perspective on where you've been and a grand view of the topography of this area.

Golfers will enjoy Golf Mont Orford's eighteen-hole, Scottish-designed course (3074 chemin du Parc, Orford; 819-843-5688).

It's time to return to Montréal. Get on Autoroute 10 Ouest (west), and in less than an hour, you can be back in the city.

Places to Stay in the Eastern Townships

AYER'S CLIFF

L'Auberge Ripplecove
700 rue Ripplecove,
J0B 1C0;
(819) 838-4296 or
(800) 668-4296
www.ripplecove.com
An upscale country inn with a four-diamond restaurant serving house-smoked salmon. This twelve-acre lakeside property ensures privacy.

CHAMBLY

À la Claire Fontaine
2130, ave. Bourgogne,
J3L 1Z7;
(450) 447-7940 or
(800) 447-5888
www.alaclairefontaine.ca
Built from cut stone in 1910 as a doctor's home located a few steps from Fort Chambly and close to the riverside trail.

EASTMAN

Entre Cimes et Racines
80 chemin Simard,
J0E 1P0;
(450) 297-0770 or
(866) 297-0770
www.entrecimesetracines
.com

Nine gorgeous cabins called "écogîtes" (a fitting name) tucked into a woodland setting where you can ski/snowshoe/hike on 15 km of nature paths, plus stroll a forest labyrinth.

LENNOXVILLE

Bishop's University
(819) 822-9600 ext 2685 or
(877) 622-4900
www.ubishops.ca
Family accommodations on campus available seasonally from May through Sept, single $57.50, double $67.50. This includes tennis, sauna and, indoor and outdoor pools and is a great deal; 438 rooms, 10 apartments.

PIOPOLIS (NEAR LAC MÉGANTIC)

Hébergement aux Cinq Sens
250 rang des Grenier, G0Y 1H0;
(819) 583-0885;
www.auxcinqsens.ca
Snowshoe or walk through woods to your private *yourtes* (yurts—modeled after nomadic Mongolian's tents). In winter, a cozy wood stove awaits.

SUTTON

B&B Vert le Mont
18 rue Maple;
(450) 538-3227
www.bbsutton.com
Pretty 1916 Loyalist style home with friendly and welcoming hosts. Want more privacy? It's possible to rent the house for a group if you are traveling with friends or large family.

Places to Eat in the Eastern Townships

CHAMBLY

La Maison Bleue (The Blue House)
2592 Bourgogne Ave.;
(450) 447-1112
This picturesque heritage (1815) home specializes in French cuisine, notably fruits de mer (seafood).

EASTMAN

Haut Bois Normand (Normand's Sugar Bush)
426 Chemin George Bonnalie;
(450) 297-2659
www.hautboisnormand.ca
Experience a genuine Québécois experience at this traditional maple sugar shack during March when the sap is flowing. Take a sleigh ride, tube the snow-clad hills, or try the *tire sur neige* (literally: pull through the snow), where warm maple syrup is poured on fresh snow. Dip a popsicle stick into it, then sample oh-so-sweet taffy.

THE OUTAOUAIS: NATURAL SPLENDOR →

Pronounced *Ooo-tah-ways,* this spectacular sector of Québec includes the almost-unknown westernmost region called the Pontiac, whose natural beauty beckons at every twist and turn of the road. Rushing rivers allowed fur traders to penetrate the hinterland throughout the Outaouais. The historic Ottawa River, which extends from the St. Lawrence River to the Great Lakes, here meets its mightiest tributaries. (In fact, the Ottawa River is affectionately called the first Trans-Canada Highway.) Québec's famous triple play of rivers—the Noire (Black), Dumoine, and Coulonge to the west—as well as the Gatineau, Rouge, and Blanche to the east, all drain into the Ottawa within this region.

Hugging the rivers are thousands of miles of forests punctuated by pristine lakes—wild country where deer, wolves, and bears still roam. You'll find pastoral fields dotted with grazing cattle, corn "as high as an elephant's eye," and prosperous farms. Villages here reflect the pattern of immigration to the New Land. There's Luskville, named for Irish immigrant Joseph Lusk; Shawville, honoring Englishman John Shaw; Fort Coulonge, an early French fur-trading post; Maniwaki, a village with an Algonquin

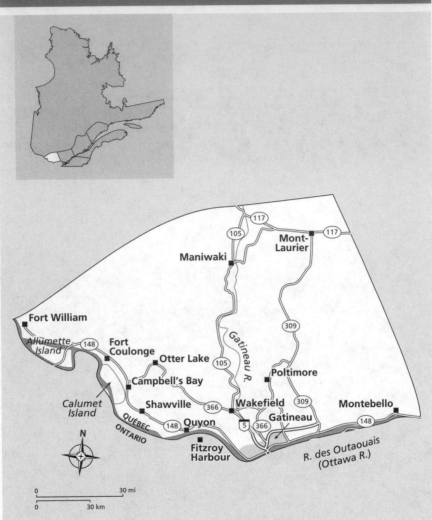

Mont-Laurier

Maniwaki

Fort William

Allumette Island

Fort Coulonge

Otter Lake

Campbell's Bay

Gatineau R.

Poltimore

Calumet Island

Shawville

Wakefield

Montebello

QUÉBEC
ONTARIO

Quyon

Gatineau

N

Fitzroy Harbour

R. des Outaouais
(Ottawa R.)

0   30 mi

0   30 km

name; Ladysmith, formerly Schwartz, a German settlement dating from the mid-1800s; and Papineauville, too, for Louis-Joseph Papineau, leader of the Rebellion of Lower Canada in 1837. Indeed, this region of Québec is truly a microcosm of Canada: Poles, Lithuanians, Germans, French, English, Scots, and Irish all settled here.

Peppered throughout the Outaouais, alternative communities are part of the ebb and flow. Some are vestiges of circa 1850s communities, such as the area north of Shawville and Otter Lake called the Polish Hills, named for the many Polish immigrants who settled in the area. In the 1960s communes were established on inexpensive land in these back-of-beyond spots. More recently, escapees from more hectic city life have renovated old farms in the Pontiac region. Like the first wave of back-to-the-landers, these former urbanites have chosen what they hope will be a more community-minded, "natural" place to live and raise their families.

chiefpontiac

The Pontiac area of the Outaouais region is named for First Nations chief Pontiac, who led a rebellion against the British in 1755. He was the chief of the Odawa people from Michigan and died in Illinois. The Odawa gave their name to Ottawa, the capital of Canada, and also to the Outaouais region.

And there's another aspect to the Outaouais: It's largely federalist. During the referendum of October 1995, more than 90 percent of the population voted an emphatic *Non* to the question of Québec separation from Canada. English is spoken freely here. You'll see English in signs and hear it in announcements made at country fairs, sometimes to the exclusion of French. In the Pontiac, although proud to live in Québec, Anglophone and Allophone residents are equally and fiercely proud of their English-speaking (or other) backgrounds and ancestry. Truly, the Pontiac is a microcosm of a multicultural Canada.

AUTHORS' FAVORITES IN THE OUTAOUAIS

Château Montebello	Norway Bay Pier
Coulonge Chutes	Shawville's self-guiding walking tour
Esprit Rafting	Spruceholme Inn in Fort Coulonge
Gatineau Park: Luskville Falls hike	Wakefield
Mackenzie King Estate	

Intimately wedded to the capital of Canada, Ottawa, the south-central section of the Outaouais is part of the country's National Capital Region that extends south into Ontario. Because of its proximity to Ottawa, the region is a bedroom community for federal government employees. Many federal offices are in Gatineau, an initiative started when the late Pierre Elliott Trudeau was prime minister during the early 1970s. Because of its great natural beauty, the Outaouais is the capital's recreation Mecca, also providing superb conference along with cottage retreats.

We love Québec, but especially the remote, wild countryside in the western Pontiac region of the Outaouais. We moved here in 1989 to our farmhouse snuggled against Gatineau Park. On a summer's night, with the canopy of stars twinkling overhead, we can sip a glass of wine on our front porch and hear the wolves howl, from one ridge to the next. And if we want to take in a show or meet with a client, we can be in Ottawa–Gatineau in less than an hour. It's a little corner of heaven. Come on out and get yourself a hearty Outaouais welcome!

Special note: In June 2001 "Gatineau" was selected as the new name for the amalgamated cities of Gatineau, Hull, Aylmer, and the neighboring rural areas of Buckingham and Masson-Angers. Many citizens of the smaller villages decried the change as revisionist and anti-heritage because its creation eradicated villages with names recalling English-speaking settlers. Despite objections, amalgamation became official on January 1, 2002. As a result, villages are swallowed into the French name "Gatineau," thereby further erasing the region's rich heritage of multiracial names.

Exploring the Outaouais

The Outaouais is best accessed from Montréal or Ottawa–Gatineau. Generally, the road system in this large territory follows the river systems used by the native people and voyageurs of days gone by. To the west of Gatineau, the Pontiac region stretches along the Ottawa River, with rolling farmland and sometimes dense bush surrounding both it and other wild rivers. To the north, the Gatineau Valley extends far up into the rugged Canadian Shield of the Laurentian plateau. To the east, the influence of the seigneurial system of land allotment is still visible in the long, thin farms of Papineauville and La Petite Nation, which extend from the river's banks.

Fluently bilingual staff at **Outaouais Tourism** will happily answer questions (103 rue Laurier, Gatineau; 819-778-2222; www.tourismeoutaouais.com).

If you use the Gatineau area as a base to explore this vast territory, be sure to spend some time in nearby Gatineau Park.

Seigneurial System

The French king gave large tracts of land called *seigneuries* to *seigneurs*, landowners (often nobles), who subdivided it to *les habitants* (tenant-colonists). This system was introduced into Nouvelle France by Cardinal Richelieu in 1627. Typically, *seigneuries* were strips of land extended about a mile back from a water frontage of 540 feet, with central parcels set aside for a mill, the seigneurial house, and the church.

Based on the feudal system in France, tenants paid taxes to the seigneurs and had to give three days of work every year, plus perform road or bridge maintenance if needed. To ensure tenants' needs would be looked after, seigneurs were required to live on their estates, and were vassals of the King of France. As well, common land extended along the river frontage, and both the mill and Church (both being crucial to the development of community) were centrally located.

After the fall of New France during the Conquest of 1759, the seigneural system was kept by the British—but was abolished by Canadian Governor General Lord Elgin in 1854.

Gatineau Park

Managed by a Crown corporation called the National Capital Commission (NCC), *Gatineau Park* is a jewel of the National Capital Region. Over 200 kilometers of groomed trails welcome skiers in winter, while other trails are open to snowshoers. In summer a shared network of trails welcomes mountain bikers and hikers; other paths are only for hikers. *Lakes Lapêche, Philippe, and Meech* offer excellent canoeing, and camping is delightful at Lac Lapêche and Lac Philippe. Ask the Visitor's Centre (819-827-2020) about the overnight accommodations at Brown Cabin. The parks people are continuing to develop hut-to-hut hiking and skiing. In addition, the park's National Trail connects to the Trans-Canada Trail.

Also in the park is the *Mackenzie King Estate,* once the residence of our tenth prime minister William Lyon Mackenzie King, who bequeathed his three properties (Moorside, Kingswood Cottage, and The Farm) to the people of Canada in his 1950 will. Today the NCC operates the first two as interpreted historical sites where visitors can learn about the life and times of this prime minister who believed in the spirit world. He held seances to commune and confer not only with his late mother but also with his three Irish terriers—all named Pat. (In fact, new at the Estate since 2008 are Ghost Walks, where actors depicting historical characters lurk in the woods . . . 819-827-2020; or, if you opt for dinner and a night tour, 819-778-2530.)

Other areas in the park, such as the ruins of Thomas "Carbide" Willson's generating station and Canada's first super-phosphate fertilizer plant on Little Meech Lake, are of significance as heritage sites but have only a couple of interpretive signs. The dearth of signage is perhaps due to bare sightings. No, we don't mean "bear sightings." The old mill, as the site of the fertilizer plant is erroneously yet affectionately known by locals, has been adopted by nudists. Signs put up by the NCC assert that nudism is an offense. Well, some signs seem fated to be ignored, and such is the case with these. Nudism is alive and well at this site, so either go in the dead of winter or in the height of bug season if your sensibilities will be offended.

Gatineau Park is accessible by car through five main entrances. To the south, enter via Taché Boulevard in Gatineau. From the southwest (via the Eardley-Masham road) as well as the northwest, entry is to the Lac Lapêche sector. From the north, access Lac Philippe camping via Highway 366 at Sainte-Cécile-de-Masham. To find the park visitor center or rent a bike or other equipment, head north on Highway 5 from Gatineau and take exit 12 at *Old Chelsea.* Proceed west on Meech Lake Road through the village; turn right on Scott Road.

they're off and running

Philip McGinnis was a racetrack reporter from Huntingdon, Québec. He invented a wire starting barrier that could be raised at the starting post of horseraces. Although eventually replaced by electric starting posts, McGinnis's invention quashed many an annoying squabble precipitated by horses that broke ranks when anticipating the dropping of the flag, which had hitherto indicated the start of a race.

Continue for a moment: immediately on your left you'll see the *Gatineau Park Visitor's Centre* (30 chemin Scott, 819-827-2020; www.capcan.ca). Park for free and head inside to the small museum. There is a small boutique, too, where you can get trail maps as well as ski and hiking passes; purchase books (such as *Historical Walks: The Gatineau Park Story* written by Katharine); bird-watching lists; and literature about guided walks or lectures given by Friends of Gatineau Park.

Return to Old Chelsea. As you drive, first note on your left the heritage mid-1800s square-cut log home at the corner of chemin Padden. It recalls early pioneer days where such homesteads hewn from the surrounding woods would have resembled this solo survivor. Continue to the corner of Meech Lake Road: across from you note the flat-roofed home sided with tin. In the mid-1800s it was Dunn's Hotel, one of five "stopping places" (tavern-inns) all run by Irishmen here in the village. The village housed a couple of mills and a tannery: all have gone.

TOP ANNUAL EVENTS IN THE OUTAOUAIS

MID-FEBRUARY

Gatineau Loppet
(819) 243-2330
www.gatineauloppet.com
Join 2,500 skiers from twenty countries in cross-country ski races in Gatineau Park.

JUNE

Pontiac Artists' Studio Tour
Pontiac area west of Gatineau;
(819) 647-6365
www.pontiacartists.com

JULY 1

Canada Day
celebrations throughout the region.

AUGUST

Les grands feux du Casino
near Gatineau's casino
(819) 771-3389 or (888) 429-3389
www.feux.qc.ca
Fireworks from international competitors light the sky.

Musiqu'en Nous (August Music Festival)
in Saint-André-Avellin and area; in the streets, churches, and bars;
(819) 983-3273
www.musiquennous.ca

SEPTEMBER

Shawville Agricultural Fair
(819) 647-3213
www.shawvillefair.ca

Artists in Their Environment Studio Tour
Wakefield;
(819) 459-3233
www.arttourchelseawakefield.com

SEPTEMBER/OCTOBER

Coloris automnal (Fall Rhapsody)
Come and see the fall colors in Chelsea and Gatineau Park; exhibitions, interpreted walks, family activities.
(819) 827-2020
www.capcan.ca

DECEMBER

Festival of Lights
Admire the stunning Coulonge Chutes waterfall boiling its way through a spectacular, craggy gorge—illuminated by thousands of lights; north of Fort Coulonge, Pontiac.
www.chutescoulonge.qc.ca

Now for something completely different: a pioneer cemetery stroll. Turn right on chemin Meech Lake Road and immediately left on chemin Kingsmere. Proceed, keeping a lookout for the *Old Chelsea Picnic Grounds* which appears almost immediately on your left. Park for free. Walk through the picnic-table-strewn grass, descend steep stairs to a wooden bridge spanning Chelsea Creek and ascend the opposite embankment. You emerge into the quiet oasis of the *Old Chelsea Protestant Burying Grounds.* In summer the grass is purple because flowering (and fragrant) creeping thyme blossoms here. Stroll about, visiting the final resting place of such notables as the pioneer doctor, and Congregationalist Minister, **Asa Meech,** for whom Meech Lake road and lake are named.

Check out **La Cigale** (Old Chelsea; 819-827-6060). Entrepreneurs George Claydon and his wife, Chris Kaarsberg, opened an ice-cream parlor and fresh-squeezed juice bar, a delectable stopping place that serves up homemade ice cream made from natural ingredients. It's a don't miss, truly; open seven days a week, noon to 9 p.m. weekdays and 11 a.m. to 9 p.m. weekends from May through mid-Oct. (At time of writing in late 2009, a move to a larger location opposite the NCC Visitor Centre on Scott Road was being planned.)

smokin'

Boucanerie Chelsea is another "don't miss" because this Chelsea Smokehouse serves local (and quite rare) smoked sturgeon and other delicacies (706 Rte. 105; Chelsea [not Old Chelsea: confusingly, there are two!] 819-827-1925). A great spot to buy picnic fixings.

Before leaving Gatineau Park and Old Chelsea, we recommend you indulge at **Le Nordik Spa Scandinave** (16 chemin Nordik, Old Chelsea, J9B 2P7; www.lenordik.com). The Scandinavian-inspired system of hot followed by cold spa treatments invigorates tired muscles regardless of whether you've been sitting in the car for too long or skiing or hiking for hours. You can stay overnight here at the lodge or simply spend the day going in and out of hot tubs, cold-or-lukewarm pools, steam baths and saunas. As well, there is an excellent restaurant on-site overlooking the outdoor pools.

Our best tip for Le Nordik is to visit at night and also, in winter because especially during the Christmas season, delicate lights illuminate some of the forest trees and lanterns light the pathways. Moreover, the images of steam curling up towards the canopy of stars amid the snow-draped woods is unforgettable.

Gatineau and Beyond

We'll start our exploration of the Outaouais using Gatineau (formerly named Hull prior to the 2002 amalgamation) as our leaping-off point. Poised as it is on the north side of the Ottawa River across from the nation's capital, the city is unknown to many. To the relief of many, Gatineau is now outgrowing its old reputation as a "drinking town."

Gatineau was founded by New Englander Philemon Wright, a republican who came here from Woburn, Massachusetts in 1800. He and his party of intrepid settlers struggled north using ox-drawn sleighs, navigating frozen waterways as their highways. Once established in Wrightsville, as their agricultural settlement was first known, Philemon soon recognized that the very trees they were felling for their farms and villages would be their ticket to prosperity.

In 1806, when Napoleon blockaded the Baltic, Great Britain was cut off from its timber resources. How could the Royal Navy's ships be built? As British eyes cast about for trees, so did Philemon's: in fact, just about all he could see was trees. So he set to work, and in 1807 he and his sons floated their first raft of timber downstream to Québec. This historic trip founded the timber industry that was to make his fortune and that would enshrine the Outaouais and Ottawa Valley regions as Britain's primary source of square timber for its shipbuilding.

When the days of the square-timber trade waned, the sawn-timber industry took over. Huge piles of planks were stockpiled in Ottawa and Gatineau, products of the sawmills powered by the water of mighty rapids such as the

Outaouais Geology

At the Chaudière Falls rapids in Gatineau, you can see the Ottawa River pouring through jutting layers of limestone. This is intriguing to the geologist because this exposed rock is younger than the sinuous ridge of the Eardley Escarpment, which rises just to the north. The ridge is the most ancient rock in the world: Pre-Cambrian rock that formed the weathered roots of a range of mountains once higher than the Rockies. Weathering, glacial action, and faulting conspired to erode them to their present size. The fault line along the base of the ridge is the boundary to Gatineau Park and the northernmost edge of a huge rift valley, extending into the Appalachians of New England.

Successive eras of glaciation covered most of North America, scouring the mountains, depressing the land, carving valleys, and depositing moraine (earth and stone) as the glaciers first grew, then receded. About 20,000 years ago the last ice sheet started to melt and, as it did, the Champlain Sea covered the land. The Eardley Escarpment was its northern boundary. As you stand on the Champlain Lookout in Gatineau Park, your feet firmly atop this ridge, look due south over the flat Ottawa Valley plain. In the distance the Ottawa River flows past, but if you had stood here 12,000 years ago, water would have lapped at your feet. Whales, seals, and other marine creatures dwelt here in saline waters.

Looking out over the plain from the vantage of the Eardley Escarpment is one thing. It's just as intriguing to drive through geological history. As you drive west on Highway 148 from Gatineau toward Quyon, you will pass several terraces, old beaches formed when the Ottawa River was receding. Keep your eyes peeled for these ancient landmarks.

Chaudière. Most of the lumber went to the new market, the United States, whose bustling cities such as Boston and Philadelphia had an insatiable appetite for construction materials. Gatineau was razed by flames in 1900. It started as a chimney fire, but sparks borne by the wind landed on both sides of the Ottawa River. The ensuing conflagration destroyed most of the old city of Hull and burned much of the capital, too.

Enough reading: let's get exploring! We'll start at the **Chaudière Falls,** where Champlain and countless, nameless river traders before him portaged round the rapids the Algonquin called **Asticou,** (*Chaudière* in French, or Boiling Kettle). First Nations traders hauled their canoes onto the limestone rocks here and paused before paddling upstream. Champlain's journal of 1613 records their tobacco ceremony, practiced on the shore beside the rapids. Native peoples tossed offerings of tobacco into the boiling waters to placate the river spirits and to seek safe passage upstream, to the Great Lakes.

You'll find the falls and **Voyageur Park** on Taché Boulevard in Gatineau, at the junction of rue Montcalm, overlooking the Ottawa River. Saunter inside the park's iron gates and approach the edge of the river. An iron sculpture suggests the hull of a boat, while others depict wolves. Standing at the rushing water's edge, it's easy to understand how the cascading series of rapids represented an impassable barrier. Perhaps Champlain stood right where you're standing, observing the tobacco ceremony!

To your immediate left is the stone Eddy Mill, named after American entrepreneur Ezra Butler Eddy, who arrived in Gatineau in 1851 from Bristol, Vermont. Eddy became the "match king" of the British Empire, building mills here that produced more than a million matches a day. A devastating fire in 1875 wiped out his first mills spanning the Chaudière; the new ones were similarly wiped out in 1900. As a measure of his perseverance, he rebuilt after both fires, and when he died in 1906 his mills were in the black.

Continue west (heading right) on the paved pathway alongside the Ottawa River to **Brewery Creek.** Yes, there used to be a brewery here, as well as a sawmill and gristmill. In 1947, in order to free himself from the stresses of the post-war years, British high commissioner Malcolm Macdonald used to enjoy paddling across the Ottawa River, then along this creek. An amateur naturalist and avid birdwatcher, he chronicled the species he observed here in his classic (and out-of-print) book *The Birds of Brewery Creek.*

Look upstream to spy an island in the midst of Brewery Creek. Here stands **Théâtre de l'Île,** (Island Theater). Locals luxuriate on its grass in summer, "catching the rays" during our fleeting Canadian summer. On a gentle summer's eve, take in the live theater; all performances are entirely in French (1 rue Wellington, Gatineau; 819-595-7455).

A stroll along the creek's boardwalk brings you to the *Les Brasseurs du Temps* (170 rue Montcalm, Gatineau; 819-205-4999; www.brasseursdutemps .com). Not only is the heritage stone building a former water charming, this micro-brewery makes hand-crafted traditional-styles of beer. For example, the brewery makes an unfiltered wheat beer, *le bouillon de la Chaudière*, which takes its name from the Chaudière rapids nearby. There's a restaurant here, and also, special events which include beer tastings plus pairings with foods such as cheeses ($25 per person—check Web site for dates, details). In autumn of 2009, an on-site museum promises to chronicle the history of brewing.

champlain's astrolabe

French explorer Samuel de Champlain lost his astrolabe, used to calculate the location of celestial bodies, in 1613. A farmer discovered it in his field, near Cobden, Ontario, and sold it to an American. Today it's back in Canada, and you can see it displayed at the Canadian Museum of Civilization in Gatineau.

It's now time to leave urban sprawl behind. Head west on Taché Boulevard, which soon becomes Route 148 Ouest (West), leading toward the former village of *Aylmer,* and ultimately into the Pontiac region.

En route, opposite a Harvey's fast-food restaurant in Gatineau, you'll find one of the five entryways into Gatineau Park on your right. Carefully look to the north (right-hand side) for a large stone surrounded by evergreens. It is the last remaining original milestones of the *Old Britannia Road*—the old name of the footpath, then road that were precursors to today's Route 148, connecting the former towns of Hull and Aylmer.

The Britannia Road was once simply a series of portage tracks connecting the string of settlements on the river's north shore. Although the Ottawa River was the primary transportation route, steamboat passengers had to disembark and portage both themselves and their goods around three impassable rapids: the Chaudière, Deschênes (Oak), and Petites Deschênes (Little Oak). It didn't take long for enterprising folks such as the Klock family to build/operate stagecoaches along the roadway along which you are driving—but not before landowners whose property fronted the path reluctantly agreed to "road duty" to maintain the road along their boundary. Those tempestuous days are recalled in modern times: in 1997, the stretch of Route 148 passing through Aylmer was widened and local residents lobbied to save the magnificent old maples and oaks lining the thoroughfare. Thankfully, in most cases the grand trees still grace the route.

Continue west on Route 148 until you reach a major intersection with signs pointing left to Ottawa. Get into the left-hand turn lane and descend to the next set of lights. Ahead of you is the Champlain Bridge leading to Ontario and Ottawa. Do not proceed across the bridge; instead turn right onto what is called the Lower Aylmer Road (chemin Lucerne). (*Special note:* Cyclists will enjoy bicycling along the Ottawa River on a paved path extending some 11 kms from the Champlain Bridge to the old village of Aylmer—now the westernmost sector of Gatineau. For maps contact the National Capital Commission's Visitor Centre at 90 Wellington St., across from Parliament Hill in Ottawa, or the Gatineau Park Visitor Centre at 33 Scott Rd., Chelsea; 819-827-2020.)

isabelle duchesnay: icedancer

Born in Aylmer in 1963, Isabelle and her brother Paul wowed the world with their innovative ice dancing. Renowned as avante-garde skaters, they received so much criticism here that they left Canada for France, where Paul had been born. Continuing their innovative excellence, they won a world championship in 1991 and a year later, a silver Olympic medal—for France.

Continue driving and, on your left, just before the first set of traffic lights (intersection with chemin Vanier), you'll find a long, old limestone wall, with a gap behind which is a parking lot and limestone buildings. One of the buildings is home to a treasure of a restaurant that is only open for dinner: ***L'Échelle de Jacob (Jacob's Ladder)*** (27 blvd. Lucerne, Gatineau; 819-684-1040; www.lechelledejacob.ca). After parking, turn to look at the cut-limestone buildings; you'll note a grassed gap and walkway between them. Walk up here and turn left to enter the door leading upstairs to the restaurant. Ask for the table d'hôte menu, and always inquire about the specials. Ask to hear tales of the history of the building, which was once the terminus for streetcars that took passengers from Aylmer to Gatineau. It also served as an axe factory.

If you wish to explore the riverfront, do so by heading south on any of the streets here (Vanier's a good choice). A riverside path frequented by cyclists, skateboarders, dog-walkers allows access to the river. Take care:

Reconnect to Route 148 by proceeding along the Lower Aylmer Road (chemin Lucerne). Off to the left is the Ottawa River. Eventually the road curves right and connects with the highway. Turn left at the lights at rue Principale (Main Street); a little fountain and park mark this corner, on your left. For now, continue through the old part of the former Aylmer until you glimpse the river ahead.

On your right, at a bend in the road, you'll see what was once the ***Symmes Hotel***, a magnificent cut-limestone building with white, double-story front, and back wooden porches. Artist W. H. Bartlett's engraving of this old hostelry was published in London in *Canadian Scenery Illustrated,* in 1842. The picture shows the frozen expanse of a widening in the Ottawa River behind the hotel. The hotel exhibits classic Québécois architectural features, with a bell-shaped, sweeping roofline designed so that snow will slide off instead of accumulating. It was built by Charles Symmes, a son-in-law of Philemon Wright's, in 1832 as a hotel for the steamboat passengers who needed accommodations prior to pressing on upriver. Nowadays, it is home to the **Aylmer Museum** (1 rue Front, 819-628-0291)

Park your car at the **Aylmer Marina** (1 rue Principale, Gatineau; call 819-684-9288 for information about the marina as well as the on-site restaurant and bar). Wander its grounds or, in summer, find the sandy beach behind and to the right of the main building. Not only is **Aylmer Beach** a good place to swim, it's a noted windsurfing mecca. Even if you don't do this sport yourself, it's awesome to watch and photograph the photogenic athletes looping and blasting.

Cyclists: note the bicycle path, which you can explore equally enjoyably on foot or by bike. It will return you, eventually, to Voyageur Park in central Gatineau, passing along the waterfront and through pretty woodlands.

In front of the marina (and beside the Symmes Hotel) is the totally delightful **Parc l'Imagier,** the creation of art lovers, Pierre Debain and his late wife, Yvette Debain. Wander the grassy, out-of-the-way park immediately opposite the marina's parking lot to discover all sorts of unlikely art and folk art "installations." For example, you won't be able to miss seeing the oversized picnic table which has been decorated by local artists, many of whom (such as Marcio Melo) participate in annual studio tours. It is inspiring to watch kids dashing about, swinging on the park's small swing-set and slide and playing amid (if not on) the art. Also look for the saucy couple who are permanently enjoying a bath in an old-fashioned bathtub. They are located in the back garden of your next destination: an art gallery which is indelibly linked to this park. To find it, walk to Front Street.

bikingthepontiac

Rails-to-trails movements throughout the world are transforming old railbeds to recreational trails for bicyclists. In Pontiac, the **PPJ Cyclopark** (800-665-5217; www.cycloparcppj.org) extends 72 km from Wyman (just outside Quyon) to Waltham along the bed of the former Pontiac Pacific Junction Railway line. We were dismayed when, in the 1990s, landowners connecting the Quyon to Aylmer (Gatineau) section of railbed refused to participate. Their decision orphaned the Pontiac section of bike trail from the capital of Canada and Trans-Canada Trail network. Sad. Nonetheless, biking from Wyman to Waltham is attractive and fun, linking villages, B&Bs and restaurants.

Pontiac: A Vibrant Artistic Community

Artists often choose to live in peaceful, less expensive communities which can be way off the beaten track. When Eric and I moved to the Pontiac, we quickly integrated into a multi-layered community of artists, writers, and artisans, many of whom are now close friends. After I moved here in 1989, six other women and I founded the Pontiac Artists' Studio Tour, which occurs two weekends in June (www.pontiac artists.com).

Since then many artists, craftspeople and writers have joined the tour, such as potter and papermaker Valerie Bridgeman and pen-and-ink artist Michael Neelin. What's great fun is that every year, new artists bring their energy and unique creations to the tour—and because artists exhibit at their home studios, visitors get to travel the backroads of Pontiac, exploring its beauty and discovering how people live and work here.

If you like arts and crafts as well as exploring back roads and country places, plan to coincide with the Pontiac Artists' Studio Tour. Admission is free, and you will be warmly invited into each creator's space to view (and possibly buy) their work.

Hot tip: Want to take a workshop with an artist? Explore the Pontiac Artists' Studio Tour Web site and click on individual participants' Web sites. Many, such as potter Clément Hoeck, offer workshops—but you must register in advance. And if you cannot visit in early June, contact the artists because most will welcome a pre-arranged visit.

—Katharine

La Centre d'Exposition l'imagier Art Gallery (9 Front St., Gatineau; 819-684-1445; www.limagier.qc.ca) is located in a board-and-batten chocolate brown house sporting a flirtatious hot-pink trim. Over a span of three decades or so, proprietors Yvette and Pierre have been tremendously supportive of the regional art scene. In fact, it was the Yvette who encouraged the former City of Aylmer to create the magical park you have just seen, so the public could appreciate *l'art en plein air* (art in the fresh air).

Once back in your car, drive northwest (left) on Front Street (past the gallery) to rejoin Route 148. Turn left (west) toward Luskville, Quyon, Shawville, Fort Coulonge and beyond. Watch for a blue tourist sign announcing *Potager Eardley* (Eardley Kitchen Garden; www.potagereardley.com), and on your right (after the intersection of chemin Perry, also on your right) find a pretty ox-blood-red barn with white windows. Park (free) and enter to find local agri-food producers products, soaps and balms, honey and beeswax candles, as well as seasonal gelatos, frozen yoghurt, and ice cream. As well, in summer and early autumn you can pick vegetables and fruits grown here, including eleven varieties of strawberries.

Continue west: now you leave built-up streetscapes behind as you drive into the **Pontiac region** of the Outaouais, where spectacular nature is your companion. Look left to the mighty Ottawa River flowing downstream to Ottawa and Montréal. Imagine: 5,000 years ago native copper traders would be paddling by; in 1613 Champlain canoed upstream, searching for a route to the Orient; and 200 years later, steamers plied the waterway. These days in summer, sailboats dot the river while during winter you can see clustered "villages" of ice huts, where hardy types fish through holes they've cut in the metre-thick ice.

The drive offers panoramas of agricultural life. Keep your eyes peeled: not only will you see beef and dairy cattle but also draught horses, such as Belgians, which many farmers here still raise, primarily because they love them. At country fairs you can watch teams of up to eight of these gentle giants, proudly pulling gaily colored wagons.

Watch for **St. Augine Church,** an old stone church converted to a private dwelling perched right beside the highway, atop a hill, about ten minutes out of the former city of Aylmer. This is **Ghost Hill,** a local landmark where tales

Legend of Ghost Hill

Stories of murder, ghostly sightings, and buried treasure mark Ghost Hill, a lonely stretch of highway west of Aylmer, at Breckenridge. Once the village had a store, post office, sawmill, railway station, water tower, and cluster of homes. Today it's a hill, a bend in the road, and a bridge over Breckenridge Creek. Blink your eye and you've missed the memory.

But once upon a time, what's now Route 148 was a simple dirt track wide enough for a traveler's horse and cart. Trees, marsh, and mist were their companions. One blustery night, as his horse plodded home, one such fellow was aching to get home. Half asleep, roused by a sudden bellowing noise, he recoiled in fear. Dashing straight toward him was the oddest-looking cow he'd ever seen. With fear as his guide, he pointed his rifle and shot. Jumping from the cart, he inspected the horrible apparition: his best friend lay at his feet, dressed in the skin of a calf.

It's not only the soul of the practical joker that haunts Ghost Hill. It's the ghost of the Armenian peddler, too. The peddler roamed the countryside, as did many folks, buying and selling what he could from his cart. Tall tales of his wealth grew, until one day, he felt sure his life was in danger, so he buried his bag of gold—on Ghost Hill. Sadly, his premonitions proved accurate, and he was brutally murdered. Weaving such legends together over the years are the reported sightings of ghosts at Ghost Hill. Skeptics say it is merely the will-o'-the-wisp, or marsh gas. But on a dark and stormy night, when the skeletal limbs of the trees are a-groaning, who's to deny that anguished souls are crying . . . on Ghost Hill?

of ghostly sightings, murder, and mayhem abound. The descent is abrupt and winding: take care. At the bottom is a marsh where people have occasionally seen will-o-the-wisps, that bouncing ball of wavering light created by marsh gases—or the ghost of a lost soul, pending your sensibilities. You pass over a small stream, Breckenridge Creek, which once sported a sawmill, gristmill, and general store. Today it's merely a bend in the road.

Continuing on Route 148 Ouest, this section of the drive brings geology to life as you traverse the flat Ottawa Valley plain. To your left is the Ottawa River, to the right is the Eardley Escarpment, the ancient roots of the Laurentian Mountains.

Route 148 suddenly and seemingly inexplicably widens to a short four-lane stretch at Luskville—apparently the result of an election promise! The road used to be quite narrow and winding, and there had been a couple of fatal accidents. The incumbent promised to improve the road if re-elected, but postponed action until just before the next election.

In this four-lane section, there are two interesting destinations: one is Luskville Falls, a waterfall and hike to the north (right-hand-side) of the highway; the other is a lavender and winery on the left.

First watch for the brown National Capital Commission sign pointing right to Gatineau Park and **Luskville Falls** picnic ground. Turn right onto chemin Hôtel de Ville Road (immediately after the Luskville town hall, also on your right). Here find a picnic ground, barbecue pits, and a splendid, heart-healthy hike 300 metres up the steep **Eardley Escarpment** alongside the falls. The 5 km return hike takes approximately two hours if done at a leisurely pace and allowing for a picnic stop at the summit. There are outstanding lookouts from the ridge over the Ottawa River Valley and interpretive panels explain the history, geology, and flora. Take binoculars as you often will see raptors (birds of prey), such as the red-tailed hawk or turkey vulture, soaring on updrafts of air along the ridge. Bald eagles and golden eagles nest along this ridge. The "baldies" are a relatively common sight; "goldens" are rare.

After the Chutes Luskville, return to the highway. Now, cross it but turn left (temporarily heading back east towards Aylmer/Gatineau) and watch carefully for Doug Briden and Joanne Labadie's farm, **Ferme Lavender Ridge** (1983 Rte 148, Luskville, 819-455-2544). The white farmhouse has a jaunty red roof and in summer, you might spy Houdini wandering about. (That would be their escape-artist goat!) As the name implies, Doug and Joanne grow lavender which they transform into salves, soaps, and such inventive products as insect repellant.

But these agri-food producers also have one of Pontiac's few wineries. They established both the lavender fields and vineyards in 2006, and while they've enjoyed a real learning curve adapting to new varieties of both plants, they are also enjoying successes. Call ahead to ensure they're there to welcome you, or, as Joanne says, visit them "by chance." Either way, both Doug and Joanne are informed if not inspiring Pontiac agri-producers.

To return to Route 148 Ouest, you'll have to do another "U" turn. To accomplish this, head right (east) from Lavender Ridge Farm; watch carefully for the next left-hand turn at chemins Tremblay/Creigheur. Carefully turn left and left again, to "do the U" turn; then proceed west on Route 148, again.

Back on Route 148 Ouest, continue until you reach the second exit to the village of Quyon (pronounced Kwee-Yon or, as locals say, Kwee-Oh). Quyon is well-known in the National Capital Region because a seasonal ferry operating from this little village crosses the Ottawa River to Fitzroy Harbour, Ontario. (And it makes a great little circuit drive when the ferry's operating, from Gatineau-Quyon-Ottawa, a route allowing you to explore the rural part of the twin cities of Gatineau and the capital of Canada.)

To visit the village, cross the highway carefully to **Quyon.** Just before crossing the Quyon River note the old flour mill, M&R Feeds, on your right; then stop at the T intersection with Rue Clarendon. If you want to visit the fair-grounds for *JamFest* (annual July music festival featuring country music singers such as Gail Gavan; www.quyonjamfest.ca) turn left on Clarendon. At rue Saint-John, look left to find **Gavan's Hotel** (1157 Clarendon St., 819-458-2354). This tavern is renowned for its March 17, St. Patrick's Day bash, but you can catch live country music here every weekend. As you might have guessed, it

How to Find a Brazilian Artist's Studio Really Far from Brazil

Want to head into the back of beyond? From Route 148 at the second exit to Quyon, turn right immediately after Mohr's Garage onto paved chemin Lac de Loup. Follow it for about 10 kilometers as it gains elevation. Immediately after it bisects a cornfield, it turns into a gravel road. Remain on it for about 2 kilometers, then turn left onto another gravel road, Twelfth Line, which forms a T intersection here. This abrupt turn is marked by a stand of tall white pine and, immediately to your right, a small cottage. Descend the Twelfth Line for 1.4 kilometers, cross a little bridge, and immediately turn right into the lane to *Marcio Melo Studio.* (8 Twelfth Line, Bristol; 819-647-3416; www.marciomelo.com). This funky farmhouse, picturesquely perched beside Moffat Lake, is full of Marcio's brilliantly colored, whimsical watercolors and acrylics. His partner, Ted Fort, makes tasty wildflower honey from his own beehives. Although you can visit them during the Pontiac Artists Studio Tour in June, both fellows welcome visitors throughout the year—but please do call first.

belongs to local country singer Gail Gavan's family—and mark our words, it's one of the Ottawa Valley's landmark watering holes! Where is the fairground? Turn right on the next street, Onslow Lane, opposite Marcottes' gas station and *dépanneur*, and you'll find it on your immediate left.

At the foot of Onslow Lane at the Ottawa River find the "Beach Barn" or Lion's Hall, a large Quonset hut. There's free parking, a dock, plus a small children's playground complete with pirate boat and swings. It's a good spot to stretch your legs and perhaps have a picnic of fresh foods you purchased from Potager Eardley en route.

Quyon's seasonal ferry or *Traversier Saissonnier* (www.quyonferry .com), takes roughly 10 minutes to cross the Ottawa River to Mohr's Landing and Fitzroy Harbour, Ontario (early Apr to late Nov or Dec pending weather; $7.50—contact ferry hot line for times, dates of operation: 819-458-2286). *Cautionary tip:* please respect the no swimming sign: At the confluence of the Quyon and Ottawa rivers there is a nasty current so swimming is forbidden.

However, canoeists can launch their canoe onto the river at the beach immediately left of the ferry docks (at the Beach Barn). You must wear lifejackets as you paddle. By paddling upriver, you will come to a generating station constructed in the 1930s. It creates power from what was once a formidable 4 km stretch of rapids known as *Chats Falls* (loosely translated as Wild Cat Rapids). Be cautious here: signs on buoys in the water delimit how close you should get to the dam.

Why canoe here? Because this is a pretty paddle: watch for common loons, kingfishers, white-tailed deer, painted turtles, and other wildlife. But also, you are visiting an historic route where First Nations' peoples, explorers like Samuel de Champlain, plus Hudson Bay and North-West Company fur traders had to portage the treacherous rapids. Where to stay? If you wish to take the ferry to the Ontario (south) side of the Ottawa River, you can camp overnight at *Fitzroy Provincial Park* (www.recreationontario.com).

Reconnect to Route 148 by retracing your route: return to Rue Clarendon and continue west by turning left on it. This used to be the main highway, but now it passes through the center of the village and past some heritage homes. At the junction with Route 148, turn left. After roughly 10 kilometers watch for a highway sign pointing left to *Norway Bay.* This is a tiny cottage community where picturesque cabins (many now being four-season homes) nestle beside the Ottawa River, beneath towering Norway pines. Come summer the fragrance of pines in the hot sunshine evokes many a Canadian cottage memory.

Proceed on River Road (note the road signs are predominantly in English) through Norway Bay to *Wharf Road* and turn left to find the *Norway Bay Pier* and a shady park with picnic tables. There is a safe, sandy beach with very shallow water, and is excellent for youngsters. In the late 1800s, today's landscaped pier was home to a ferry which linked the Pontiac to Sand Point, Ontario. Now it serves as a public boat launch and dock—plus there are benches so you can sit and savor river views and breezes. Locals like us enjoy diving off the pier and swimming in the river.

Return to River Road and turn left toward **Bristol.** Drive slowly, as the road provides a good surface for leisurely strolls for four-footed and two-footed walkers. Coming up soon is the 1930s family resort and golf course known as **Pine Lodge** (6 Pine Lodge Rd., Bristol; 819-647-2805; www.pine-lodge.ca). Not only is there a restaurant and lodgings here. You can also play golf on the nine-hole course or else laze on the sandy beach with a good book.

Back on River Road, turn left towards the small community of Bristol. On your right you'll see the Graham family's **Cidrerie Coronation Hall Cider Mills** (206 River Rd., 819-647-2547; www.coronationhall.com). Formerly a popular 1930s dance hall (it still boasts its sprung dance floor) the Grahams transformed the premises into a *cidrerie* (cider hall) because of their nearby operation, Third Line Orchards. The family now produces apple a range of apple ciders: sweet (Le Bristol), sparkling (William King) and an ice cider, (le Nordic) in honor of the ferry that used to cross from Norway Bay to Sand Bay. In fact, enjoy all things apple here, from cider presses to apple pies and other treats served at the tearoom and gift shop. Check their Web site or telephone for the wide variety of events such as film nights and apple pressings, where you can watch fruit being transformed into cider.

shawville

With a population of 1,634, Shawville is the only town of its size in Québec that does not have a Roman Catholic church. The Pontiac may be the biggest county in Québec, but it has only one traffic light—in "downtown" Shawville.

Now we'll introduce you to Shawville, the "shopping center of the Pontiac." Turn right on the Bristol Road and reconnect to Route 148; turn left. Shawville soon appears on your right. Turn right on Centre Street and find parking near the white building labeled **The Equity,** the home of a newspaper of the same name that has been "the voice of the Pontiac" since 1883 (133 Centre Street, 819-647-2204; open 8 a.m. to 5 p.m. daily, 9 a.m. to noon Sat; closed Sun). Publisher Heather Dickson operates this family-run business, which publishes the primarily English-language weekly. Step inside to discover regional books for sale written by local authors and to soak in the feel of a real community paper. Ask for copies of Shawville's **self-guided walking tour.**

Continue north on Centre Street to the next intersection. Aha! You've discovered the only set of traffic lights in the Pontiac! Turn left here, onto Main Street. Park and stroll to *Café 349*—at 349 Main (819-647-6424; www.cafe349 .com; open Mon to Wed 8 a.m. to 4 p.m., Thurs through Sat 8 a.m. to 8 p.m.; closed Sun). Proprietor Ruth Smiley-Hahn is true to her name: you'll find a warm welcome here where you can sit down at linen-clad tables and enjoy a delicious home-cooked meal, latté or chai. If you're there for breakfast, try her (enormous) bumble berry or pumpkin muffins. Ruth is also a keen supporter of the arts, and the walls of her establishment serve as a permanent gallery with oft-changing exhibits featuring local artists' creations (photographs, oils, watercolors, or perhaps mixed media).

After visiting this delightful haven, stroll Shawville to discover its quiet ambience. If you've procured a copy of the town's heritage walking tour at *The Equity,* now might be a good time to stretch your legs.

Whether you have the booklet or not, you can walk east (left out of Café 349) along Main. Visit *L'Artizan* (324 rue Main, 10 a.m. to 5 p.m. Mon to Sat; 819-647-3032). Jam-packed with art, crafts, quilts, books, local preserves and beeswax candles, this artists' co-operative is a fabulous spot to get a feeling for the Pontiac's artistic community. Business cards, posters, and brochures allow you to connect with regional artists and cultural events, too.

Continuing your appreciation of art, cross Main Street and, on the east side of the large parking lot, find printmaker Raymond Sander-Regier's gallery and press, *Impressions* (305-F Main; 819-503-8004; www.raymond.sanderregier .com). Raymond operates a gallery here and, in the basement, you'll find his printing presses, artworks, and art supply shop.

Back outside, continue east (left) on Main. After leaving Shawville's shopping district you'll get to its residential section. What's architecturally very unusual about Shawville is its Victorian red-brick houses built for bank managers, wealthy merchants, and doctors in the late 1800s. Bricks came from two

Country Fairs

Throughout Québec are many country fairs, and the Pontiac region is no exception. During the first week of Sept come to the *Shawville Fair,* largest in the region, where horses are featured. English and western competitions as well as old-fashioned heavy horse pulls are popular events that draw city and country folk alike. You'll find a giant pumpkin competition, as well as vegetable and flower arrangement contests where platters of eggplant and scarlet tomatoes gleam beside vases of locally grown flowers.

Navigable Water Route

Entrepreneurs such as engineer Thomas Keefer in the late 1800s envisioned the Ottawa River as becoming the major water route connecting the St. Lawrence River to the Great Lakes for shipping. Accordingly, canals, bypasses and locks were partially constructed. The keyword is "partially" because the St. Lawrence Seaway gained supremacy and funding thereby dashing these entrepreneurs' hopes.

Today, a 500-kilometer navigable water route solely for recreational boats (not including houseboats) enables boaters to enjoy the Ottawa River from Arnprior, Ontario (50 kilometers west of Ottawa) to Témiscaming (Québec). Dams and rapids are bypassed by a series of boat ramps and hydraulic towing by four-by-four vehicles. The river is navigable by pleasure boats of 30 feet and pontoon boats up to 28 feet. For information about the seasonal (summer-only) system of boat launches call (866) 224-5244; www.ottawariverwaterway.com.

nearby brickyards. Also of interest are the ***Mill Dam Park*** (you can still see the stone foundation of the old mill by the edge of the creek) and the town's large agricultural fairgrounds. Many events are held there, including July 1 Canada Day celebrations, an Antique Machinery Show during the third weekend in Aug, and the Shawville Fair held during Labor Day weekend (the first full weekend in Sept).

Return to Route 148 and head west (right). On your right, you pass a gas station and small strip mall. Opposite, on your left (south side of the highway) look for the ***Tigre Géant*** (Giant Tiger) discount store. On its eastern wall is a mural depicting the history of the Pontiac region, from the early days of exploration and logging to a celebration of agricultural life. Inside, find locally raised agri-food products such as organic beef from ***Rolling Acres Farm*** and trout from ***Ferme Cedar Creek Farm***. Special note: if you want to fish for your own trout in a pond, contact Ferme Cedar Creek Farm at 819-647-2428; www.cedarcreekfarm.ca).

Just a bit farther west on Route 148, you'll come to a flashing yellow light. Turn left to ***Portage du Fort,*** which was a significant portage and stopping place in the late 1700s for *coureurs de bois* ("runners of the woods"—independent, unlicensed fur traders). There used to be a North West Company fort here, which transferred to the Hudson Bay Company during their merger in 1821. The village was the shopping center of the Pontiac until a devastating fire in 1915 destroyed its bustling commercial district. Shawville then superseded its position in the region, not only because of the fire but also because of the shift from water to rail and then to road transportation.

Portage du Fort is home to a summer gallery and art school. A the heritage stone school is home to **Pontiac School of the Arts** (28 Mill Street; 819-647-2291; www.pontiacschoolofthearts.com; classes during July) as well as the **Stone School Gallery** (open 1 May through 31 Oct). During summer, walk outside to the back of the school where you'll find a tiny library. It used to serve as the town hall. It has an old cabinet in which are housed a few historical artifacts of the village and area.

Even if you're touring when the gallery and school are not open, Portage-du-Fort is still well worth a visit because of its heritage architecture. The fire did not destroy the stone buildings, so you'll find both homes and edifices

WORTH SEEING IN THE OUTAOUAIS

Canadian Museum of Civilization
100 Laurier Street,
Gatineau;
(819) 776-7000 or (800) 555-5621
www.civilization.ca
Designed by internationally renowned Canadian First Nations architect Douglas Cardinal, this building's "bubbles and curves" suggest the rapid-filled Ottawa River which courses by. The museum's First People's Hall presents more than 2,000 artifacts to celebrate native peoples' traditions and culture. Of special note is their contribution to Canadian—and hence world—culture. Although the Grand Hall celebrates west-coast Canadian native art and life, ask to see the small, permanent exhibit nearby, *Kichi Sibi* ("great River" in Algonquin), featuring native artifacts found along the Ottawa River, including the Outaouais. As well, there is an excellent Canadian history exhibit presenting the history of European contact, exploration, fur trade and settlement. A must-see which could easily take a day.
The on-site **Canadian Children's Museum** is open the same hours but closes at 5, 6, or 7 p.m. on Thurs, depending on the season.

Celebrate Art throughout the Outaouais
From artists' workshops to studio tours, to galleries and summer school courses, the Pontiac is a thriving cultural community. Visit **Association des Artistes du Pontiac Artists' Association** (www .pontiacartistsassociation.com) for a listing of annual activities and events throughout the Pontiac region. Chelsea and Wakefield are other thriving centres for the arts with a popular annual studio tour (www.arttourchelseawakefield.com).

Entrepreneur Deborah Bradley hosts primarily classical music events in a repurposed horse barn at **Venturing Hills Farm** (440, Cregheur Rd., Luskville; 819-455-2574; www.venturing hills.ca; year-round events).

For avant-garde projects designed by dancer Tedd Robinson find your way to **The Barn at Lac Leslie** (69 Lake Leslie Rd.; www.tengatesdancing.ca; summer only; no phone, so check Web site for driving instructions, events, times and registration). Dances may be indoors, outside—or a creative combination.

such as the town hall and two churches. After exploring, grab a bite to eat at **Sonia's Pizzaria** (10 Main Street; 819-647-6222; www.soniasrestaurant.com).

Check out the **Chenaux Dam** spanning the Ottawa River here, and the remarkable rocks below it that you can view (with caution) from it. (Note: take great care if you explore the surrounding rocky outcrops because poison ivy is rampant here. And do not venture onto the rocks below the dam as river levels can be suddenly altered by Hydro Québec.)

Return to Route 148 by driving north on Highway 301 Nord (north). Here you'll find a family restaurant, **Auberge Mont Blanc** (37 Calumet; 819-647-5303).

Now continue west to Bryson. Here, turn left to visit *Île du Grand Calumet*. This pastoral mostly agricultural island is home to kayak school and outfitters **HorizonX** (819-648 2727, 866-695-2925 www.horizonx.ca). Not only can you kayak/camp with HorizonX, you can also book a unique-to-Pontiac full-moon kayak on the Ottawa River with them.

Just before you arrive at the village of **Grand Calumet**, you will find a noted Pontiac landmark: a cairn marking the resting place of a *coureur de bois* named Cadieux. Legend has it that the tragic *Lament de Cadieux* was written here, where he and his band of Algonquin companions were ambushed by a roving band of Iroquois in the 1600s. His pals fled, and when they returned they discovered Cadieux's half-buried body. The rather tall story goes that he erected his own wooden cross, wrote his own eulogy, and half-buried himself before expiring. These are his words:

> *Lament of Cadieux*
> *Little rock of the high mount*
> *I've come here to end my days*
> *O, sweet echoes, hear my sigh*
> *I'm sinking fast and going to die.*

Here you have a choice: to return to Route 148 or explore the island. You can visit artist Dale Shutt at her way-off-the-beaten-path studio, **Island Design**. A silk painter, Dale has a studio open by appointment only. You must call her (21 chemin Berry, Île-du-Grand-Calumet; 819-648-2441; www.dale shutt.com) not only to arrange a convenient time to visit but also to get clear directions: It is easy to get lost on the island's gravel back roads. Her remote studio is at the north end of Calumet Island, in an old homestead's original barn. Inspired by fantastical dragons (ask her about the dragon living beneath her hill) as well as by natural, organic forms, Dale's silk paintings, whimsical hanging fish, and dragon sculptures are a delight. She has lived here for more than thirty years and has interpreted her landscape on silk, glass, and canvas for as long.

Dale can direct you to the campgrounds and picnic spots at **Parc Rocher Fendu.** *Rocher Fendu* means "split rocks," and the rocky islands here rise dramatically from the Ottawa River. This park is managed by a Native alliance, L'Alliance Autochtone (819-648-5514). Rocher Fendu is one of the few public access vantage points where you can actually get down to the water. But take care, because the water can be swift and high. If you like spectacular scenery, it's well worth the drive on gravel roads, especially if you enjoy canoeing, swimming, or rustic picnic and camping spots. Note, however, that in recent years kayakers have claimed this park "as their own." If you're a kayaker you'll fit in 100 percent. If you're a family or other tenting and nature enthusiast, be forewarned that there may be many kayaks in the water here.

Return to Route 148 at Bryson and turn left. The next stop is Campbell's Bay, another village on the Ottawa River with an interesting set of redbrick heritage buildings fronting the river. Near the turnoff to the village find **Café GiGi** (819-648-5050; breakfast and lunch only) where local artist show their work. In the village itself, you can eat family-style foods like club-house sandwiches at **Restaurant La Jonction** (2 McLellan, 819-648-2400), overlooking the river.

What's new in "the Bay?" Motor bikes! **Bikes in the Bay** (www.bikesin thebay.com) is a June event for motor bike enthusiasts where you'll discover special bike events, live music, and good fun.

Mishipashoo: God of River Rapids

The ancient peoples who traded copper and tobacco along the Ottawa River paid homage to the god of rapids, Mishipashoo. In Algonquin, mishi means "big," and pashoo means "cat." Old pictograms drawn on cliffs depict a being with a dragon-like head, complete with horns and a writhing, serpentine body.

Mishipashoo controlled the rapids, being respected but feared by navigators, who understood that the safety of all on board was dependent not only on their skill but also on the capricious will of Mishipashoo.

So it was that all who ventured on the river gave Mishipashoo a portion of their treasured possessions. In 1613, when he paddled the Ottawa, Samuel de Champlain and his Algonquin guides gave gifts of tobacco to the Mishipashoo at Chaudière Falls. Gifts of tobacco and copper, the most important trade items in the ancient days, were left on the riverbank. Distracted, Mishipashoo crawled out of the river to claim his due, while the clever river-runners sped past.

Back on Route 148 and a few miles beyond Campbell's Bay, spy the steeple of a large church at Vinton. The fieldstone church seems far too big for this tiny hamlet, but when built in 1896, Vinton was a thriving Irish settlement with several hotels and schools, a sawmill, and a cheese factory.

Farther west, **Fort Coulonge** soon approaches, originally another trading post along the Ottawa, built to protect the interests of the North West Company. Today this predominantly French village is noted for its three historic stone mansions, all built by George Bryson Sr., for his family. Bryson Sr. was a renowned Ottawa Valley timber baron, first president of the Bank of Ottawa (now the Bank of Nova Scotia), and a representative of Pontiac in the Legislative Assembly in Québec City in the mid-1800s. Another Bryson construction is the lovely **St. Andrew's Presbyterian Church,** opposite the stone homes on Rue Principale.

To visit Fort Coulonge, you'll travel through history if you proceed on Route 148 until you see a red covered bridge (also known as a kissing bridge) spanning the river on your left. Drive through it. The **Marchand Bridge** is the longest covered bridge in Québec, built in a matter of months by Augus Brown and his teams of horses and men during the winter of 1898. (The same industrious fellow, by the way, was the first to construct and operate a ferry at Quyon.)

Follow this road as it gently curves, returning you toward the village of Fort Coulonge to **Spruceholme Inn** on your left. In 1996 Glenn and Marlene Scullion purchased one of the Brysons' cut-limestone residences and commenced a major renovation project. In a phenomenal seven months, they opened this stately mansion as Spruceholme Inn (204 rue Principale, Fort-Coulonge; 819-683-5635; www.spruceholmeinn.com). Here you can stay in truly luxurious B&B surroundings that are chock-full of family heirlooms, including a woolen wall tapestry from Paisley, Scotland. Marlene did the tasteful period renovations, and we know you'll enjoy chatting with her. The Scullions are well informed about Pontiac tourism events and history. We highly recommend that you stay here. Spruceholme's accommodations include the "Carriage House," at the rear of the inn. This separate self-catered unit features a kitchenette, fireplace, and accommodates 2 to 4 people.

Return across the bridge to the highway and proceed west toward Davidson and Waltham. Immediately on the right you'll see the heritage building, **Maison Bryson House,** built by family patriarch George Bryson Sr. as his own home in 1854. It is an architectural anomaly here, being an example of a style far more common in the Eastern Townships. It once stood on a prosperous farm boasting seven barns. The farm grew crops that nourished the teams of men laboring in the bush at Bryson's lumber shanties dotted throughout the

The Black River

Want to head still farther upstream? About 15 kilometers west of Fort Coulonge and just before Waltham, turn right onto the *Chemin Rivière Noire (Black River Road).* The road almost immediately becomes gravel, winding through very old pastures and clearings. You'll pass by old log cabins, now much-beloved private cottages. A bit farther along and, off to your left, you'll catch glimpses of the old logging river, now popular for its recreational canoeing. Roughly 14 kilometers upriver you'll come to the quaint—read very rustic—*Black River Inn Outfitters.* Here you can rent a very basic room, play a game of pool, and catch the yarns as the lads spin them out over a few pints of beer. (Watch out: our brew is way stronger than American beer!) Phone (819) 771-5108 or visit www.blackriveroutfitter.com for information.

hinterland. This unique agricultural complex of home and outbuildings was restored and achieved designation as a Québec Heritage Trust in 1982. Today it is home to the modest **Bryson House Museum** and the stone outbuilding—a former Bryson office building—houses an art gallery showcasing the work of local artists. In 2009 a small *farmers' market* started here during summer (for times: 819-683-1632).

Don't miss a visit to the spectacular 150-foot waterfall on the Coulonge River, **Coulonge Chutes** (100 promenade du parc des Chutes, Fort-Coulonge; 819-683-2770; www.chutescoulonge.qc.ca), about 7 kilometers farther west off Route 148. Turn north on Rue des Bois-Francs and venture up the winding gravel roads to the Chutes' parking lot and Visitor Center. There is a thrilling aerial park here which lets you zoom you through the forest on cables, then down over part of the 2,500-foot canyon.

In 1835 George Bryson built a 3,000-foot water chute for timber from the top of the falls, extending along the canyon wall. It carried logs and prevented them from being smashed in the raging Coulonge Chutes and the rock-strewn rapids below. The logs descended to the Ottawa River and floated down to Ottawa and Montréal prior to being shipped to Britain. (The last raft of square-cut timber sent down Ottawa's slide in 1909 was from the Coulonge. Another lumber baron of the day, John Rodolphus Booth, charged admission to watch that historic raft go by.) *Tip:* Ask to view the black-and white historic video depicting teams of men and horses felling and transporting timber at the Visitor Center—and don't miss the self-guided walk with bilingual interpretive signs and several spectacular viewpoints over the falls.

Return to Route 148 from the Chutes. Turn left to backtrack on Highway 148 for a kilometer or so and follow the right turn to **Davidson.** Drive through this former lumber sawing town which is still dominated by a mill. It opens and closes with the fortunes of the forestry industry, leaving both villagers and regional workers extremely concerned about their futures in this highly unstable economy. Drive through the village (about 5 kilometers) on Chemin Thomas Lefèbvre, where you'll curve along the Ottawa River waterfront.

Watch for the sharp left-hand turn to **Esprit Rafting** on Pointe Davidson. From early Apr through Oct you'll find owner-operator Jim Coffey primed and ready to pitch you into the heady world of river adventure. (Call 800-596-7238 year-round for information. The operation moves to Mexico from Oct through Apr, or contact Esprit at 3 chemin Esprit, Davidson, J0X 1R0; www.espritrafting .com; camping is $10; hostel dorm is $16.) Ever-popular Tuesday-night International dinners are held *al fresco* where the bonus is the sunset over the Ottawa River.

Chemin Thomas Lefèbvre continues past Esprit to rejoin Highway 138. Almost immediately after turning left at the highway, watch for **Base Macrocarpa,** a camping site right on the waterfront (515 Rte. 148, Mansfield J0X 1V0; 819-683-1330 or 866-683-1729; www.basemacrocarpa.com). There are thirty sites for camping. Enjoy nature walks, an interpretation center on white-tailed deer and in winter, cross-country ski trails.

Back on Route 148 and proceeding west, you'll cross the Black River. Look upstream to see the old Waltham Power Plant. Built in the early 1900s, it was Canada's first commercial power plant.

Zipping through the Canyon

Our niece from British Columbia and I decided to brave the Aerial Park at Chutes Coulonge. After our guides fitted us with helmets and gear and introduced us to the safe use of caribiners, we clambered up a ladder lashed to an immense white pine to a small platform where we clamped the pulleys securely to the cable. Then, waving to Katharine below us, we swooshed through the forest's canopy from one platform to another.

The forest zips built our confidence for the *pièce de resistance*: with the boiling waters of the Coulonge River below (and the sound of the frothing waterfall behind us) we fastened our caribiners securely and whoosh! Off we went, over the river, to land on a secure platform on the far side of the chasm. Returning was no simple feat: Celina and I crossed the river on two spindly logs suspended over the river, then climbed the cliff face using the metal footholds secured into the rock.

And what was Katharine doing? Shooting us . . . with her camera of course. With vertigo, she perhaps wisely stayed on terra firma . . . But if you are up for an aerial adventure, in my opinion, this tops all others I've experienced.

—Eric

Sustainable Tourism: Esprit

I believe Jim Coffey of Esprit is particularly commendable for his leadership in sustainable tourism—and I'm not alone. In Nov 2007, the company was voted the #1 ecotourism outfitter in North America and #2 internationally, in a *National Geographic Traveler* magazine survey. Such achievement is deserved. I've been on many so-called ecotourism adventures and destinations throughout the world: Jim both walks the walk *and* talks the talk.

Not only does Esprit follow leave no trace guidelines and other environmentally-friendly (and hence, sustainable) activities, Jim tries to make environmentalism a way of living. He specifically seeks to hire and train Pontiac youths who become whitewater survival training guides through to hostel managers. He brings his Mexican staff here to the Pontiac in summer so they can learn English, French and North American culture. He also takes Pontiac employees to Mexico. Therefore, it's not too much of a stretch to say that Esprit attempts to foster cross-cultural understanding.

It's always smart to give Esprit a call prior to planning a visit because Jim is full of energy and ideas. You never know what's going on here: sometimes he invites notable environmental leaders such as Elizabeth May, the leader of Canada's Green Party, to speak at Esprit. So call to find out what's going on prior to planning your exploration of the Pontiac.

—Katharine

Past Waltham on Route 148, cross a bridge onto *Île des Allumettes* to explore the village of Chapeau. First Nations' peoples vied for this territory because of its strategic position in the Ottawa River. From this vantage point, passersby could be levied for taxes or trade items, for whomever was camping here held command of all who passed.

Champlain visited the then-Algonquin settlement in 1613 during his attempt to discover the Indies led by "the boldest liar" (Champlain's own words recorded in his journal) he'd ever met, Nicolas Vignau. This young adventurer falsely claimed to have previously made it to the Indies via this route. Neither of us can quite imagine how thoroughly disgusted Champlain must have been to discover Vignau's deception.

These days Chapeau is well-known for its August agricultural fair—operating since 1861—as well as its winter carnival. But go and explore any time. You'll easily find the way to St-Alphonsus-de-Liguori, a beautiful church built in 1885 which towers over the village. Get out to wander the old cemetery and read the story of this settlement through the gravestones. After exploring, find *Karl's Bakery* (100 rue Saint-Jacques; 819-689-2259), where you can buy 100 percent organic whole wheat bread, Chelsea buns, sugar pie (try this traditional Québec delight), and other treats. Stay overnight at *Marieluise B&B* with well-informed host Marieluise Taube (1509 Chapeau, Sheenboro Rd., Chapeau; 819-689-5500).

SunBacktrack to Route 148 and turn left to pass through Chichester. Proceed to the "end of the road," as *Fort William* is known. Although it began as a French trading post named Fort-des-Allumettes, it was renamed in honour of the North-West Company's director, William McGillivray, in 1821. Come summer there's a long sandy beach to welcome you here. Truly off the beaten path, the scenery here is spectacular. You'll find basic accommodations during summer only and a restaurant/bar at the *Hotel Pontiac* (819-689-2605). These days, Fort William has a population hovering around 170 persons on a hot summer's day, where 95 percent claim English as their first language.

From here, you must retrace your travels east on Route 148 to return to Campbell's Bay. Once there, you will turn left onto Highway 301 to Otter Lake, home of *Belle Terre Botanic Garden and Arboretum* (120 chemin Milliken East, J0X 2P0; 819-453-7270). Owners Joyce and Wayne Keller purchased an old homestead and property here in 1971 and have been developing the gardens ever since. Today their summer greenhouse sells a variety of hardy perennials. All are organically grown, and Joyce takes particular pride in following the Steiner method of biodynamic gardening. Footpaths enable you to explore the garden and teahouse.

Also near Otter Lake is our favorite public campground, *Parc Leslie* (460 Belmont Rd., J0X 2P0; 819-453-7382; www.parcleslie.com). Signs point the way, but once at Otter Lake look for Belmont Road, turn onto it, and follow it to the end. You'll find 158 campsites here, some on remote, extremely quiet lakes. There are kilometers of excellent hiking paths and good fishing here.

Now head south on Highway 303 to *Ladysmith.* Formerly known as Schwartz, this tiny community was founded by German immigrants. Just as Shawville is predominantly English and Fort Coulonge French, this settlement was home to Eastern Europeans who fled religious persecution in the mid-1800s. The cemetery has interesting German headstones.

Northfork Country Kitchen B&B

The Pontiac is full of remote, intriguing destinations. For instance, visit this out-of-the-way country farmhouse inn to dine on trout (252 Ancien chemin de Nichabau Old Rd.), Chichester; GPS coordinates: N45.95102 W77.09181; 819-689-2588). You absolutely must call first to reserve a place for dinner as well as your overnight accommodation: there are only 4 units and this place is popular. Horse drawn sleigh rides are available.

Québec Anomaly: Swisha

"Swisha" is a uniquely fascinating little village. First, because we English couldn't pronounce *Rapides-des-Joachims,* the little settlement located on an island a few kilometers upstream of Deep River, Ontario, became known as the far-more pronounceable "Swisha." Second, although located within Québec, Swisha is only accessible by driving through Ontario and crossing a rare single-lane interprovincial bridge. Once a stopping place for steamers plying the Ottawa River, Swisha is now a community of 200 or so.

Why go? Because there's a funky auberge here called **That Canadian Lodge** (175 rue principale; 613-586-9353; www.thatcanadianlodge.ca). In 2009, innkeeper Jim Gibson was elected Swisha's mayor—so you'll be regaled with local lore and politics when you rent a rustic cabin or room from him.

That Canadian Lodge pulls no punches: its rustic lodge and cabin accommodations evoke an appealingly "old-time feel." The handsome inn overlooks the Ottawa River and an easily accessible boat launch. It's a favorite with fishermen who annually make the trek to Swisha from the USA, UK as well as Canada to relax while catching pickerel, walleye, catfish, and bass. Still others fish Swisha's inland lake—McConnell Lake—for trout from May through Nov.

Jim's partner, Tina Michaud, is a vivacious personality and extremely well-informed about Pontiac events and history, as well as a very talented artist. Visit her art gallery, art workshop space, and boutique **Gallerie-Gallera** in the lodge. (For art classes and gallery info, call Tina at 613-585-3308.)

Also at Swisha, there are hiking and skiing trails. Come prepared to linger in truly unique, out-of-the-way solitude. *Tip:* Bring your canoe or kayak: Tina encourages her students to paddle after classes—and don't forget binoculars because bird watching is awesome here.

—Katharine

Turn left (east) onto Highway 366 at **Hotel Ladysmith** (2144 rte. 303; 819-647-6797) where owners Cathy and Ernie Pasches' operate a tavern and restaurant. The rooms sport wild animal heads throughout: this is a real country place, very popular with hunters come autumn. But whatever the season, the Pasches' warm hospitality and hearty cooking serve up a true Pontiac welcome. Join locals there quaffing beer and munching chicken wings during the Pasches' popular Thursday "Wing Nights."

Always held the weekend before Canadian Thanksgiving in early Oct, **Oktoberfest** is celebrated with great enthusiasm in Ladysmith. The town hums to music, dance competitions, and art shows, accompanied by superb German fare cooked by the loving hands of local residents. Starting on Fri night, celebrations continue through Sun evening. (For information: 819-647-5306; www.ladysmithoktoberfest.ca.)

Continue driving east on Highway 366. The gravel road changes to pavement at *Lac des Loup (Wolf Lake).* Continue to the hamlet of *Sainte-Cécile-de-Masham,* where there's another entry through a covered bridge into *Gatineau Park.* Enter here to hike or ski such trails as *Kennedy Road* or to swim, camp, or hike at *Lac Philippe.* This is also the access point to *Lusk Cave,* a noted geological feature of the Outaouais. If you explore this cave, be sure to wear old clothes that you don't mind getting wet. And don't forget a flashlight: you'll need it. The main park information center is located at *Old Chelsea* (819-827-2020).

québectrivia

Nicolas Gatineau dit Duplessis was a Québec-based notary who got bored. Yes, he forsook his office existence, and in the early 1600s became an explorer. In search of the best beaver pelts, he paddled north for adventure. Legend has it he drowned in the river that now bears his name.

After Sainte-Cécile-de-Masham, you'll see the junction with Highway 105. Turn left to descend into Wakefield Village. At the foot of the hill you'll need to make a choice: turn left to continue on Highway 105 to Maniwaki; turn right to explore the village of Wakefield; or go straight across the bridge over the Gatineau River toward Val-des-Monts and the Laflèche Cavern.

We'll turn left, north, taking Highway 105 toward *Maniwaki.* This is such an extraordinarily beautiful drive that we understand why many Ottawa residents live up here and commute to the capital. The road literally hugs the Gatineau River—and what vistas you'll see! The natural beauty challenges you to pay attention to your driving, as the road twists and turns amid the great views.

You pass the little hamlets of Alcove, Brennan's Hill, Low, and Venosta before the intriguingly named Kazabazua. Here you'll come across the junction with Highway 301 Ouest (West) to Otter Lake—now you know there's another route to that community! Past "Kaz" you'll pass through Gracefield, Blue Sea Lake and its cottage country, and the River Desert Indian Reserve. You hug and then lose sight of the Gatineau River, passing through rugged bush and spectacular cliffs and then through a sandy region of glacial till.

At Maniwaki visit a unique forestry museum, *Centre d'interpretation Château Logue* (8 rue Comeau; 819-449-7999; www.ci-chateaulogue.qc.ca). It highlights not just the logging industry but also forestry protection techniques and technologies. An online connection to the nearby forest-fire monitoring center displays up-to-the-minute information about lightning strikes and fires

québectrivia

For a horsey adventure, call Craig Clost, who will take you on hourly or up to five-day horseback riding and tenting adventures at *Captiva Farms* (189 chemin de la Montagne, Wakefield J0X 3G0; 819-459-2769; www.captivafarms .com).

over a vast area of eastern Canada and the northeastern United States. Originally a residence built in 1887 by Irishman Charles Logue, the Second-Empire house is built with locally quarried limestone and was refurbished in 1988. Today it houses the museum, the local library, and an art gallery.

The museum is open Tues through Sun (Mon by reservation only) from 10 a.m. to 5 p.m. late May through mid-Oct. Call to arrange a special tour from Nov through Apr. Admission is $5 adults, $3 students. The on-site fire observation tower was moved from its original location on a hill near Lake Matapédia, where it once allowed fire wardens to look for fires from a height of 518 metres above the surrounding forest.

Also in Maniwaki is the *Parc du Draveur/Raftsman's Park* (171 rue Principale South; 819-449-6627), which celebrates the life of the raftsman with several interpretive panels and an immense steel statue of a river man (log driver). And to further celebrate the former logging industry which saw timbers floated downriver, take a tour on the Pythonga tugboat, which towed millions of cubic feet of logs on the Baskatong Reservoir. (For details on the park and tugboat tour, browse the Chateau Logue Web site.)

Maniwaki began as a trading post at the confluence of two of the major Outaouais rivers, the Desert and the Gatineau. The town was established in 1851 by Catholic priests from Les Oblats de Marie Immaculée order, and even then logging had become its mainstay industry. Today, Maniwaki is the outpost leading to the *Parc de la Vérendrye (La Vérendrye Park)* and to two ZECs (*Zone d'exploitation contrôlée,* or controlled hunting and fishing zones): the *Pontiac* and *Bras-Coupé Desert.* Maniwaki has many well-qualified outfitters who can help you explore the hinterland by canoe, on foot, or during winter on snowmobile or skis.

You can return to Wakefield on Highway 105 Sud (South). For a circuit, however, we recommend continuing on Route 107 to Highway 117. Turn east toward Mont Laurier and watch for the right turn onto Route 309. This good paved road takes you beside sandy rivers to Val-des-Bois and Route 307. Follow Route 307 through Poltimore and Saint-Pierre-de-Wakefield, where you can visit Laflèche Cavern or follow Route 366 back to Wakefield.

To really go into the true "back of beyond," continue north on Highway 105 to Grand Remous and then head northwest on Highway 117 through La Vérendrye Park to the mining town of Val-d'Or. This is a long trip, and you'll either need to return via the same route or continue on through Rouyn-Noranda to Ontario. This region is a canoeist's heaven. The rewards will be many here, such as the sight of a moose and her calf. But be sure your car is in great shape to enjoy this trek.

Drive to Abitibi-Témiscaming

We took three rather rushed days to drive a 1,200-plus km circuit to explore Québec's Abitibi-Témiscaming region, west of the Outaouais. (Tip: take longer for this exploration than we did! Also note that sometimes on maps and brochures you'll find Témiscaming is spelled with a "k" not a "c".)

This often-overlooked region is along an alternate way to enter (or leave) Québec from the west: Highway 117 is part of the Trans-Canada Highway, and offers a shorter route along less-traveled highways. You can also connect with this drive from St. Jovite (see Montréal and Its Northern Playgrounds section).

From Maniwaki, we drove about 30 kms north on Highway 105 to connect with the northern Trans-Canada Highway (Route 117) at Grand-Remous. This good all-weather highway takes you northwest through *La Vérendrye Wildlife Reserve,* home to the headwaters of the Ottawa and Coulonge rivers. Here you'll find the "great divide", the height of land where watersheds change their course to flow north to Hudson Bay and south to the Ottawa River.

Thousands of lakes and rivers make La Vérendrye a naturalist's paradise (www.sepaq.com/rf/lvy/; 819-354-4392; registration centers along Highway 117 are open seasonally). We did not have the time to do so but we could happily have lingered here to canoe, tent, and "lose ourselves" to wilderness camping (www.canot-kayak.qc.ca for canoes). At minimum, as we did, enjoy lunch and a stroll at a roadside picnic grounds.

At the mining town of Val d'Or, delve 91 metres underground at *Val d'Or* (Valley of Gold) to learn about gold at the historic *Lamaque mine* at what is called *La Cité de l'Or,* (90 ave. Perreault; 819-825-1274 or 877-582-5367; www.citedelor.com; daily June 21 to Labor Day; see Web site for rate packages). Examine the shafts and learn about gold extraction both below- and aboveground. Closed-in footwear is mandatory, plus, do have warm clothes since it is only 8°C inside the mine.

You can continue west from Val d'Or to Rouyn-Noranda, but we suggest you head north on Route 111 through Amos and west to Taschereau, a small village on a lake of the same name where the *Gîte Cassiro* awaits (380 Kirouac Ave., Taschereau; 819-796-3395; www.cassiro.qc.ca). The owners enjoy sharing information including brochures and maps about the many activities nearby. We stocked up on delicious black currant products made on the premises (*cassis* means black currant), then drove south on good secondary roads to **Parc d'Aiguebelle** to explore the watershed divide (1702 rang Hudon, Mont-Brun, J0A 2Y0; 819-637-7322; 800-665-6527; www.sepaq.com/pq/aig/). Challenge any vertigo you might have by walking the 64-metre-long suspension bridge 22 metres above the lake, or by climbing up the fire tower.

More secondary roads lead west through rolling fields and the village of Clèricy before you turn south at Highway 101 to arrive in **Rouyn-Noranda.** To orient ourselves, we visited the regional tourism information centre, **La Maison Dumulon** (191 ave. du Lac; 819-797-7125; www.maison-dumulon.ca). It started life as a log cabin and one of its former functions included serving as a post office. Heritage photos depict how Rouyn-Noranda grew in the 1920s from a shanty town to become the cultural and business centre servicing this region. This tidy museum also sells local crafts, soaps, books and art. You'll need to register here for some specialty tours.

And that's the case if you want to explore the **Horne Smelter** (101 ave. Portelance; 819-787-3195; 888-797-3195; open June 24 to Labor Day, 9 a.m. to 3 p.m.; reservations mandatory; www.xstrata.com or, far more helpfully, www.abitibi-Témiscamingue-tourism.org). The free two-hour tour of this industrial site reveals how 180,000 metric tonnes of copper ore is smelted here annually. Perhaps because we use computers almost daily, we were particularly intrigued with their on-site, huge recycling centre which reclaims copper from computers and wiring. Note: Closed-in shoes, trousers and long sleeves are mandatory.

Many of the earliest miners in Rouyn-Noranda were Russian. Therefore, in the 1950s the 600-or-so strong community erected a Russian Orthodox Church, completed in 1957. **L'église orthodoxe russe St-Georges de Rouyn-Noranda** is well worth a visit—and reminds us Québec is home to many more cultural groups than merely French- and English-speaking peoples (201 rue Taschereau O.; 819-797-7125; open daily 8:30 a.m. to 5 p.m., free; 1-hour 15-minute guided visits at 9 a.m. and 1:30 p.m. from late June through Aug, $7 adults).

Leave Rouyn-Noranda on the Trans-Canada Highway, also signed as Highway 101. Note: If you are leaving Québec, turn west at Amtfield to connect with Highway 66 in Ontario; otherwise, stay on Highway 101 south.

Because we like cheese, we ventured to **Montbeillard** to visit the artisinal **La Chèvrerie Dion** (Dion's Goat Cheese Farm; 128 Rte. 101; 819-797-2617; www3.telebecinternet.com/chevreriedion). Madame Dion proudly showed us products her family has been making since 1982, including feta, parmesan, Montbeil (a marvelous soft cheddar), and an assortment of creamed goat cheeses. We couldn't resist buying fresh yoghurt, curds and some of the Montbeil, then visited the family's sixty or more kids, nanny goats and Billy goats.

We particularly enjoy hands-on explorations of Canadian historical sites. Hands-down, our favorite destination in this region was ***Fort Témiscamingue*** (834 Chemin Vieux-Fort, Duhamel-Ouest; 819-629-3222; www .pc.gc.ca/temiscamingue/; early June to Labor Day, daily 9 a.m. to 5 p.m.; $4.90 adult, $4.15 senior, $2.90 youth, $11.70 family). Located in Duhamel-Ouest on the shores of Lake Témiscaming (which is part of the Ottawa River watershed), the fort commemorates the history of the fur trade and Christian missions in Québec. Don't miss the First Nations' exhibit, where birchbark canoes are being constructed. Canoe-builder Mike Chevrier demonstrated how to make a bow from cedar while we watched. There's a beautiful picnic area on Lake Témiscaming here, and statues dotted about outside recall the *coureurs de bois* and other characters from the past.

Highway 101 continues south through large farms and forested areas, with occasional glimpses of the nearby Ottawa River, to end in Témiscaming. Located in the village's original 1927 railway station, ***Musée de la gare*** depicts this region's other resource industry, forestry, and its pulp and paper mills (15 rue Humphrey; 819-627-1846; www.temiscaming.net; June 24 to Labor Day, $5 adults). Outside, stroll the paved bicycle path to Donald River Falls or, either by bike or on foot, complete the 9 km loop, then walk to a lookout overlooking Lake Témiscaming.

Where to stay in Témiscaming? ***Auberge Canadienne*** (819-627-3111; www.aubergecanadienne.com) is comfy and clean, and we ate well at the

Cold? No Kidding!

Extreme temperatures are not unusual in the Outaouais. Winter temperatures average well below freezing, but can reach -40 degrees, where Celsius and Fahrenheit are the same. Fairly shallow lakes and watersheds fed by precipitation warm up quickly in the spring and are great for swimming by summer when the air temperature can approach 100°F.

When my family moved to this area from mild British Columbia in 1966, we found relief from the summer heat in the lake at our rustic cottage near the Black River. In mid-Feb of the first winter, we made our way up the road—well maintained in winter to let the logging trucks through in those days—and stopped at the edge of the frozen lake. After some debate, my parents agreed to let the six of us cross the lake on the ice— but only if we carried long poles in case the ice broke. We headed out in pairs, walking gingerly until my brother Steve and I came across giant fresh tracks: a bulldozer! We flung the poles aside and joined arms to jump up and down, to the consternation of our parents farther back, until they too saw the tracks. The ice was almost 3 feet thick.

—Eric

on-site family restaurant. (We chose a room in the 400-series wing, being furthest away from the tavern, which as a matter of fact was not noisy when we were there.)

To return to Ottawa-Gatineau, cross into Ontario to Highway 63 towards North Bay, then east towards Mattawa on Highway 533 southeast, there linking to Highway 17 to Pembroke. You can cross the Ottawa River here to re-enter the Outaouais on Highway 148.

Wakefield Village

For those of you who don't choose to head north to Maniwaki, turn south on Highway 105 to **Wakefield** on River Road. It's a pretty little village that once was a major service center to the Irish, English, Scottish, French, and German settlers who homesteaded here. Wakefield is rather too well-known to still be considered a "secret" gem but nonetheless, for newcomers to Canada's National Capital Region, it has much to offer. Only twenty minutes from the twin cities of Gatineau/Ottawa, it's an excellent base from which to explore the region.

First you pass the German-style inn **Alpengruss** (831 Riverside Drive; 819-459-2885; www.alpengruss.ca), which also has an excellent restaurant. If you like German comfort food, sample tasty schnitzel, cabbage, and beet dishes.

Just past the inn, turn right across the old railway tracks on Chemin Pont Gendron and proceed to the end. Here you'll find one of the old "kissing bridges," or covered bridges, spanning the Gatineau River. Closed to vehicular traffic, this community-built bridge is nonetheless a proud reminder of the original, which perished at the hands of an arsonist. Parking is tight.

roadsidesprings

Often you'll see little drainpipes gushing water at the roadside. These are roadside springs (called *source* in French), and locals flock to them to gather drinking water. You'll find one outside Wakefield Village. Want some water? Not only can you get tasty, potable water here, it's also a great place to gossip and hear the latest news 'n' views.

Return to your car and drive up Sully Road, perhaps half a kilometer, and look out on your left for the little gravel driveway marking the studio and gallery of potters David McKenzie and Maureen Marcotte. **Galérie McKenzie Marcotte** (26 Sully; 819-459-3164; www.mckenziemarcotte.ca) not only features their whimsical plates, wall sconces, lamps, and mugs but also other artists' works. Maureen tells us that an appointment isn't necessary. "Just tell folks to drop in!" she says enthusiastically. You won't regret meeting this creative, supportive couple, and we bet you'll purchase at least one cup and saucer.

Return to River Road. You'll pass the terminus and turnaround for the **Hull Chelsea Wakefield Steam Train,** an old Swedish train, complete with dining car. Tours depart from Gatineau and take half a day, including a two-hour stopover in Wakefield (165 rue Deveault, Gatineau; 819-778-7246; www .steamtrain.ca). Operates mid-May through Oct; in July and Aug departs at 1:30 p.m. Sun through Thurs, 10 a.m. on Fri and Sat; dinner trains on Fri and Sat evenings in June through early Sept. Call for departure times for other months. Adults $45, seniors and students $41, children twelve and under $20, one-way fare $41.

Wakefield is best explored on foot. With the steam train terminus behind you, walk south along River Road. Enter country shops, like **Jamboree** and the **Wakefield General Store.** Then a white clapboard Victorian house appears. This charming establishment is an 1896 doctor's home, now **Les Trois Érables (The Three Maples)** B&B, owned by Joanne Hunter and Jim Fitzgibbons (801 chemin Riverside; 877-337-2253 or 819-459-1118; www .lestroiserables.com). It's an oasis of tranquility, set on a generous lawn and surrounded by an airy wraparound porch. The proprietors keep the five-bedroom inn open year-round—a welcome change for this beautiful old home.

Farther along Riverside Drive, at the corner of Mill Street, pop into the popular **Auberge Mouton Noir (Black Sheep Inn)** (420 Riverside Dr.; 819-459-3228; www.theblacksheepinn.com). Over the years, music-loving owner, Paul Symes, has created the hot spot in the National Capital Region to hear great local bands, from jazz to folk to blues. Call ahead: you may need reservations and, depending on the band, you may need to purchase tickets. The inexpensive and very basic rooms at the inn are very popular with younger travelers, cross-country skiers, and mountain bikers.

New in Jan 2009 is the on-site **Bistro Rutherford** which serves what cooks James, Jordan and Mackenzie call (and, we quote) "kick-ass poutine."

Now follow Mill Street and the gurgling Lapêche River up the hill to get to the Wakefield Mill and what's left of the Maclaren mill complex.

In 1838 Glaswegian William Fairbairn petitioned Sir John Colbourn, governor of Upper and Lower Canada, for permission to erect a mill where the Lapêche River tumbled over a falls en route to the Gatineau River. Permission was granted, and the clever businessman built a prosperous gristmill. Six years later, the Maclaren family, also Scottish, bought the mill and expanded the complex to include a sawmill and woolen mill, general store, brickyard, and lodgings for their laborers. In 1865 or so, the family built **Maclaren House,** a fine Victorian brick home overlooking the **Maclaren Mill.** When our first edition was published back in 1999, the old mill and so-called "bachelor's house" were languishing from neglect, and we were fearful both might suffer demolition. Thankfully, along came entrepreneurs Robert Milling and Lynn Berthiaume, who recognized a potential country inn and conference facility in the making. Their dream was realized in spring 2001, and now the two buildings offer a total of thirty heritage rooms and suites beside the Lapêche River waterfall that once powered the mill complex.

The *Le Moulin Wakefield Mill Inn and Spa* (60 Mill Rd.; 819-459-1838 or 888-567-1838; www.wakefieldmill.com) offers a calming destination. It's soothing to sleep with windows open, where the falls' cascade lulls you to sleep. Reservations are a must at the mill's restaurant, which prides itself in stocking unusual wines from around the world.

Adjacent to Maclaren House is a road leading up a pleasant hill. Ascend to the Maclaren Cemetery, where former Liberal prime minister Lester B. Pearson is buried. On July 1 (Canada Day), 2001, then Prime Minister Jean Chretien dedicated the cemetery as a National Heritage Site. A Canadian flag proudly snaps in the wind here.

If you want to head into Gatineau Park for an exhilarating hike, find the little gravel roadway opposite Maclaren Hill and walk up it, beneath the overpass beside the Lapêche River. The roadway soon starts to climb into the woods, entering the park trail system. (Katharine's first book, *Historical Walks: The Gatineau Park Story,* is still the only guide to the trails of the park. It's

"My" Gatineau Park

Gatineau Park is "my" park. The wild ways and spaces of this park outside Gatineau are dear to me, perhaps because it's where Eric and I spent a lot of time when we first began dating. One of our first dates was to McCloskey Trail, which pitches down the back of the Eardley Escarpment to Meech Lake. It was my first time on cross-country skis. You know the drill: all were close friends, and here I was, new to both the sport and group. As soon as we hit the trail, Eric and the rest vaporized in a cloud of snow, leaving me to slip and slide uphill as best I could. I finally took my skis off, turned around, and murmured black remarks. I figured I'd just head back to the car. Suddenly a group of skiers started running uphill toward me. Meanwhile, I had sunk knee-deep in snow. With tears of frustration pouring down my face, I found myself peering into the face of the leader of this athletic group. In disbelief he looked at me, saying, "What are you doing here? If you don't know what you're doing, you'd better get back down." With this, his group dashed off, uphill, leaving me floundering. Somehow I negotiated the descent and, somehow, Eric and I are still together, happily surmounting other challenges.

—Katharine

available at shops in Wakefield and details the network of hiking paths you can enjoy from here.)

Return to Riverside Drive and, turning right at the Black Sheep Inn, next find *Jamboree* (740, chemin Riverside, 819-459-2537). Owner Shirley Brown operates this "country store" chock-full of gardening and nick-nacks.

Continue south to the flashing red light. At the corner is a charming, connected series of clapboard buildings known as *Place 1870,* which house a variety of shops. Explore them all: each has its own charm. Katharine's favorite is *La Tulipe Noire* (715, chemin Riverside; 819-459-3847). Here you'll find everything from Indian tablecloths to local artisans' and jewelers' specialty goods.

While we're mentioning our personal faves, when we dine in Wakefield we head to totally funky *Chez Eric,* named after the fish from that oddball movie *A Fish Called Wanda.* Find it (and Eric, in this instance, the chubby goldfish) a few doors down from Place 1870 in another old frame house. We enjoyed being served on the backyard picnic table. (We don't know if Eric the fish approves of fish entrées, but Eric the co-author enjoyed his grilled salmon sandwich here.) Chez Eric is a very popular local hangout and it's very small, so call ahead for a reservation (28 Valley Dr.; 819-459-3747; www.cafechezeric.ca).

For a heady detour, return to Highway 105 and, heading southeast toward Gatineau (about 3 kms) find *Great Canadian Bungee* which boasts Canada's highest bungee jump. You too can terrify yourself by jumping into the old quarry. Owner Matt Lawrence tells us it's fun, but so far we've not managed to convince ourselves. Perhaps you'd like to try? (Great Canadian Bungee, Wakefield; 819-459-3714 or 877-828-8170; www.bungee.ca.)

Exploring the Eastern Edge of Outaouais

Return north on Highway 105 through Wakefield to where the bridge spans the Gatineau River. Turn right and cross the river, following Highway 366 Est (East), then Highway 307 Nord (North) toward *Saint-Pierre-de-Wakefield.* Your destination now is the 20,000-year-old, geologically fascinating *Laflèche Adventure—Cave and Aerial Park* (255 rue Principale, Val-des-Monts; 819-457-4033; www.aventurelafleche.ca), the largest known caves in the Canadian Shield rock, discovered in 1865 by a hunter while tracking a bear. The bruin disappeared into the rock and, investigating, intrepid tracker Joseph Dubois was astounded by his magnificent find. He was actually less intrigued by the amazing stalactites and stalagmites than by the glitter of gold.

Ecological reserve

Forêt-La-Blanche (White Forest) is an ecological reserve set up to protect 2,052 hectares of woods containing both typical and uncommon species of plants. As well, it's home to a large heronry colony where great blue herons nest. More than 20 km of trails are superb for walking and snowshoeing. There is a small visitor's centre and signs identify trees along the trails. Located in the Municipality of Mulgrave Derry (*very* Irish) this area was also settled by German immigrants in the mid-1800s. (300 chemin Saddler, Mayo; 819-281-6700; www.lablanche.ca; open fall, winter, spring, Fri, Sat, Sun and Mon 10 a.m. to 5 p.m. in fall, winter, and spring; daily 9 a.m. to 8 p.m. in June, July, and Aug.)

He bought the property, visions of wealth dancing in his head. Alas, it was pyrite—fool's gold—and the caves languished until the 1920s, when they became a commercial success. In 1937 Zephyr Laflèche took them over until 1960, when again they were abandoned. Unfortunately, vandals destroyed the most spectacular formations, apparently including several columns created when some of the ancient stalactites and stalagmites eventually joined. Reopened in 1995, the Laflèche caves are well worth exploring. Bilingual tours are available. (As you venture farther east in the Outaouais, English translations are less easy to come by.)

Halloween is a particularly spooky time to go into the caves. Guides dress up and give you the fright of your life. Mind you, the rest of the year, such ghouls are not about, so it's safe to go spelunking. For the price of admission you get your own battery-powered miner's light firmly affixed to a hard hat. There are two tours: the ninety-minute general tour and one called "wild caving," which promises a three-hour exploration of special cave-galleries. Even in winter the Laflèche caverns are spectacular, with sparkling formations of ice along with (actually very hard to find) hibernating, upside-down bats. And speaking of winter, there is an annual Christmas "crescendo choir" here where *a capella* choirs sing medieval Christmas songs. Their voices mixed with flickering candlelight create a magical seasonal mood.

In the past few years, many destinations boast aerial parks and the Laflèche Caves also bought into the craze. So after you explore "down under" you can strap carabiners and gear onto yourself and scoot through the canopy of the forest.

From here, if you wish, you can return to Gatineau on the east side of the Gatineau River via either Highway 307 through Cantley or Highway 366 through Val-des-Monts. However, we'll continue exploring Québec's side of Canada's National Capital Region.

Now we drive through the easternmost region of the Outaouais, known as *La Petite Nation (Little Nation),* home of the stunning *Fairmont Château Montebello* (329 Notre-Dame, Montebello; 819-423-6341; www.fairmont.com/montebello). Admittedly not truly off-the-beaten-path, it is such a quintessentially Canadian lodge that it really is a must-see. Made from cedar logs, the building takes the form of a star with a massive stone central fireplace marking the centre. Rooms are strung along the "arms" of the star. It's heavenly to sink into cozy armchairs either with a book or a single malt scotch and, on the second floor balcony overlooking the lobby, find board games such as chess and backgammon waiting for you.

Dine at the Fairmont's signature and indescribably delicious buffet, plunge into the swimming pool (while floating on your back gaze at its hand-painted ceiling), and pamper yourself at the spa. Whatever activities you choose, the Château is a slice of heaven. Come winter, choose from a variety of sports offered here: sleigh rides, dog-sledding trips, ice-fishing, cross-country skiing, and snowshoeing are all possible here, as is curling on the Château's private rinks. And at maple sap time (mid-Mar through very early Apr pending on the weather) check out the seasonal activities where horse-drawn wagons take you through the forest so you can get the sense of old-time sap gathering, not to mention maple delicacies back at the Château.

québectrivia

The Château Montebello is the largest log cabin in the world—and it took only four months to build in 1930 on the grounds of a 1700 seigneury.

To get to Château Montebello, follow Route 148 east toward Montréal. Pass through Thurso—with its sometimes smelly pulp and paper mill—to Papineauville and the village of Montebello. The entrance to Fairmont Château Montebello appears on your right, through a grand log gateway.

The Château's grounds were once the home of Québec patriot Louis-Joseph Papineau. Parks Canada now operates his 1846 mansion as the *Manoir Papineau,* a museum (500 Notre-Dame, Montebello; 819-423-6965; www.pc.gc.ca/papineau). We cannot think of a better eastern bastion of the Outaouais.

North of the Château Montebello on Highway 323, you first pass *Parc Omega,* a wildlife park (Route 323, Montebello; 819-423-5487; www.parc-omega.com; open daily 9 a.m. to 5 p.m.; adults $17, children six to fifteen $12, children two to five $5). As you drive through the grounds, you'll spy such animals as bison (buffalo), white-tailed deer, and wild pig.

Farther north on this road is **Kenauk** (1000 Kenauk Rd., Montebello; 819-423-5573; www.fairmont.com/kenauk). This is a little-known seigneurial preserve owned and operated by the Château Montebello and originally was part of Papineau's seigneurial holdings. Kenauk now offers private cabins on secluded lakes: this is a pricey but unforgettable Outaouais destination. Just ask about their "blue trout," a mouthwatering delicacy.

Continue to the village of Saint-André-Avellin to visit **Musée des pionniers (Pioneer Museum)** in Saint-André-Avellin (20 rue Bourgeois, Saint-André-Avellin; 819-983-1491; open daily June 24 through Labor Day weekend from 9 a.m. to 5 p.m.; $3 adults, $1 students).

Return via Route 148 to Gatineau, or continue east to Montréal. Gatineau is becoming increasingly well known for its annual and extremely whimsical **Gatineau Hot Air Balloon Festival** (800-668-8383 or 819-243-2331; www.montgolfieresgatineau.com). Since 1987 this popular festival has been held at Gatineau's **Parc la Baie** during Labor Day weekend in Sept. It's a fantastic display of brilliantly colored, fancifully shaped balloons depicting everything from a Walt Disney castle to a Holstein cow.

Whether it's hot air ballooning in Gatineau, running river rapids with Esprit Rafting, or hiking the trails in Gatineau Park, the Outaouais offers nature at its best. Enjoy it.

Places to Stay in the Outaouais

GATINEAU (OLD HULL)

Les suites Victoria
1 rue Victoria,
131 rue Laurier,
J8X 1Z6;
(819) 777-8899
www.suitesvictoria.com
Right downtown with kitchenettes so you can prepare your own meals.

Auberge un pied à terre
245 rue Papineau,
J8X 1W9;
(819) 772-4364
www3.sympatico.ca/unpiedaterre
Near Museum of Civilization on a residential street.

GATINEAU (OLD AYLMER)

Gîte Enchanté B&B
32 rue Lakeview,
J9H 2A1;
(819) 682-0695
www.giteenchante.ca
Chat with artist Rita Rodrique; tranquil Ottawa River views.

BRISTOL

Woodhaven B&B
88 Pine Lodge Rd.,
J0X 1G0;
(819) 647-5858
www.woodhavenontheottawa.com
Stunning log home overlooking the Ottawa River in quiet cottage community.

CHELSEA

Le Nordik Nature Spa
16 chemin Nordik,
J9B 2P7;
(819) 827-1111 or
(866) 575-3700
www.lenordik.com
Indulge in the Nordic system of hot-cold spa cycle,

then dine and collapse into well-deserved rest.

DUHAMEL (NORTH OF MONTEBELLO)

Auberge Couleurs de France
Chemin du Lac Doré Nord;
212 chemin des Jonquilles,
J0V 1G0;
(819) 743-5878
www.chaletcouleursde
france.com
Complete with Nordic spa
this remote chalet over-
looks Petit Lac Preston.
Rent skis and head off into
the surrounding forest.

MANSFIELD (NEAR FORT COULONGE)

Les Cabines de la Chute
538 Chemin de la Chute,
J0X 1V0;
(819) 683-3469 or
(866) 883-3469
www.lescabinesdelachute
.com
Well-kept, comfortable
cabins overlook the Cou-
longe River.

SHAWVILLE

O'Neil's Bed & Breakfast
C64 Calumet Rd. East,
J0X 2Y0;
(819) 647-6674
www.oneills-bedandbreak
fast.com.

Places to Eat in the Outaouais

CHELSEA

Les Fougères
783 rte. 105;
(819) 827-8942
www.fougeres.ca
Absolutely delectable
regional cuisine paired to
fine wines by well-informed,
friendly wait staff.

OLD CHELSEA

L'Orée du Bois
15 chemin Kingsmere, Old
Chelsea;
(819) 827-0332
www.oreeduboisrestaurant
.com
Log "cabin" tucked into the
woods beside Gatineau
Park. Good food after a
long hike/bike/ski.

GATINEAU

Le Twist
88 rue Montcalm;
(819) 777-8886
www.letwist.com
Since 1986; great ham-
burgers; terrace in summer.

La Ferme Rouge
1957 rte. 148;
(819) 986-7013
www.fermerouge.ca
Popular buffet includes
nightclub show. (The night
we dined there, one of the
"can-can-girls'" high-heeled
shoes became launched
into the crowd. Every-
one ducked and laughter
rocked the rafters!)

SHAWVILLE

Café 349
349 Main St.;
(819) 647-6424
www.cafe349.com
Excellent homemade
lunch, dinner in tastefully
decorated environment.
Breakfast of coffees, teas,
scones and immense muf-
fins. On-site art gallery.

EXPLORING THE COASTAL REGION

→

Our proposed circuit—to explore the coasts of Québec—mixes mountains and rivers, oceans and saltwater breezes. Starting from near Matapédia, we'll take you east on the coast to New Richmond. Then, instead of following the coast to Percé Rock like most people do, we'll head north on an inexplicably underutilized road hugging the Cascapédia River. It's lovely: the road eventually gains substantial elevation as it climbs through the *Chic-Choc* and McGerrigle Ranges, extensions of the Appalachians that are now part of the 802-square-kilometer Parc de la Gaspésie. The highest elevation is Mont Jacques Cartier, at 1,268 meters. We'll take you to an agate mine hidden among its ancient hills and, if you hike or ski the Chic-Chocs, you could even find some caribou that live in the park's tundra-like habitat.

Quite apart from water and mountains, this coastal drive introduces you to a part of Québec settled by the Acadians, Loyalists, and Basque, French, English (many from the United Kingdom's southern isles of Guernsey and Jersey), and Scottish peoples.

Jacques Cartier is far too often credited with "discovering" this land in 1534, but historical and archaeological evidence

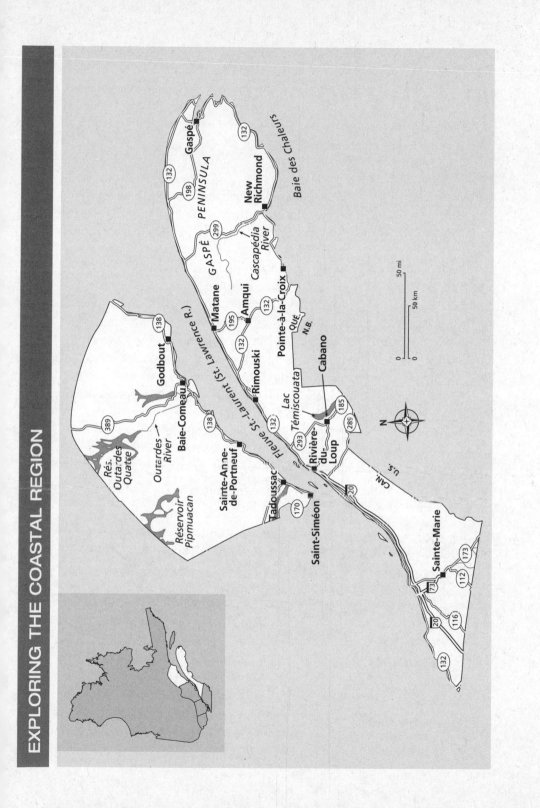

indicates otherwise. In the early sixteenth century, Portuguese, Basque, and French came to fish the great schools of cod on the Grand Banks, but it would be another hundred years before any attempt at permanent settlement was made. Conditions were just too harsh. It was far easier for fishermen to erect temporary shelters, fish all summer, then return with their catch stowed in their holds, ready for the European market.

But for more than 8,000 years, Native peoples dwelt here. During the time of Cartier, Montagnais were living a good life, following the herds of caribou and hunting the prolific deer and moose. Around the 1500s these people were driven north, to the north shore of the St. Lawrence (which we'll explore on this drive), by the Micmacs, a name given to the tribe by the French, possibly meaning "allies."

The Gaspé Peninsula region is rich with the history of its settlers. There are some excellent museums here, including La Bataille de la Ristigouche parc historique national. It depicts the Battle of the Restigouche—another classic battle between French and English, but this time a naval, not land-based, fight. If you want to learn the history of British settlement in the Gaspé, don't miss the heritage village and museum in New Richmond, a superbly interpreted village where you can also stay overnight, with advance reservations.

Yet another museum, in Bonaventure, explains the impact of the tragic Acadian Deportation of 1755, the year before the commencement of England and France's Seven Years' War. Because these hardy, successful pioneers refused to give an oath of allegiance either to the French or British Crown, neither the British or French wanted them around. (Ironic, isn't it? Who knew what trouble those pacifists would be?) The French King was undoubtedly delighted that the happenstance of history meant it was the Brits who were the

AUTHORS' FAVORITES IN THE COASTAL REGION

Battle of the Restigouche National Historic Site

Camping Bon-Désir

Cascapédia River

Fort Ingall and the Témiscouata Rose Gardens

Gaspésien British Heritage Village (also known as "Britville")

Mont Lyall Agate Mine

Pointe-aux-Outardes (near Baie-Comeau)

Salmon ladder at the Mathier-D'Amours Dam in Matane

ones to forcibly evict 14,000 Acadians from their extremely productive farms. Their homes were razed.

Where were they taken? Some fled. Others were put onto prison ships and transported to the Thirteen Colonies, primarily—where some made it as far as Louisiana. (Ever wondered why this state has a thriving French-speaking, or Cajun, heritage and culture?) Some Acadians returned to their original farms after the Treaty of Versailles in 1763. However, they discovered that United Empire Loyalists had taken over their homes and businesses. What happened to them? They cleared more land and established new settlements, such as the town of Carleton, across Cascapédia Bay from New Richmond.

The Acadian Deportation sparked a fierce pride among *les Acadiens*. Today their ancestors, who live throughout the Maritime region of Canada as well as throughout the country, celebrate their ancestry.

The late 1700s to mid-1800s saw waves of Scots and Irish immigrants to these shores. These were the times of the Scottish Clearances, when landlords evicted poor tenants from their crofts in the Highlands. Their crofts were burned to make more grazing land for sheep. This was also the time of the Irish potato famines. In fact, the years between 1846 and 1855 witnessed the largest mass migration of these peoples to Canada. Names such as the Scottish Cuthburt, the Irish Duthie, the Acadian Leblanc, and the Loyalist Pritchard have blended over the years to create the rich cultural heritage you will enjoy today.

québec'srooster

Weathervanes are true folk art born from religious iconography. They recall the Bible story, where Christ's disciple, Peter, was told he would deny knowing Jesus three times before a rooster crowed. Québecors were raised as devout Catholics: thus, cockerel weathervanes reminded people not to ignore their Christian faith and duties.

Today's Gaspé region is a blend of all these peoples, though French is by far the majority language spoken here. Our major tip regarding this region? If you are interested in the Loyalist, Acadian, and English-speaking peoples' history and genealogy in the Gaspé, visit New Richmond's Gaspésien British Heritage Village (also known as "Britville").

We propose a "water route" as you explore this area of Québec. You'll visit the seaside towns hugging coastlines along the St. Lawrence River and Gulf of St. Lawrence. As we explore inland, we will traverse the banks of two classic salmon fishing rivers, the Matapédia and Cascapédia.

Finally, we suggest that you really "get wet" by crossing the St. Lawrence River to traverse its north shore. Several ferries ply its waters. Pack your binoculars, because you'll likely see whales. When we made the crossing in

FEBRUARY

Pohénégamook Haut en couleur Festival d'hiver (Pohénégamook Winter Festival); Pohénégamook (on Highway 289); from snowmobile drag racing and ice fishing to fireworks, this is a wild 'n wonderful winter festival; (418) 859-2222; www.pohenegamook.net

Festival Opti-Neige (Snow Festival); Matane; end-Feb; snow-sculpting competitions with fireworks at night, horse-drawn sleigh rides in daytime; (418) 562-4665; www.tourismematane.com

JUNE–JULY

Festival de la chanson de Tadoussac (Song Festival of Tadoussac); Tadoussac; mid-June; village bursts into song with roughly 40 acts on eight stages; (418) 235-2002; www.chansontadoussac.com

Symposium de peinture de Baie-Comeau (Baie-Comeau Painting Extravaganza); Matane; end-June/ early July; painting *al fresco* where artists from Europe and North America congregate to paint, exhibit their work, and hold workshops; (418) 296-8300; www.sympobaiecomeau.com

JUNE–SEPTEMBER

International Garden Festival; Reford Gardens, Grand-Métis; avant-garde garden design, information, and display of flowers and shrubs. Historic Reford Gardens really shouldn't be missed; (418) 775-2222; www.refordgardens.com

JULY

Annual **Montagnais native powwow** in Essipit; shows, fireworks, bonfires; (418) 233-2266; www.essipit.com

Matane Country Western Festival; folk music, shows and dances, kid's activities; (418) 562-6821

AUGUST

Festival Musique du Bout du Monde (World Music Festival); Gaspé; throughout Aug; rock to world beat music and dance, then take in workshops, participate in jams, and find musical instruments to purchase; (418) 368-5405; www.musiqueduboutdumonde.com

SEPTEMBER

Festi Jazz International de Rimouski (Rimouski International Jazz Festival); Rimouski; early Sept; whether it's in the bars or on the streets come here for great jazz; (418) 724-7844; www.festijazzrimouski.com

OCTOBER

Festival La Virée (Celebrate the Arts Festival); Carleton; month of Oct; regional artisans demonstrate, sell, exhibit their works; (418) 364-6822; www.festivallaviree.com

Festival d'automne de Rimouski (Rimouski Fall Festival); Rimouski; early Oct; since 1980, this has grown into Québec's biggest fall festival showcasing artisans and featuring regional cuisine, also a night parade, competitions, children's events; (418) 732-0101; www.festival-dautomne.ca

early August, we thrilled to the sight of pods of belugas—those smiling white whales—from the ferry crossing between Saint-Siméon and Rivière-du-Loup.

Once on the north shore, you will drive south, through coastal villages such as Les Escoumins to touristy towns like Tadoussac. In fact, Highway 138 is known as the **Route des baleines** (Whale Route). Blue-and-white signs identify it. And if you are really up to something rugged, Eric has a truly wild 'n' woolly suggestion that will take a bit of planning on your part: after crossing the St. Lawrence, you could head east and end up on a ferry to Newfoundland, then back to the Gaspé via Nova Scotia.

Since this route involves catching ferries, you must make reservations. This inevitably means that you'll need to plan your trip carefully, giving yourself enough time to reach ferry docks a full hour or more in advance. Also, it requires setting yourself a schedule and booking accommodations at or near the ferry.

We start this exploration of Québec's "maritime" coast at Pointe à la Croix, near the New Brunswick border town of Campbellton. Have a good look at a route map to orient yourself: you could make a variety of circuits here. You can also custom-design your trip to head north to Rivière-du-Loup and then, after crossing north to Saint-Siméon by ferry, continue west to Québec City.

The Gaspé Peninsula

The first town we propose visiting is **Pointe à la Croix (Point of the Cross),** situated on the Québec side of the interprovincial bridge spanning the Baie des Chaleurs, across from Campbellton, New Brunswick, via Highway 11. The Point of the Cross refers to a cross the Micmacs once erected to denote the boundaries of their territory.

As soon as you cross to Pointe à la Croix, proceed along the Boulevard Interprovincial and, for now, turn left onto Route 132 Ouest (West). On your left you'll see a federally operated museum, **La Bataille de la Ristigouche parc historique national (Battle of the Restigouche National Historic Site)** (418-788-5676 or 888-773-8888; www.pc.gc.ca/ristigouche; open daily June through mid-Oct 9 a.m. to 5 p.m.; $4 adults, $10 family). It is fully interpreted in English and definitely should not be missed, as it sets the context for the history of the Gaspé region.

This battle was one of the "last hurrahs" for New France. The facts are well explained at the museum in a series of fascinating exhibits and in an English-language video. British forces numbering 1,700 well-disciplined soldiers and sailors routed the 400 French equivalents with their allies the Micmacs and some 1,000 Acadians. This dramatic naval battle saw French admiral Giraudais, in his frigate, the *Machault,* as well as two other French ships, the *Bienfaisant* and *Marquis de Malauze,* defeated by the British frigates, *Repulse* and *Scarborough*, plus an armed schooner, on July 8, 1760. The French had drawn the British farther and farther into the Baie des Chaleurs, taunting them with glimpses of the *Machault*. Giraudais had attempted to secure his position by sinking several ships in the bay. But the hoped-for blockade of sunken hulks proved no defense against the skilled British navigators, and the needed French reinforcements never came.

This museum provides insight into our current politics as well as that battle of so long ago. Step outside the museum entrance to look out over the Baie des Chaleurs, where the *Machault* sank. Then, inside the museum, find actual pieces of the ship that have been brought from the depths, restored, and displayed.

Now return eastward along the coast toward **Pointe-à-la-Croix.** Need a spot to stay? You mustn't miss the red-turreted **L'Auberge du Château Bahia** just south of Route 132. This place is the realization of a dream: "On April 9th, 1976" Jean Roussy suddenly decided to build a castle. So his family and friends came to help dig foundations into the side of a hill . . . and today, the wooden castle has twenty-two rooms and even a banquet hall—but you can also camp or stay in hostel-like accommodations. You can even stay for free if you're prepared to work! With trails for hiking or biking, swimming, and with English, Dutch, German, and French being spoken, you've no excuse not to stay at this true "dream castle." (152 blvd. Perron, Point-à-la-Garde; 418-788-2048; www.chateaubahia.com).

Continue about 20 kilometers east on the highway to another museum of a completely different kind. Turn right onto Route Miguasha Ouest (West) and follow the signs to the 1999 designated UNESCO World Heritage Site **Parc de Miguasha** (231 rte. Miguasha Ouest, Nouvelle; 418-794-2475; www.sepaq .com/pq/mig). This spot is internationally renowned for its rich fossil deposits, and no wonder: they are stunning. Discovered by Dr. Abraham Gesner in 1842, the spot didn't really gain much scientific interest until 1879. During the next seventy-five years, archaeologists and paleontologists discovered twenty-three fish species, four invertebrate species, nine plant species, and sixty-six varieties of spores.

Not only can you wander around amid 370 million years of natural history here, you also can walk through the museum's grassy lawns to descend a sturdy staircase to the beach. As you wander along the coastal cliffs you'll be able to see an astonishing concentration of fossils. Please: You must remember that *none* may be removed. When you've completed appreciating this natural wonder, or perhaps an oceanside picnic, return up a second, more easterly set of stairs, where you can now start the 1.9-kilometer Evolution of Life clifftop walk. The park museum has a snack bar and, when we were there, a local singer was playing both French and English folk songs on his acoustic guitar. There's also a good boutique here with lots of literature and good post cards featuring fossils.

You can either return to Route 132 by following the road across the Miguasha Peninsula to Nouvelle or, if you'd like to stop for the day, follow the coastal road to **Camping L'Érabliere** (28 rte. Miguasha Ouest, Nouvelle; 418-794-2929; www.campinglerabliere.qc.ca) near the tip of the peninsula. This pretty site has chalets and camping overlooking the bay.

We pushed on to the 1756 Acadian settlement of Carleton-sur-Mer (also just called "Carleton"), where we were hoping to set up our tent at **Camping Carleton** (418-364-3992; www.carletonsurmer.com) on the sand-spit called Banc de Larocque on the east side of town. This site is famed for its nearby bird sanctuary, and we were eager to see terns and herons. However, we were thwarted. Little did we know that this pretty village *au bord de la mer* (beside the sea) is one of Québec's most popular holiday spots. Nearby you'll enjoy golf, summer theater, boating, and loafing on the sweep of beaches. The campground was full to overflowing, and we joined many travelers who were given special permission (for $4) to camp at the municipal park. Be smarter than we were. Reservations do have their merits. Nearby is a 35-kilometer network of hiking trails, and, if nothing else, the view of the *Baie du Chaleur* (which means "the warm bay" in English) and mountains from an observation desk is superb.

The night we were in Carleton was the start of **Maximum Blues,** an annual five-day international blues festival held in early August. With thirteen different sites, the place was hopping with large and happy crowds (418-364-6008; www.maximumblues.net). And when we awoke, we saw more than a dozen blue herons in the bay just in front of our tent.

WORTH SEEING IN THE COASTAL REGION

Percé Rock,
Percé (on eastern tip of Gaspé Peninsula)

Forillon National Park,
on eastern tip of Gaspé Peninsula, is the end of the Appalachian Mountain chain

Besides excellent bird-watching, there are several hikes around Carleton. As you approach town, you'll see a sign pointing left at Route de l'Éperlan (the French word *éperlan* refers to a small, fish resembling a smelt) to walking paths called *Sentiers pédestres de l'Éperlan* on 613-meter-high **Mont Carleton.** In town, just past the quay, find Rue de la Montagne, leading to **Mont Saint-Joseph** (555 meters), for more hiking. Get details at the Tourist Information Center, on your right just east of the turnoff to Mont Saint-Joseph. The fluently bilingual staff is extremely helpful, and there's a little exhibit on the bird life you'll possibly be able to see on the coast. If hiking or lookouts interest you, ask for the brochure and map called *Carleton-Maria: Réseau de sentiers de randonnée pédestre,* which gives a detailed description of the trails that also hook up to Maria, the next town to the east. You can get some spectacular views of the ocean from the summits of these mountains.

If you are camping, there's a very good fish store in town, **La Poisson-nerie de la Gare,** at the corner of Route 132 and rue de la Gare, where you can purchase, then cook a local catch. There are many places to stay here— but reserve ahead or get there early if your visit happens to coincide with the Maximum Blues Festival like ours did!

At 211 rue du Quai in Carleton, you'll come across a boat dating from WW II, the *Saint Barnabé*. We were told that owner Pierre Landry purchased it for $1 in Québec City and floated it here. But apparently it took over 150 men and a bulldozer to haul it up onto the beach. Now it's a very trendy bar, **Bar St-Barnabé** (211 rue du Quai; www .stbarnabe.com). Apparently the beer is stored belowdecks, where it is kept chilled by the insulating sand.

québecfolkart

The tradition of wood carving in Québec probably springs from long winter nights in the bush or beside *la mer*, where men took to whittling wood and women to rug hooking, rug braiding and quilting. The province is renowned for its folk art, which is in many international museums. Learn more at www.folkartcanada.ca.

On the far side of the BaBar, find **Le Merin d'Eau Douce,** where you can eat the catch of the day or, if you don't care for fish, dine on other specialties of the house (215 rue du Quai, Carleton; 418-364-7602; www.marindeaudouce .com). For family dining, try **Le Heron,** overlooking the ocean atop the rise of land in the middle of town (561 blvd. Perron, Carleton; 418-364-3881).

After leaving Carleton, the next town you come to is **Maria,** appropriately named after Lady Maria Effingham, the wife of Sir Guy Carleton. If you want a hike, watch for Rang (Rural Route) 3 just west of town, and turn up this road to discover the start of the sentier (trail) that leads to pretty **Chute Grand Sault.**

All along this coast we were intrigued with the bird life, especially with the cormorants, whose characteristic stance—wings extended as they perch with their breasts facing the sunshine and wind—makes a wonderful silhouette against the ocean backdrop. Cormorants pose like this to dry their feathers.

cap-des-rosiers

The Cape of Roses on the eastern tip of the Gaspé Peninsula was named for the wild roses that once grew there. In 1759 a French officer there spied General Wolfe's fleet approaching. Immediately a messenger was sent to warn Québec City. Now the gateway to Forillon National Park, its 37-meter lighthouse, built in 1858, is the tallest in Canada.

Pause in Maria to stretch your legs at *Plage Goéland (Gull Beach)*, typically rock-strewn, with the village's homes crowding the street. On the eastern outskirts of Maria, you'll pass through Gesgapegiag, a Micmac reserve whose church is built in the form of a giant white tepee.

Immediately after the bridge over the Cascapédia River, you'll meet the end of Highway 299 Nord (North). We'll follow this route north soon, but for now follow the sign pointing right to New Richmond, and watch for the signs directing you to *Stanley House Inn (Auberge la Maison Stanley).* Please stay here if you possibly can. We'll go a step further: plan to stay here followed by a visit—and possibly another overnight stay—at the nearby *Gaspésien British Heritage Village,* which is also (and most amusingly) known as "Britville." That way, you will get both sides of the coin. A fancy overnight stay in former Governor General Lord Stanley's salmon retreat-cum-mansion and a taste of an ordinary English person's home at Britville, when its B&B is open (in season).

Follow the signs and turn right into the *Stanley House Inn/Auberge la Maison Stanley* (371 blvd. Perron Ouest, New Richmond; 418-392-5560; www .stanleyhouse.ca). Its long driveway curves through meadows and woods. Then you'll gasp: in front of you, on a landscaped lawn, stands a charming old clapboard estate with the American, Canadian, and Québec flags snapping in the ocean breeze. Step inside, and you'll know you have made a real discovery: handsome tongue-and-groove wood paneling greets you amid a cool atmosphere of calm and repose.

The home was built in 1888 as the retreat for Frederic Arthur Stanley, Lord of Preston, sixteenth Earl of Derby, who was Canada's governor general from 1888 to 1893. It is he who inaugurated the prized Stanley Cup hockey trophy in 1893. Two other governors—General Lord Aberdeen and the Earl of Minto—used the home as a summer retreat. It has had various owners, including former Philadelphia mayor John Reyburn. The Canada Council for the Arts operated it as a heavily subsidized artists' retreat from 1972 through 1984, until it became economically and politically untenable. The present owners, the LeBlanc family, have painstakingly restored it.

Madame Lucille LeBlanc is the cook, and she also designed and, in many cases, painted and sewed to create the unique look of each bedroom. What a lovely job she's done! There are eleven bedrooms of various sizes, some with an en-suite bathroom, some with shared facilities. Quite apart from the peaceful interior ambience, the grounds beckoned us. Situated on twenty-five acres of lovely lawn, woods, and cropped fields, this is a treasure of a place to walk or to curl up with a good book and enjoy yourself. There's a pretty descent to the wind-tossed 1,500 feet of private beach, where you can sit in the sun on picturesque driftwood logs, watching the gulls on the breeze and the statuesque herons fishing. Across the bay is Carleton.

Almost next door is the historic village of New Richmond's ***Village Gaspésien de l'héritage Britannique (Gaspésien British Heritage Village)***—affectionately known as "***Britville***"! (351 blvd. Perron Ouest, New Richmond; 418-392-4487; www.villagegaspesien.com; open June 24 through Aug 22 daily 10 a.m. to 5 p.m.; $7 adults, $5 students and seniors, $15 family). This living museum is a collection of homes once lived in by British settlers to this region. Don't make the mistake of assuming that everyone who's British is specifically English. Here there are Irish, Scots, Jersey, and Guernsey folk—as well as English. As you'd expect, this center hosts many festivals and special events in summer, all of which celebrate cultural diversity. Check their Web site to see what's on. Do not miss this superb village, which is being developed carefully and well.

The museum was the brainchild of a group of concerned citizens who wished to celebrate the bicentennial of the Loyalists' arrival here. In 1984 they formed the Cascapédia Bay Loyalist Village Corporation, with the express purpose of preserving their British heritage in this region of Québec. Fourteen buildings were selected and moved to this site, to re-create a village ambience in the British style. It works well. Volunteers dressed in period costume wander about, animating the experiences of early settlers and their links with the other founding communities of Mi'gmaq and Acadians. In fact, it was the Mi'gmaq who first called this area home. They referred to the point of land overlooking the ocean as *Nsweg* (the Lookout) because of the clear views from its promontory.

Today, the entire museum stretches over 82 acres of woods and meadows. To explore the site, either walk or hop on convenient shuttle carriages. You will time-travel from the 1700s to early 1900s, visiting such dwellings as the George Harvey home, built circa 1890 after the American colonial style. There's also ***Willett House,*** being revamped as a B&B (scheduled for completion in 2010; call to reserve). Loyalist William Willett came to the Gaspé after his father was killed in the American Revolution. Behind J. A. Gendron's General Store (the first village structure), don't miss the delicious local treats served at Darlene's Tearoom. If you are like us, you'll be pleased to find some books written in English describing the legends and history of Québec and Gaspé. We found several here, including the amusing *Grandma's Kitchen Favourites,* a local recipe book. Some recipes, such as the Queen of Puddings, date to the 1600s. The book also spins many colorful anecdotes about life here "in the good old days."

Allow yourselves a good three or four hours to explore these heritage buildings. Genealogists will surely want to spend time here, for the center is renowned for its Loyalist records, the most extensive in the Gaspé. If you call, any one of the management team is willing to answer questions about the region and its history.

You may want to proceed through New Richmond about 40 kilometers to ***Bonaventure,*** where you'll discover the ***Musée Acadien du Québec (Acadian Museum of Québec).*** Another bilingual museum, it explains the history of the Acadians, the dreadful deportation years, and their proud resettlement of this region (95 ave. Port-Royal, Bonaventure; 418-534-4000; open daily year-round with differing opening hours; $8 adults, $6 seniors, $5 students, $13 family; www.museeacadien.com).

Grandma Says

Here are some quotes from *Grandma's Kitchen Favourites,* an old recipe book from New Richmond that's loaded with far more than just recipes. "The first Jewish mayor of a municipality in Québec was Mr. Isaac I Iyman, who was mayor of the municipality of Cap des Rosiers for about forty years. He was the son of William Hyman who founded a fish farm in Grand Grève in 1844."

"When the Loyalists arrived on the coast they were without equipment and provisions. The Gov't, however, offered assistance: each family received an axe, hammer, saw, hoe, spade, seeds, a quantity of nails, a pair of door hinges. Each group of 5 families received a shipsaw for making planks and a gun for hunting. They were also to be supplied with some foods for three years."

"One of the first pre-fabs in Canada was Lorne Cottage on the Cascapédia River. All the lumber was pre-cut to size and was floated down from Ottawa. It was to be the summer home of Princess Louise (daughter of Queen Victoria) and her husband the Marquis of Lorne. It was at this cottage that the hymn 'Unto the Hills' was written by the Marquis of Lorne in 1877."

Now head north, taking the road beside the church in the town of Bonaventure, to the village of **Saint-Elzéar.** Here you'll find two interesting sites.

First, find **Hydro Canomore** (305 rue Principal, Saint-Elzéar; 418-534-3522), Gaspé's only private hydroelectric plant, which dates from 1928. Of particular engineering note is the splendid arched dam. The station produces 1.1 megawatts of power, and the magnificent setting, surrounding the Hall River, is best appreciated while walking the site. Bring food; there are picnic tables here (open June 24 to the beginning of Sept).

Nearby find the oldest cave in Québec, **La Grotte de Saint-Elzéar et le Musée des Cavernes** (189 rte. de l'Église, Saint-Elzéar; 418-534-3905; www .lagrotte.ca). This cave is worth visiting. It has many large rooms, and the stalactites and stalagmites are spectacular and numerous. Be sure to wear comfortable clothing, particularly flat-bottomed shoes such as sneakers or hiking boots. Note that a descent of 12 meters is necessary.

Because the temperature is a constant 4 degrees Celsius, you'll require a cozy jacket or sweater. Allow four hours for your tour. If you want to explore the ice fracture caves, allow three hours more. The fee is not insignificant: $37 for adults, $27 for ages six to seventeen. We think this is reasonable, particularly since this is a guided tour. Do not miss the museum, which features bones discovered inside the cave.

To continue our basic circuit, from Saint-Elzéar retrace your route to Bonaventure; from there return to New Richmond. Now head north on Highway 299. This pretty road skirts the Cascapédia River, past some beautiful old

The Phantom Ship

Joan Gow has seen it. Twice. The first time was when she was fourteen. The second time, she called her husband to her side, and he too saw the Phantom Ship of Chaleur Bay.

You see, once upon a time there was a pirate ship that was running hard against the wind, pursued by a man-of-war with all guns a-blazing. While desperately trying to evade capture, the renegade burst into flames, and all hands were lost.

The phantom, seen over the years by hundreds of people, appears suddenly, out of nowhere. Some describe the sea as boiling when the apparition strikes. Most, like Joan, say that you can clearly see the sailors running to and fro, up and down the rigging, while the captain stands on the foredeck, with a woman in white.

Say what you will, many people in this area believe this tale, and the *Northern Lights* newspaper of nearby Bathurst, New Brunswick, even has photos of it.

farms, farmhouses, and villages such as **Grande Cascapédia.** We noted St. Andrews United Church, established 1899, and realized that all the names on post boxes and even streets were of British derivation. Canadian flags flew in the breeze.

Watch for the **Musée de la rivière Cascapédia (Cascapedia River Museum),** at 275 rte. 299, Cascapédia (St. Jules) (418-392-5079). Here are permanent and traveling exhibits depicting one of the most famous salmon fishing rivers in the world.

As you leave the settled land of Grande Cascapédia, you drive north into what becomes a stunningly beautiful section of countryside. The **Cascapédia River** tumbles over boulders on your left, and all along the riverbank are pull-offs for salmon fishing, all of them named. We stopped at Number 27, Big Jack, which had a picnic table, like many of the others that we saw. After preparing a picnic sandwich, we took the little rocky trail to the water's edge and sat down to eat lunch. Canoeists paddled past, and the river invited us to take a dip. Brisk, though, that water!

You absolutely must have a fishing license prior to fishing here. What's more, fishing holes such as Big Jack are designated to particular fishermen, reserved when a fisherman registers. You'll see signs advising you: *Pêche avec réservation seulement* (meaning that fishing is permitted only by reservation). While we were enjoying lunch, a river warden stopped by to ensure that we were not fishing. Respecting these rules helps preserve our Atlantic salmon and other fish.

As we traveled north, we wondered about the many fishing holes along the river with such names as "Maple" or "Lower Joe Martin." Who were the people named? We also reflected on the days of old when the river was the private stomping grounds of the governors-general like Lord Stanley, whose retreat we just saw. How peculiar and absurd it must have seemed to the First Nation's people to think of one person "owning" such a river territory.

Continuing north on Route 299, we arrived at a gas station called **Le Relais de la Cache,** where you can get fishing licenses and where you must report your catch.

Past it on the right are some horrid examples of clear-cutting, a rare sight in the Gaspé region, and on the left you'll see towering mountains. Suddenly the road becomes steep, and road signs advise caution. The elevation is 533 meters here, and the road twists and turns around the bedrock, which glints with mica.

Roughly 75 kilometers from Bonaventure, watch for a sign pointing to your right to the agate mine and to **Murdochville.** Five kilometers down this road (1.5 kilometers of it is gravel), look for the right-hand turnoff onto

Chemin des Tresoirs and proceed a farther 900 meters up a very bumpy road to the *Mine d'agates du Mont Lyall (Agate Mine)* (41 Village-de-l'Anse, Cap-Chat Est; 418-786-2374; www.mont-lyall.com). Here, for $30, you get a pair of safety goggles, a geologist's hammer, and a big bucket and off you go, up the side of the mountain, to prospect for geodes and agates for three hours. (The mine is open mid June through Sept daily from 9 a.m. to 6 p.m.; if you simply wish to view gem exhibits, the cost is $8 for adults, $5 children.)

We had a ball collecting. No one, we feel sure, could come away without finding some sort of treasure. The day we were there, the sun was beating down on the white rocks of which this part of the mountain is formed, so make sure that you have sunscreen, sunhat, and sunglasses. Crowds of people were working the mountainside. Kids were excitedly jumping up and down, shouting "I've found one," while adults—also far from calm—were making their own finds.

taiga

The vegetation known as taiga makes up the transition between arctic tundra and the boreal forest, covering hundreds of square kilometers between the 52nd and 56th parallels. Spruce and fir, along with dwarf shrubs and trees, represent the flora here. But it is the rich lichen growth that provides sustenance to herds of caribou in Québec's taiga regions. Taiga is also found in Les Grands Jardins and Gaspé Parks, both of which also support rare herds of caribou.

Return to the paved Route 299 Nord and turn right, into the *Parc national de la Gaspésie.* The countryside becomes increasingly mountainous, and here you are traveling through the northernmost limit of the Appalachian Mountain Range. Québec's highest peaks are here: Mont Jacques Cartier is 1,268 meters; Mont Albert is 1,154 meters high. At the highest levels, the habitat is tundra. Here in the *Chic-Choc Mountains* are one of the last remaining herds of caribou. (They're very shy; people see them mostly in winter, while skiing in remote areas.) Here you'll find the *Réserve faunique des Chic-Chocs (Chic-Chocs Wildlife Reserve).*

After 15 kilometers, on your right you'll see a campground: *Camping Mont-Albert.* This is a good spot to stop if you intend to stay overnight and do a hike or two. Just past the campground, you can't miss *Le Gîte du Mont-Albert* (2001 Rte. du Parc, Sainte-Anne-des-Monts; 418-763-2288 or 866-727-2427; www.sepaq.com). This white clapboard, black-roofed inn has forty-eight rooms and several cabins in the woods (although the cabins are open year-round, the main lodge is only open mid-June through Oct, and late Dec through early Apr). Pick your spot, dine on fine cuisine, and swim in the sunshine. Don't be fooled by the modest *gîte* in the name; this is a first-class hotel, with a pool and an excellent restaurant. The campground is also oper-ated by Le Gîte du Mont-Albert, so call them for reservations for either the gîte or camping.

About 1.5 kilometers away is the **Centre d'interprétation de la Parc de la Gaspésie (Gaspésie Park Interpretation Center)** on your right (418-763-7811; open daily from June through Sept). By this time you will have passed the start of at least one hiking trail—Sentier du Diable (Devil's Trail)—but we suggest you procure a copy of the Parc de la Gaspésie map before starting a hike.

There are some outstanding hikes here at the northern terminus of the Appalachian Range, including one that is a full-day trip that takes you up the north face of Mont Albert. This is a strenuous ascent; you'll climb more than 800 meters and cross the mountain's open, plateau-like summit, where you will find arctic-alpine vegetation such as red alpine campion. Prepare in advance for what can be extreme conditions of wind, sun, heat, and cold here. For instance, you'll need a backpack (at minimum a day pack) so that you can carry enough clothing for layer-ing appropriately. Pack not only extra clothing but also a wide-brimmed sunhat, plenty of water, sunscreen and, throughout the summer, bug repellent. If bugs really like you, consider using a repellent containing DEET.

gillesvigneault

Chansonneur (singer) Gilles Vigneault—born in Natashquan, Québec, in 1928—stirred the pride of Québécois when he penned and sang "Mon Pays" ("My Country") in 1964.

Many people come to the Chic-Choc Mountains year-round, on skis or else on foot, in the hopes of spotting the elusive caribou. Once this area's herd of indigenous creatures was 1,600 strong. Now the herd is reduced to 250, and their status is listed as "menaced." They feed on "old man's beard," a lichen that grows only in old-growth forest and is their winter staple. Ask the park interpretation staff about them. The staff here is fluently bilingual. Also ask for the binders containing English-language information when you explore the interpretation center's exhibits on geology, flora, and fauna; there's also a slide show in English.

In addition to trails for hiking in summer, there are fourteen lakes for trout fishing. Salmon fishing (with a permit) is popular, too, in park rivers, either from canoe or by wade-fishing in their watery pools. There are mountain bik-ing trails on Mount Logan, guided sight-seeing tours of moose in their habitat, as well as guided plant and geology walks, just to mention a few of the many activities. Come winter, try snowshoeing and cross-country, telemark, and alpine skiing, as well as snowboarding. There also are some great remote hikes where you can really and truly be off the beaten path. Consider your abilities, check out the options—and go for it!

After exploring the park, we drove north to the south shore of the St. Lawrence, to *Sainte-Anne-des-Monts,* where we soon turned west, rejoining Highway 132, which circumnavigates the entire Gaspé Peninsula. The descent to this village is spectacular, with the wide mouth of the river directly in front of you, its vastness pierced by the steeple of the inevitable Catholic church. Continue our "water theme" here by crossing the junction of Route 132 and proceeding "on top of the water" onto the fishing pier.

kayaking "lamer"

There's no better way to get "up close and personal" with la mer than by sea kayak. Get a guide or rent equipment (remember the wind—it's chilly and strong here at Cap-Chat) from *Valmont plein air* (10 rue Notre-Dame Est, Cap-Chat; 418-786-1355; www .valmontpleinair.com).

It's so pretty here—and a completely different landscape from the mountainous terrain we've just been enjoying. Gaily colored fishing boats bob on the tidal swell as local residents fish for capelin (a small fish). Pick up the friendly banter, the lilting accents, and try your French. Your generous smile and a *"Bonjour!"* will reap its rewards. While you're there, look back at your route, up at the Chic-Chocs; then turn around 180 degrees to look at the north shore, then west to the next destination, *Cap-Chat.*

Before proceeding by car, find *Explorama, la mer à découvrir,* at 1 rue du Quai, Ste.-Anne-des-Monts (418-763-2500; www.exploramer.qc.ca), where marine life is revealed in ten aquariums—an intriguing contrast to the tundra and boreal forest information you've seen in the Chic-Chocs!

Now start driving through a dramatically different and immensely appealing "maritime" landscape. At times it seems as though the tides will lap into your car, you're just that close to *la mer* ("the sea," as the Gulf of St. Lawrence is called here). Meanwhile, on your left, cheerful cottages hug the road, including a pink clapboard home with an emerald green roof and trim: astonishingly pretty. What a spectacular view these homes enjoy in summer—and what blustery exposure come winter.

In fact, "bluster" is a running theme for this coast, for the wind blows steadily here. As you drive west, almost immediately you'll note an apparition in the distance, atop a hill. It's the "giant eggbeater"—the *Éole Cap-Chat* (Cap-Chat Wind Turbine). Cap-Chat is enchantingly pretty, situated on a sweeping beach on a protected cove. Route 132 is briefly elevated here, so you can look down on a typical man-made harbor of rocks, with a clutch of boats bobbing on the water.

If you want to stay right on the coast, you can camp at **Camping au Bord de la mer** (Route 132, Cap-Chat; 418-786-2251; www.campingauborddelamer .com; eighty-two sites, from $13.30 for tent camping, call for other rates, showers available). Or on the western outskirts of town, stay at the **Auberge au Crépuscule** country inn (*crépuscule* means "twilight"), with proprietors Jean Ouellet and Monette Dion (239 Notre-Dame Ouest, Cap-Chat; 418-786-5751; www.aucrepuscule.com). Nearby attractions include the small museum dedicated to Father Germain-Lemieux, who collected Canadian folk songs and music.

As you ascend the hill at the far side of town, watch for the right-hand turn off the highway to **Centre Vents et mer** (Le Tryton Wind and Sea Centre; 9 route du Phare, Cap-Chat; 418-786-5543; open daily from mid-June to mid-Sept 8:30 a.m. to sunset). A multimedia show depicts the legend of Cap-Chat, of an Indian maiden and her lover, and of the "crouching cat" formation in the rocks that supposedly gives the village its name. (We couldn't see the resemblance at all.) You'll learn about the early settlers, many of whom were seafaring Scots and Irish, who along with the French made wooden boats to fish these once-rich waters. You will also hear of the 1976 fire that devastated the town. Now people are "farming the sea" with fish-culture ventures along this coast. Ask for headphones to hear the English translation of this multimedia show.

Afterward, walk down to the 1871 lighthouse that is now the **Germain-Lemieux Museum** and wander along **Le Jardin des Brumes (The Garden of Mist)** hugging the sea cliffs. There is also a little cafe overlooking *la mer*. At the museum we were told that "everyone here used to be pirates." The museum guide spun the tale of how, in days gone by, locals would light fires along the rocky coast, luring vessels to shore. Once close to the rocks, the ships were destroyed, their goods cast upon the waves in kegs and trunks. A

Riding on the Beach

Are you a horse nut like I am? (Katharine here . . .) If so, contact Matane's **Centre Équestre du Phare Ouest (Equestrian Center)** at 2043 ave. du Phare Ouest; (418) 562-4218; www.centreequestrephareouest.ca.

Ride through the spectacular countryside or—how lovely this is—ride by moonlight and enjoy a campfire and chat. Or ride alongside *la mer*. Heaven! Also, these guides can tour you around the windmill park or a cattle-breeding outfit!

famous pirate here was Frenchman Charles Le Moyne d'Iberville, who plied the coast, plundering booty as he could.

From days of old and swashbuckling images of pirates, look to what may become the way of the future: wind technology. Much hope and great aspirations gave birth to the ***Éole Cap-Chat (Cap-Chat Wind Turbine)*** (Route 132, Cap-Chat; 418-786-5719; www.eolecapchat.com; bilingual tours daily from mid-June through early Oct or by reservation). Watch for a well-signed left-hand turn just west of the interpretation center off Highway 132. Unfortunately, the astonishing 110-meter-high *éole* (vertical windmill) sustained permanent damage during particularly strong winds. We're told that it probably won't be fixed. Nevertheless it is an impressive sight, particularly "up close and personal," so don't miss going on a forty-five-minute tour of the tallest windmill in the world.

Indeed, the éole (named after the Greek goddess of the wind, Éole) was strategically built at Cap-Chat due to the constant, steady winds striking the coast here. On the windmill tour the guide explains how we can harness the power of the wind. The tour is particularly intriguing because you go inside the windmill itself to see how the technology works.

paperproducts

In the late 1800s, major North American newspapers were producing dailies. The industry created an insatiable demand for newsprint, and the *Chicago Tribune* established a plant in Baie Comeau. In 1907 the Bromption (Québec) Pulp & Paper Company of East Angus was the first to produce kraft paper. From the German word meaning "strong," this is the sturdy paper used for cardboard boxes. Because it could be made from a variety of woods, it was an important discovery for the Canadian forestry industry.

Adjacent to the éole is a windmill farm named ***Le Nordais Windmill Park***—the largest of its kind in Canada. Windmill vanes mounted on giant 55-meter-high poles spin in the steady maritime winds, generating more than 100 megawatts of power—enough to provide 5 percent of the Gaspé region's household energy needs. In fact, Nordais sells its power to Hydro Québec, so wind energy becomes part of their grid system.

When we first visited Le Nordais in 1998 for the first edition of this book, there were 76 windmills—and the technology was still quite new. In 2004 we cruised past the farm on a ferry and were both astonished and delighted to see how the farm had expanded to more than 133 windmills along this part of the coast. In our travels throughout the world, we've been intrigued at the rise in wind farms: we've seen wind turbines in use in California, Wales, and Scotland. Their presence is not always welcomed. In fact, Welsh environmentalists expressed grave concerns to us about wind turbines being erected in the path of birds' migration routes. As well, many people dislike their intrusive appearance on the landscape. Nonetheless, along with experimentation involved with getting power from ocean waves, wind energy represents an interesting alternative technology.

Return to Route 132 and drive west toward **Matane,** where you can book car passage on the ferry to the north coast. En route, you'll pass an astonishing private residence called Castel des Galets, a turreted and brilliantly colored fantasy to the left of the road.

As you enter Matane, drive over the bridge spanning the Matane River. We were checking in at **Auberge la Seigneurie** (621 ave. Saint-Jérôme, Matane; 877-783-4466 or 418-562-0021; www.aubergelaseigneurie.com). We immediately turned left after the bridge onto Rue Saint-Jérôme; the *auberge* is just on the right. Our hosts Guy Fortin and his wife, Raymonde, installed us in Anne's Room. Although the auberge itself is lovely, we don't recommend this particular room as it is noisy because of its location near the shared bath and shower rooms. But the breakfasts are generous and delicious. Abandon caution and enjoy the homemade jams, jellies, and strawberry butter (*beurre aux fraises*), which is divine spread on croissants.

Matane is a fun spot to spend some time. We first went to the Tourist Information Center, which is located right on Route 132, in the old lighthouse immediately west of town. The center has a tiny nautical exhibit (plus, rather incongruously, a stuffed beaver). Fluent English is spoken here. In the parking lot we found a giant shrimp: **Pincette,** the town mascot, is a female crustacean mounted on a wagon, ready for her appearance in the annual shrimp festival in mid-June. We were told that a festival favorite is the equivalent of shrimp poutine: fried shrimp with cheese curds and sauce. Ask to see the current copy

Matane Mermaid

Once upon a time, a Matane fisherman spied a mermaid hopelessly tangled in his herring net. When free, she beseeched him to take her home with him. So he walked through the streets of Matane with the mermaid draped over his shoulder so that her tail wouldn't drag on the ground. The priest took one look at the bewitchingly beautiful mermaid and scolded the fisherman, demanding that he return her immediately to la mer. Fearing excommunication, the fisherman reluctantly complied—but not before his neighbors got a good glimpse of his catch. So this is how the good folk of Matane spied a mermaid. (From Jean-Claude Dupont, *Légendes de la Gaspésie et des Îles-de-la-Madeleine,* Éditions J.-C. Dupont, Québec, 1995.)

of *Guide vacances Matane et région (Matane and Region Vacation Guide),* which is full of other attractions.

No one should visit Matane without seeing the **salmon ladder** at the **Mathier-D'Amours Dam.** Return to Rue Saint-Jérôme and drive about a kilometer to the dam. Park and explore the river's edge with its lovely walkway, the **Promenade des Capitaines (Captain's Walk).** At the west edge of the dam, find the salmon ladder (418-562-7006; open daily mid-June through Aug, 7:30 a.m. to 9:30 p.m. and 8 a.m. to 5 p.m. during Sept; $3 adults, ages twelve and under free). Salmon are measured and counted as they pass by two large glass windows in the fish ladder observation post on their way upstream to spawn. On the summer evening when we first visited, friendly and bilingual museum guide Sylvain Benoit told us that because of the day's heat, he'd seen only 4 Atlantic salmon (versus the 200 he might normally see)—but these specimens were a metre long. So, keep your eyes peeled and perhaps you'll spy such immense fish.

There are many places to dine in Matane. Sylvain recommended two spots: **Le Vieux Rafiot (The Old Shipwreck)** on Highway 132 near the ferry docks (1415 du Phare Ouest, Matane; 418-562-8080), and the **Hôtel Belle Plage,** famous for its smoked salmon made on-site in their own smokehouses (1310 Matane-sur-Mer, Matane; 888-244-2323 or 418-562-2323; www.hotelbelle plage.com). We stopped to examine the smokehouses (and salivated over the enticing smells).

For a short side trip from Matane, here's something unique. You can visit a wild 'n' wacky house *drôlement colorée* (whimsically colored) in **Saint-Ulric,** approximately 10 kilometers west of Matane. Owners Léonace Durette and Colette Michaud welcome visitors to M*aison Pin d'Épices* (a quirky, fun *double-entendre* on *"pain d'épices"* which means "gingerbread house", but here, *"pin"* means pine, so the couple have called their home the "House of Pine"). It is a one-and-a-half-story affair that is totally covered with brightly-colored "found objects" (51 Ulric-Tessier, Saint-Ulric; 418-737-4762). Because the owners live here, understandably it is not always open for visitors. However, if they're in, spend the nominal admission to see their astonishing collection of "everything under the sun." Madame Michaud (who only speaks the tiniest bit of English) says they not only collect objects, but they also paint and make use of literally almost everything else that can be recycled for the home. You'll agree—even if you can only view the exterior!

It was difficult leaving Matane. Some places really make you want to linger, and this is one of them. But we had to make our 8 a.m. ferry reservation for the 2½-hour crossing to Godbout. After Raymonde Fortin's delicious breakfast, served to ferry passengers at a prompt 6:15 a.m., we made the

On the Road to Labrador

Here's something that will impress the folks back home: a drive to Labrador! In fact, with a suitable vehicle, you can use this as a unique way to get to the island of New-foundland. The road is very rough in places, and four-wheel-drive is recommended. Stop at the Tourist Information Center in Baie-Comeau to pick up current information about road conditions and services. Expect to drive for eighteen hours to cover the 1,100 kilometers from Baie-Comeau to the ferry terminus at Goose Bay—and reserve the ferry accordingly.

Highway 389 Nord takes you along the Manicouagan River, past the Manic-2 and Manic-5 hydroelectric generating stations (free 105-minute tours daily from June 24 through Labor Day; 418-294-3923). The road follows the eastern shores of the 8,000-square-kilometer Manicouagan Reservoir—the remnants of a huge meteor crater now filled with water held back by the *Daniel Johnson dam* at Manic-5—to Labrador City across the still-disputed border between Québec and Labrador. From there, it is all gravel to Goose Bay, and the section from Churchill Falls is recom-mended for four-wheel-drive only.

From Goose Bay, the thirty-five-hour, twice-weekly **Sir Robert Bond** *ferry* (Labrador Marine; 709-535-0810; www.tw.gov.nl.ca/FerryServices/) will take you to Lewisporte, Newfoundland.

eight-minute trip to the tetrapod docks. (Tetrapods aren't beings from outer space. They are man-made, four-legged concrete "stabilizing rocks" used to build secure water-based structures such as docks and quays.)

Société des traversiers du Québec (Society of Québec Ferries) oper-ates daily ferries to Godbout and Baie-Comeau from Matane year round. The trip takes two hours and twenty minutes. For vehicles or passenger group reservations call 418-562-2500 or 877-562-6560 (www.traversiers.gouv.qc.ca/). Ask about schedule and rates, which change annually.

As you cross, watch for whales and compare the difference between the populated coastline you leave behind and the rock cliffs of the Canadian Shield ahead.

Îles de la Madeleine

Îles de la Madeleine—once called Magdelen Islands—is a fish-hook shaped archipelago of a dozen islands in the Gulf of St. Lawrence located 215 kilo-meters from the Gaspé Peninsula, 105 kilometers northeast of Prince Edward Island. The landscape is otherworldly: the islands are rimmed by glorious, blond, sandy beaches that stretch as far as the eye can see. Salty flavored grasses wave in offshore breezes (sometimes, strong winds) in fields where contented cows graze. Houses take on an old-style charm, being gaily painted, often surprisingly contrasting colors such as purple with a turquoise trim or pumpkin with a crimson trim.

All these features conspire to transport you to another time, of maritime ways, and of a seemingly relaxed lifestyle. However, although les îles offers this to you, the locals work hard in agriculture, salt mining (les Îles produces more rock salt used for roads in winter than any other place in North America), and in the fishery. For example, lobster fishing is a coveted profession here, and procuring a license is highly competitive, involving hundreds of thousands of dollars to purchase the permit and boat. You can get superb food here, from local specialties such as Canadian cow cheeses to seal bourguignon or even flipper pie . . . Of course, mussels and lobster are delicious, too, in season.

timeout

Time it right: Les Îles de la Madeleine are one hour earlier than the rest of Québec because they are on Maritime, or Atlantic, time.

We visited les Îles de la Madeleine in a novel way: we had driven to Prince Edward Island (PEI) from our home in the Pontiac region of West Québec (see Outaouais chapter), then boarded a ferry at Souris, on PEI's northeastern shore. The five-hour crossing to *les Îles* was bracing, in ocean breezes. We stood on deck watching for whales and other marine life, scouring the horizon for our first view of L'Île d'Entrée (Entry Island) and Île du Cap aux Meules, where the ferry docks. Entry Island was spectacular, looming out of the ocean like a compact mini-mountain, and as we drew closer, the sheltering curve of Cap aux Meules, the village where we docked, became apparent.

From our hotel accommodations in Cap aux Meules, we spent four days exploring the islands. Although this lodging was entirely adequate, we recommend booking well ahead so you can stay in some of the islands' charming B&Bs. The islands offer much: bird-watching in summer is more than well-matched by seal-watching in Mar, right out on the frozen ocean! Because of the ocean breezes, wind sports are very popular. For those who want to chill out, rent lodging for a week and bicycle, read books, shop and dine on superb French maritime cuisine, les Îles couldn't be a better choice.

A word on exploring and ferries. There are some taxis but to explore as we did, a car is the best option—and you can bring your own from either PEI or other parts of Québec. We booked the *CMTA N.M. Vacancier* from les Îles (catching it at the ferry dock at Cap-aux-Meules) to Montréal. This ferry-cum-cruise ship stops at Matane, on the Gaspé Peninsula, and cars can board and de-board here. It also stops at Québec City, but only foot passengers can get on or off here. We drove our car off at Montréal to return home. (Information and schedule: Groupe CTMA, 435 chemin Avila Arseneau, Cap-aux-Meules, G4T 1J3; reservations: 888-986-3278; 418-986-3278; www.ctma.ca).

Tips: (1) Although ferry staff were very obliging and friendly, when we visited many didn't know much (or any) English. Most visitors seem to be French-speaking, so while on board, recognize that it's time we all practice our French. Of course, if you don't know any, you'll be fine as everyone's so helpful. (2) There's entertainment and exercise programs on board but again, when we were on board, all such activities were *en français*—it was great fun, however, to listen to the French songs and music. If it gets a little too much, simply head off to another part of the deck, pull up a deck chair and read or watch the coast slip past. (3) We were given an interior room with no ocean view and found it way too claustrophobic. If it suits your budget, ask to be upgraded to an exterior room with a porthole window. Most cabins have shared restrooms but for a price, you can get an en-suite cabin. (4) Be sure to get the schedule of scenic views from staff on board: you will get an amazing view of Percé Rock (off the tip of the Gaspé Peninsula) and also see the extensive windmill farm (*Le Nordais*) just before you reach Matane. (5) Be sure to take binoculars so you can watch for whales, seals, and sea birds and view the coastline attractions and scenery. (6) Take plenty of sunscreen, sunglasses, and a wide-brimmed hat. (7) Bring a book: the onboard library was almost exclusively French when we went. (8) Food: frankly, it wasn't the best, even though the dining room was highly recommended to us. Take snacks or use the cafeteria and treat yourself to gourmet meals when you are on Îles de la Madeleine.

Just beyond the ferry docks at Cap-aux-Meules, you'll find the helpful tourist information center where you can procure information on sights and B&B–style accommodations. However, for the duration of our visit, we stayed in **Châteaux Madelinot,** a hotel offering comfortable rooms, a restaurant, and swimming pool. It made a super point from which to explore the islands. (Châteaux Madelinot, 485 rte. 199, Cap aux Meules, Îles de la Madeleine; 418-986-3695; www.hotelsilesdelamadeleine.com). We dined at **Au Vieux Couvent,** an old convent, but it also offers rooms—try it out yourself (292 rte. 199, Havre-aux-Maisons; 418-969-2233; www.domaineduvieuxcouvent.com). Another spot we dined at but didn't stay in (rooms looked comfortable and clean) was **Auberge Chez Denis à François,** 404 chemin d'En Haut, Havre-Aubert; 418-937-2371; www.aubergechezdenis.ca.

Hop on board the *S.P. Bonaventure* ferry (C.G.R. Cyr, Etang-du-Nord; 418-986-8452 or 418-986-5705; www.traversiers.gouv.qc.ca) to explore Entry Island.

There is an exhilarating hike from the docks, through the villages to the highest point of land. You'll walk through farmers' fields (horses have been known to come up to walkers and beg for apples!) to the summit of the hill, then alongside the ocean with great photo opportunities as you return to the ferry.

If ocean sports are your thing, rent a kayak; sailboard; flippers, mask and snorkel; or canoe; or plan a snorkeling trip with seals with *L'Istorlet* (Centre nautique de l'Istorlet, 100 chemin de l'Istorlet, Havre-Aubert; 888-937-8166 or 418-937-5266; www.istorlet.com.

We mentioned the wind . . . Have fun with *Au Gré du Vent* if you want to try your hand at sailing a kite or even making a kite at a workshop. These folks specialize in "fighting kites" so if you want to get experience with this technique, the islands' winds will help you out! Purchase includes instruction at Au Gré du Vent, Place du Maré, Site La Cote, Etang-du-Nord; 418-986-5069 or 418-986-5000; www.greduvent.com.

Le Site D'Autrefois historical site provides a glimpse into the past through the whimsical eyes of your retired fisherman host, Claude, who charms you with his winning smile and nautical tales. He's fashioned the site into an odd assortment of collectibles plus has built a miniature village complete with graveyard, as well as staging several fishing scenes (complete with mannequins). Barns, homes, outbuildings show life "as it was." Quirky good fun. (Le Site D'Autrefois, 3106 chemin la Montagne, Havre-Aubert; 418-937-5733; www .ilesdelamadeleine.com/autrefois/). Gift shop, picnic tables, and also a nice short hike to an observation deck.

seal politics

Sir Paul McCartney lobbies against seal hunting, as do many. But here on Les Îles, it's a way of life. What do you think about this industry? There's more than one point of view and peoples' beliefs are passionately held.

Mines Seleine is the salt mine, and you can tour a small museum that explains this great natural resource, which was first mined here on April 1, 1983. Now, 2,000 tons an hour are mined: 65 percent of the rock salt is used in Québec; 25 percent on the East Coast of the United States, and 10 percent in Newfoundland. Mines Seleine is located next to the *Gateway to the East Interpretation Centre* (information center that houses the salt museum plus lots of great information on the ecology of the islands), 50 rte. 199, Grosse Île; (418) 985-2387.

The *Seal Interpretation Centre* houses interactive displays of the life and times of seals and seal hunting, which is a hot environmental issue because islanders think the "greenies" have decimated their fishing livelihood. Seals are reproducing with little control, while fish stocks are increasingly endangered. We sympathize with the seal hunters. How about you? Inform yourself at the Seal Interpretation Centre, 377 rte. 199, Grand-Entrée; (418) 985-2833 or (418) 985-2226; www.ilesdelamadeleine.com/cip/; open 10 a.m. to 6 p.m. June through Sept; $7.50 adults, $6.50 seniors, children $4, family $20.

Artisans du Sable is one of Québec's economuseums and is very different, albeit very commercial. Artisans create everything from clocks to sand candles using the beach as a resource. Artisans du Sable, 907 rte. 199, La Grave; 418-937-2917; www.artisansdusable.com. Also, in July don't miss the *Festival Sable-Eau-Vent* (Sand, Water, and Wind Festival), designed for families with acrobatic kite displays and battles, and even nighttime kite flying (check with Îles de la Madeleine Tourism for dates—see below). Also check with the tourism people about the Sand Castle Competitions held every Aug at Havre-Aubert Beach—you can even take part in a sand castle–building workshop!

Îles de la Madeleine Tourism will provide you with ample information about accommodations, dining, festivals, and sightseeing "musts." Tourisme Îles de la Madeleine; 128 chemin Principal, Cap-aux-Meules, G4T 1C5; 418-986-2245 or 877-624-4437; www.tourismeilesdelamadeleine.com. Be absolutely sure to ask for the English copy of their *Official Tourist Guide:* this is indispensable and presents all the festivals, all the major sights and lodgings.

The North Shore

The scenery is completely different on the north shore of the St. Lawrence. It is rugged here, without the quaint seaside towns that make the Gaspé coast so picturesque. Here it's a tough, wild world of forested cliffs plunging down to the water, of settlements scraped from unforgiving Canadian Shield rock.

Our drive will take us through Baie Comeau, a large industrial town with a colossal pulp and paper mill as well as an aluminum plant, and to Tadoussac, famous for whale watching. From there, we cross the Saguenay River on a little ferry to Pointe Noire, where there's an excellent (and free) marine interpretation center. From here we continue south to Saint-Siméon, returning to the south shore on the ferry to Rivière-du-Loup.

Special tip: Tourism offices and many off-the-beaten-path attractions on the north shore (*Côte Nord,* en français) do not open until June 24. Many of the telephone numbers you'll find in these next pages don't work off-season, so it's best to telephone the tourism office in Baie Comeau (418-296-8178) for information prior to June 24. Alternatively, check their Web site at www .tourismecote-nord.com. The short season and use of ferries make it particularly prudent to contact this tourism association.

The Matane ferry docks at *Godbout,* a tiny fishing village and one of Canada's oldest trading posts.

A bit farther east along Rue Pascal-Comeau, the *Musée Amérindien et Inuit (Amerindian and Inuit Museum)* has an interesting collection of items related to Native life on this rugged coast, including a traditional bread oven (134 rue Pascal-Comeau, Godbout; 418-568-7306; open daily June through Oct, 9 a.m. to 9 p.m.; $4 adults, $2 students and children). Of interest to us are the pottery and painting workshops, but because we were passing through, we had no time. You will—if you read this and plan your trip accordingly. Lucky you!

If you want to linger here, there is a place to stay near the ferry. The *Gîte aux Berges* offers cabins for just over $50 per night for two (180 Pascal Comeau, Godbout; 418-568-7816). Another interesting little spot to stay is *Gîte la maison du vieux quai* (142 rue Pascal-Comeau; 418-568-7453; www.gitemaisonduvieuxquai.com). You can fish from the wharf. Make sure you have binoculars, as you might catch a glimpse of a whale!

Our coastal route turns west here, but there is a lot to see farther east, too. For an unusual route to Newfoundland, read the description of a tour of the lower north shore at the end of this chapter.

Otherwise, turn west on Highway 138 for the 58-kilometer drive to Baie Comeau. The road is beautiful and hugs the cliffs grasping the shoreline. You'll thrill to spectacularly rugged coastal scenery with rock-strewn, narrow beaches. We've now utterly left the more gentle southern shore with its picturesque farms and villages. The sedimentary rock of the Appalachian Range is suddenly absent. You now drive through the granitic Canadian Shield, the most ancient rock on Earth, with spruce-ringed peat bogs in the hollows. You really expect to see moose. In season (early Aug) bring your blueberry pails, pull off the road, and feast!

After about 25 kilometers you'll see the town of *Franquelin* (formerly spelled Frankelin, after cartographer J. B. Frankelin, who mapped the St. Lawrence River). Here you'll find the *Village Forestier d'Antan* (16 rue des Érables, Franquelin; 418-296-3203; open daily mid-May through Sept 30, 9 a.m. to 5 p.m.; $5 adults, $3.50 students and children, kids under five free.),

paulinejulien

A singer, actress, and songwriter, Pauline Julien was born in Trois-Rivières in 1928. She studied in Paris in the 1950s and, upon her return to Canada, introduced the songs of Bertholt Brecht and Kurt Weill to Québecers. Soon she started to sing the songs of Québec songwriters Gilles Vigneault and Raymond Lévesque. An ardent feminist, she began writing her own lyrics in 1968.

a small museum exhibiting the life of woodcutters in bygone days. As you can imagine, forestry is one of the natural resource industries that opened up the north shore to economic development. They offer guided tours and "bush camp lunches" Wed through Sun; call for reservations.

Beyond Franquelin you pass the Rivière Mistassini. We stopped and immediately heard the rattling call of a belted kingfisher and enjoyed seeing its slim form skimming the surface of Lac Low. Then our attention was caught by more movement: A large, cheeky Canada Jay (also known as the whiskey-jack) swooped down to investigate us, saucily expecting a handout.

We continued through this rugged lake- and spruce-strewn countryside, marveling at its grandeur. Suddenly the stacks of the Reynolds Aluminum plant announced we'd reached **Baie-Comeau.** If you've been hankering to see a hydroelectric generating station, head 25 kilometers north on Route 389 to visit the **Manic-2** site on the Manicouagan River. Camping is available at nearby **Camping Manic-2** (Route 389, Baie-Comeau; 418-296-2810; mid-June through Sept; eighty-three sites; $18).

If you're visiting during summer, Baie Comeau hosts several festivals such as the **Symposium de Peinture (Painting Symposium)** (418-296-8300; www.sympobaiecomeau.com) held in late June, workshops included. Or check out the city's winter festival in March, which features such snowy activities as snowmobiling, snowboarding, and snow sculpture competitions.

After passing Route 389 Nord, cross the Rivière Amédée and turn left (south) onto Boulevard Blanche to **Parc de la Falaise (Cliff Park),** which provides an excellent lookout on the confluence of the St. Lawrence and Manicouagan Rivers. Proceeding farther west on Route 138, find the Tourist Information Office just before the bridge over the Manicouagan.

Our next stop, **Pointe-aux-Outardes,** was gorgeous. Watch for a left-hand turn and a 14-kilometer drive south on a peninsula of land, past a quaint, wind-tossed pioneer cemetery, to **Parc régional de Pointe-aux-Outardes** (4 rue Labrie Ouest, Pointe-aux-Outardes; 418-567-4226; www.parcnature.com; open daily June 1 through Oct 15).

québectrivia

Menfolk in the early 1800s went to work in the bush from winter freeze-up at the end of Nov through to the great melt in early April. They lived in shanties and cut and hauled logs from dawn till dusk.

Extensive white sand dunes, marshlands, spectacular boardwalks, and bird-watching towers conspire to make you want to linger. When we went, park staff here spoke only French, but an English-language tour is offered if you book ahead. If your French is not fluent enough to interpret common names for birds, find a French-English bird list, which will help immensely at this park. (Note: an "outarde" is a Canada goose.)

The windswept boardwalk hike is well balanced by a woods walk through stunted trees. The boardwalk is sturdy and, though there are a few steps here and there, most will be able to enjoy this easy stroll. Signs are all in French, but, with perseverance, someone who isn't fluent in French can still interpret some information, such as the pioneer genealogy panel overlooking the bay. Here you learn that the first settlers on the point, in 1850, were English-speaking. Names like Robinson, Marsh, McCormick, Miller, and Ross intermingled with the second wave of French settlers. On further examination of the genealogical list, you see the reality of the present and the hope of the future: for example, in 1850 Samuel Miller married Ephémie L'Italien; in 1891 David Malouin married Victoria Ross. Love, romance, and intermarriage: the potential global solution to our differences.

The dates and their significance roll on: in 1918 the first school was built at Pointe-aux-Outardes; 1925 the quay constructed; 1930 the first parish; 1931 the first sawmill (*scierie*); 1934 shrubs—the sand rose—imported from France; 1948 electricity replaced oil lamps; 1965 the potato research station; 1993 the creation of this park.

Now retrace your route back to Highway 138 and go west to **_Raguenneau._** Here, from a rocky point, you can look across the bay to the dunes of Pointe-aux-Outardes. This is a totally off-the-wall spot, with life-size dinosaurs and a giant obelisk. When the "tourist information officer" (lounging nearby with her boyfriend) was asked by a Parisian visitor about the significance of all this, she was merely told, "It's the symbol of our village." Hmm . . .

Five kilometers beyond is the Montagnais cultural center of **_Le Centre de villégiature de Papinachois,_** a good place to investigate if Native life and lore interest you. Call ahead so that they can help you custom-fit your experience. You can learn about the Montagnais language, culture, and legends and how to make traditional foods, moccasins, tents, snowshoes, and canoes (18 Messek, Betsiamites; 418-567-8350; www.papinachois.ca).

Napoleon Alexander Comeau

Ardent naturalist, fisherman, trapper, author, and guide, Napoleon Alexander Comeau is remembered today by the city of Baie-Comeau. He also wrote a book, *Life and Sport on the North Shore of the Lower St. Lawrence and Gulf* (1923) in English—a language he didn't hear spoken, some tell us, until his mid-teens.

Route des Baleines— Canada's Whale Route

The north coast is famed for its whales, and whale watching draws huge crowds here. Of the thirteen species of whales, minke and fin are particularly prevalent, and the blue whale—the world's largest mammal—can also be seen if you're fortunate. Please remember that whales are sensitive creatures and that beluga and blue whales are endangered species, while others are increasingly uncommon.

Early August is blueberry season, and little huts sell freshly picked baskets of these delicious berries all along this part of the highway. Not to be missed!

Continue the drive through Forestville, where you can catch another ferry to the south shore to Rimouski. We paused at a fish shop *Les Crabiers du Nord* (428 rte. 138; 418-238-2132) on the north side of the road at the eastern outskirts of Sainte-Anne-de-Portneuf. Here we bought some of the most delicious shrimp we've ever eaten. Half a pound was $5.72, and more tender, tasty shrimp you may never find. Watch for the pretty *La Maison Fleurie (House of Flowers)* (193 rte. 138, Sainte-Anne-de-Portneuf; 418-238-2153). Over the past hundred years or so, it has seen duty as a grocery store, theater, and post office. It is now a comfortable B&B, where host Germina Fournier can recommend local offerings such as bike rentals, sailboat rentals, or quiet beach walks.

The coast becomes an almost continuous set of salt marshes. Everywhere to your left you'll see pull-over parking spaces and little signs indicating spots to observe birds or see whales (*baleines*). In both spring and fall, this coastline is alive with birds on the move, stopping for food in the rich marshes before the next leg of their migration. The same rich food supplies bring the whales. As you draw closer to the hub of whale watching at the mouth of the Saguenay Fjord, you'll see how this popular activity is shaping a burgeoning tourism industry along this coast.

What's important when choosing an outfitter is to remember whales are sensitive creatures which communicate over vast distances underwater. And, we're talking hundreds if not thousands of miles. Before you book, ask outfitters how close they get to the whales. Motorized vessels contribute to what some oceanographers who study bioacoustics call "underwater smog" which prevents marine mammals from communicating effectively.

As you approach Sault-au-Mouton, you can't miss *L'Auberge de la Rivière Sault-au-Mouton* on Route 138. It stands on a rise of land at the confluence of the Sault-au-Mouton and St. Lawrence Rivers. Its accommodations offer forfait, package deals: phone ahead to arrange whale watching or

CRUISES/BOAT EXCURSIONS FOR WHALE WATCHING

Croisières Essipit Inc.,
46 rue de la Réserve
Les Escoumins;
(418) 233-2266
www.essipit.com
(whale watching, cruises)

Les Crosières Neptunes,
507 rue du Boisé,
Bergeronnes G0T 1G0;
(418) 232-6716
www.croisieresneptune.net
(whale watching)

Croisières AML,
167 rue des Pionniers, Tadoussac;
(418) 235-2222
www.croisieresaml.com

sea kayaking, for instance. This was a clean and friendly place—but more like a hostel than a real auberge. The $70 for bed-and-breakfast in the fairly basic rooms at the inn may seem pricey unless you plan to take full advantage of the activities and trails on the property (333 rue Principale, Sault-au-Mouton; 418-231-2214; www.aubergesaultaumouton.com).

Even if you don't stay at the *auberge,* do stop at the little park on the Rivière Sault-au-Mouton just down the hill. The well-built lookout beside the falls is a good place to watch for whales in the St. Lawrence below, and there are utterly gorgeous swimming holes in the nearby rounded, exposed Canadian Shield rock. Like in many of the rivers flowing south, the water is tea-colored from the peat. One perhaps unexpected benefit is that the water is often warmer than you might think. Below, on the west side of the Rivière Sault-au-Mouton, you'll spy the ruined foundations of a series of mills.

Farther along the coast, you'll descend into **Les Escoumins,** a pretty village in a sheltered cove where river pilots board ocean freighters to guide them through the narrowing St. Lawrence. It is also a Mecca for scuba divers: you'll see the red flag with the white diagonal bar at many of the motels and on signs along the road near here. Diving is a terrific way to explore the river's rich marine life.

Right on the riverfront, **Auberge de la Baie** (267 rte. 138, Les Escoumins; 418-233-2010; www.aubergedelabaie.com; twelve rooms, $80 to $125) is a pretty white-framed building with scarlet trim, with lots and lots of flower baskets lending a charming effect.

Les Escoumins village lives and breathes for tourism—and water-based tourism specifically. From here to Tadoussac you'll see increasing numbers of whale excursion boat companies along this sector of the Route des Baleines

(Whale Route). If you rent a boat on your own, know that anyone born after 1983 must possess a pleasure boat competency certificate to legally operate a boat with a motor. Also boaters and beachcombers alike must be aware of the tides. Call 800-267-6687 for nautical information.

The **L'Héritage I** ferry makes a daily crossing from Les Escoumins to Trois Pistoles between May 15 and Oct 15. (For information and reservations, contact La Compagnie de Navigation des Basques; www.traversiercnb.ca, 11 rue du Parc, Trois-Pistoles; 418-851-4676 or 877-851-4677.)

As you continue west, you enter the area of the Saguenay–St. Lawrence Marine Park—particularly notable, as it is Québec's first marine park. Watch for the left-hand turn off Highway 138 to the ***Centre d'interprétation et d'observation du Cap-de-Bon-Désir*** (Interpretation and Observation Center) (13 chemin du Cap-Bon-Desir, Bergeronnes; 418-232-6751; www.parcmarin.qc.ca; open daily mid-June through mid-Oct; $7.80 adults, $6.80 seniors, $3.90 youth, $19.60 family). From its rocky promontory you may be lucky to see whales such as finback, minke, beluga, or even the blue whale—the largest mammal alive. There are guided interpretive walks along the shoreline and lots of information about marine mammals and regional history. Don't miss this spot. As a part of the Canadian federal park system, it is fully bilingual.

Returning to Route 138 Ouest, we soon arrived at ***Camping Bon-Désir,*** on the left side of the highway (198 rte. 138, Bergeronnes; 418-232-6297; www .campingbondesir.com). Make reservations. It's popular all summer, especially during the weekend of the local ***Festival de la Baleine Bleue (Blue Whale Festival)*** in early August. Just about the best sites are No. 53, on a secluded spot on a pond, and Nos. 91–99, with good views of the water. Even with all 200 campsites occupied, you may be amazed at the tranquility as well as the courtesy of your fellow campers. Visitors are respectful of peace and quiet, as well as of nature. After pitching our tent we strolled down to the beach and the next morning reveled in hot showers (25 cents for five minutes). Great whale watching here—we used our binoculars and spied one in the bay.

Another good choice in the area is a gîte between Cap Bon Désir and Tadoussac called ***Gîte la Petite Baleine*** (50 rue Principale, Bergeronnes; 418-232-6756). It's in an old home with wonderful ambience. It has a little arts and crafts boutique featuring local artisans and products.

While in Bergeronnes, if you want to get out on the water to learn about the Saguenay and St. Lawrence Rivers, consider exploring the river marine park. From mid-May to mid-Oct there are guided tours by kayak, including some for beginners. Everything from half-day to overnight experiences are possible. (***Mer & Monde,*** 405 rue de la Mer Bergeronnes; 418-232-6779; www .mer-et-monde.qc.ca.)

Continue west, watching for the left-hand turn on Rue de la Mer to the *Centre d'interprétation Archéotopo* (498 rue de la Mer, Bergeronnes; 418-232-6286; www.archeotopo.qc.ca; daily 9 a.m. to 5 p.m. June through mid-Oct and 8 a.m. to 8 p.m. in July and Aug) located at the base of a quay extending into the St. Lawrence. This center exhibits the archaeology and prehistory of the immediate north coast region and gives a peek into pre-European Native life. Amerindians are known to have lived along the St. Lawrence River's north shore 8,000 years ago—Paleo-Indian times. Sea cruises are also available.

Back on Route 138, pass Highway 172 heading right, along the north shore of the Saguenay Fjord. Almost immediately, drive down to *Tadoussac,* Québec's whale-watching capital. Tadoussac is very pretty despite its commercialization. Turn left onto Rue des Pionniers and then right onto Rue Morin, to find the *Restaurant la Bolée* in the upper level of a trendy pumpkin-and-green wood frame building (164 rue Morin; 418-235-4750). Downstairs is a deli and bakery where you can buy homemade sweet temptations like *gâteau macarons,* a gooey, delicious sensation made of coconuts at $1.50 for a generous square—or pay the same price for a loaf of homemade bread.

Tadoussac is an extremely popular destination, situated as it is at the crossroads to the north and the road inland along the Saguenay River. It has such a pretty, natural setting that in 2003 Tadoussac hosted the World Congress of the Most Beautiful Bays in the World Club. (We guess there must be a club for everything!) Just be forewarned that if you go off-season, as we have done, everything's locked up tight as a drum. Nonetheless, in-season (mid-June through Labor Day) the well-informed, bilingual staff at the excellent Tourist Information Office (197 rue des Pionniers G0T 2A0; 418-235-4744; www.tadoussac.com) can advise you on what to see and where to go. In addition, this well-stocked center has good videos, maps, books, and souvenirs: a good one to visit, in other words!

Do visit Canada's first trading post, built in 1600 by Pierre de Chauvin: the *Poste de traite Chauvin (Chauvin Trading Post)* (157 rue du Bord-de-l'Eau, Tadoussac; 418-235-4657; open daily May through Oct). Here you'll learn about the Montagnais Native life and the history of the fur trade in Canada. Jacques Cartier landed upon this point of land, on what the Montagnais called *Tatoushak* ("nipple"), in 1534. Chauvin arrived in the winter of 1579 with sixteen men. Unprepared, eleven died of cold and scurvy that brutal winter. From 1600 to 1859, the trading post Chauvin built was one of the most active on the St. Lawrence. In 1603 Champlain himself came here on the first of several visits. More contemporary history, such as the business of the oil trade, is also described here.

Absolutely do not miss the CIMM—*Centre d'Interpretation des Mammifères Marins* (108 rue de la Cale-Sèche, Tadoussac; 418-235-4848; www

.gremm.com; open daily mid-May through mid-Oct, times vary; $9 adult, $6.75 senior, $4.50 children, $20.50 family). Suspended from the ceiling is a giant skeleton of a pregnant female whale, complete with skeleton of the fetus. When we were there, a marine biologist spent a relaxed twenty minutes with us, answering questions about whales. Here you'll learn how to tell the species apart, and children will enjoy the films, slide shows, and activities.

Use the Internet (www.baleinesendirect.net) to track the location of whales. *Tip:* When we were last at the CIMM, the director told us we could check the latest sightings to see whether it was worthwhile to go on a whale-watch cruise. If no whales are currently in the area, you might as well save your money!

Whether or not you take a cruise, drive to the docks. We did, in midwinter, when Tadoussac was pretty well shut down. We took an afternoon stroll along the snowy but sunny shore drawn there by the sight of an immense ice breaker tied at the dock. Behind it, ice floes dotted the picturesque harbor.

Look back to shore at the long white building with a cherry-red roof: **Hotel Tadoussac.** This three-star hotel with 149 rooms is open from early May through mid-Oct, with an unbeatable view of the bay (165 rue Bord-de-l'eau; 418-235-4421 or 800-561-0718; www.hoteltadoussac.com). Inquire at the hotel about the Surf the Saguenay Waves Package, which includes a Saguenay Fjord cruise with lunch on board the boat, plus dinner, one night at the hotel, and breakfast.

Adjacent to the hotel you'll find some easy walks. One extends along a wooden boardwalk aside the bay to the old wharf and Tadoussac Marina. Alternatively, explore the coastline during a two-hour (4 mile/6 kilometer) rambling walk at low tide by heading to the Tadoussac beach and wandering along the dunes and mud flats. Take your binoculars so you can identify the shore birds. (Tip: be sure to find out about tides from the hotel's front desk so you won't be stranded by the incoming tide!) A third walk is available starting from the dry dock, where an interpreted boardwalk takes you along the rocks at shore's edge to the tip of the Saguenay's peninsula. Panels describe the river's geography and ecology. Another extremely easy stroll leads up from the hotel to the very top of the peninsula. This rewards you with super views of the confluence of the Saguenay and St. Lawrence Rivers.

There is yet another trail only five minutes from the Tadoussac Hotel. Find the Fjord Trail's trailhead at the fish farm near the ferry dock (ask for directions at the hotel's front desk). The twenty-minute stroll affords more spectacular views of the fjord and terminates at Anse-à-la-barque.

After exploring Tadoussac, head to the ferry to cross the mouth of the Saguenay River. As you cross the Saguenay River on the free ten-minute ferry ride to the other side of Tadoussac Bay, get out on deck to scan for whales and marvel at the magnificent fjord's cliffs. The confluence of this rich estuarine delta is an important feeding ground for marine species such as the beluga. Don't miss stopping at **Pointe Noire** at the top of the hill on the west side. This excellent (and free) marine interpretation center has a boardwalk lookout with a superb view of the estuary and an informative video in English. Pointe Noire is at Route 138, Baie Sainte-Catherine; 418-237-4383; off-season 418-235-4703. Open: June to Labor Day. Naturalist-led tours available in English and French. Spectacular trail/boardwalk (stairs).

Immediately after Pointe Noire, the road toward **Saint-Siméon** can become highly congested—there's simply not enough parking for whale watchers and others.

At Saint-Siméon, take the ferry across the St. Lawrence to Rivière-du-Loup. As you descend toward town, you'll see the sandy beach and the ferry docks. Follow the signs to the ferry parking. Bilingual attendants help direct vehicles to the appropriate lanes. Boarding is first-come, first-served, and they recommend that you be there ninety minutes before departure during summer (other times, thirty minutes). During summer peak season, there were five crossings daily. Full fares: $15.30 adults, $14 seniors, $10.20 for ages five to eleven, $38 for a car. (For current fare and schedule information, contact **Traverse Rivière-du-Loup Saint-Siméon Ferry,** 199 rue Hayward, Rivière-du-Loup; 418-862-5094; www.travrdlstsim.com.)

After you park, lock up your car and wander along the beach or stop in at the snack bars and ice-cream stands. If you want to stay overnight here, try **Auberge sur Mer** (109 rue du Quai, Saint-Siméon; 418-638-2674; www.quebecweb.com/aubergesurmer), which offers motel-like bedrooms; across the parking lot is its seafood restaurant.

This ferry crossing takes just over an hour. You must get out of your car, but there's lots to do on the ferry, from reading the bilingual information panels on the estuarine life to scanning for pods of belugas. We were thrilled to spy a pod of eight feeding just off the lighthouse at **Île-aux-Lièvre.** This is

Wolf Howl?

How did Rivière-du-Loup (Wolf River) get its name? Take your pick of three legends. One tells how its name derives from the many seals basking there (called *loups-marins*—sea wolves—*en français*); another says it's from a French ship named Le Loup that overwintered there long ago; a third tale tells of a native tribe of this name. Ironically, no legend tells of the lonely howls of a wolf heard on a full-moonlit night.

only one of **Les Îles-du-Bas-Saint-Laurent (Lower St. Lawrence Islands).** It's possible to stay on some of these islands. A nonprofit conservation society manages them and offers limited access to unique activities and accommodations on them. For example, you can try the overnight escape at a lighthouse on **Pot à l'Eau-de-Vie,** rent a chalet or camp on Île-aux-Lièvre, or simply take a guided tour of the islands. All transportation starts from Rivière-du-Loup. (For a bilingual pamphlet, contact La Société Duvetnor at 200 rue Hayward, CP 305, Rivière-du-Loup G5R 3Y9; 418-867-1660; www.duvetnor.com.)

From Rivière-du-Loup, you could follow the tourist route east toward Rimouski on Highway 132. Or you could take the longer route and follow our side trip along the south shore. Note that if time is tight and you need to head south, our route will take you toward Edmundston, New Brunswick.

The South Shore

We love gardening, history, and the romantic tale of Grey Owl. So we drove south from Rivière-du-Loup to **Cabano** on **Lake Temiscouata** on Route 185 Sud (south). During the forty-five-minute drive through undulating countryside, we saw many peat bogs being harvested by what looked like giant vacuum cleaners!

Our main destination was **Fort Ingall,** the largest of several British forts constructed in 1839 to defend the critical Portage Trail, threatened by American forces. After only three years, the border dispute was settled and Fort Ingall was abandoned without a shot having been fired. Built of wood, the original stockade fort did not survive. However, the community of Cabano rallied and after ten years of research put their town—and fort—back on the map by reconstructing it in 1973, using the original plans (81 chemin Caldwell, Cabano; 418-854-2375; www.fortingall.ca; open daily 9 a.m. to 5 p.m. late June through early Sept; Mon through Fri 10 a.m. to 4 p.m. in June and until mid-Oct; $8 adults, $6 seniors and children six to twelve, $18 family; admission includes access to rose gardens).

Inside, there is a permanent exhibit on **Grey Owl,** the enigmatic Englishman whose given name was Archibald Belaney. Born in 1888 in Hastings, England, he came to Canada in 1906, traveling to Témiscaming in Northern Ontario, where he became intrigued with the old Native ways of life and livelihood, such as trapping. From 1906 to 1910 he lived among the Ojibway; after seeing military action in World War I, he returned to Témiscaming in 1925. Then he "went native," adopting the name Grey Owl and, in 1928, coming to Cabano with a Native woman named Anahareo. A year later he published his first article in an English magazine, *Country Life,* under his new name and delivered his first public lecture at the town of Métis-sur-Mer. The subject? Beavers. Perhaps you've read his books, such as *Pilgrims of the Wild* or *Sajo and the Beaver People*.

Grey Owl's story is an impossibly romantic legend that we both remembered from our childhood. We read his books and believed—as everyone did—he was an Ojibway. His tale is all the more appealing because he fooled so many people for decades. With his long black hair and hawk nose, he was every white person's caricature image of an Indian. His talk of conservation challenged all Canada—and the world—to take care of Mother Earth long before our modern-day environmental movement. Actor Pierce Brosnan came to Wakefield, Québec, in 1998 to star in the filming of the movie *Grey Owl*.

A companion project that literally surrounds Fort Ingall in flowers is **La Roseraie du Témiscouata (Rose Gardens).** Here you'll see more than 250 varieties of hardy roses: shrubs, climbing, and "ground cover" varieties, all of which can withstand the rigors of the weather here. There's a French formal garden and an English country garden, a garden of hybrids, and another of the explorer series developed at Ottawa's Experimental Farm. See which you prefer—and don't hesitate to stick your nose into the fragrant blossoms. Some varieties are for sale.

If you are leaving Québec at this point, follow Highway 185 Sud along the lake (and the strikingly beautiful farmland around **Nôtre-Dame-du-Lac**) into New Brunswick. At this village find **Auberge Marie Blanc**—said to have been designed by architect Frank Lloyd Wright and built in 1905 (1112 rue Commerciale Sud; 418-899-6747; www.aubergemarieblanc.com).

However, to return to the south shore and Route 132, turn northeast on Route 232, then north on Route 293 to **Saint-Jean-de-Dieu.** Watch for the sign pointing right toward **Saint-Mathieu** after you pass the Route 296 turnoff to **Sainte-Françoise.** Turn right on this unnumbered sideroad toward Saint-Mathieu and **Saint-Fabien,** where you'll rejoin Highway 132 Est.

This might seem like a zigzag, but is it ever worth it! These villages and roads are too picturesque for words. Clean and tidy towns all tease you to stay with countless little B&Bs dotted here and there. The countryside is folded gently here, and the little back road ambles along, transecting one of the valley floors. The farms exhibit the long, thin seigneurial lots that course down to the St. Lawrence. You'll enjoy the old homesteads that cluster together along the road, their old, mature pasture and croplands trailing after them in green and gold ribbons.

At Highway 132, turn east to **Bic National Park** (418-736-5035; www .sepaq.com/bic/). Parc Bic is very pretty: a sudden upheaval of knobby hills projects out into the St. Lawrence, with great biking trails, and bird and marine

Creating Parc Bic

Here there are so many mountainous islands offshore that a geological legend is in order. Folk tales tell of how the angel responsible for creating mountains grew tired, laden as she was with such a heavy basket. So upon arriving at Bic, the angel simply tipped the mountains out, thus forming the islands in the river we now enjoy!

life to observe. If you enjoy kayaking, Bic is a lovely destination. *Kayak Archipel du Bic* (418-736-5232; www.kayakzodiacarchipeldubic.com) rent kayaks and teach kayaking—what a great idea for planning a learning vacation right here on the water! Professional guides explain the marine life. Be sure to make reservations, as this is a popular attraction.

The park's campground, however, is squished by the highway and is totally flat and devoid of positive attributes. Instead you might try *Gîte aux Cormorans* (213 chemin du Golf, Bic; 418-736-8113; www.auxcormorans .com), a Victorian farmhouse with a large, welcoming veranda. It's just east of the campground, off Route 132 to your right, near the Thêatre de Bic right on the "seashore." Here you can rent a housekeeping unit by the week during summer and for fewer days during the off-season only.

Next stop is *Rimouski,* a very pretty city with cafes, bistros, and tons of sights to take in. Look for the cathedral and turn right onto Rue de l'Eglise, then right again a few blocks down onto Rue de l'Évêché Ouest. Almost immediately, at No. 31 on your left, is *Central Café.* Park in the rear and enter to enjoy the boisterous ambience and generous servings. We were in the mood for nachos and pasta—delicious! While you're at it, enjoy one of Québec's delicious microbrewery beers.

Now follow Route 132 Est. Everyone calls the St. Lawrence *la mer* here, and it's easy to see why. It is tidal, saline, and expansive. There are *les phares* (lighthouses), seafood restaurants, and near the picturesque "seaside" village of *Pointe-au-Père,* a museum that adds to our water theme: *Le Musée de la Mer.* Just follow the signs to the lighthouse, part of the museum site. You can even climb up the 125 steep steps of the lighthouse's circular stairway to enjoy the view and see the mechanism. Take care descending the steep and winding stairs.

Off the coast near here on May 29, 1914, the luxury ship *Empress of Ireland* was struck by a Norwegian collier and sank in fifteen minutes, taking 1,012 passengers and crew to their death. Only the sinking of the Titanic, two years earlier, resulted in a greater loss of life. The museum is a monument to the *Empress* tragedy and details the 1964 discovery of the wreck's precise location. Successive teams of international divers scoured the bottom, including the late French oceanographer and biologist Jacques Yves Cousteau.

One section of the museum emulates an actual dive, complete with video footage. The sometimes indistinct images and the sound of the diver's breathing and bubbles eerily evoke the inner exploration of the wreck. Suddenly the camera focuses on . . . a human skull! The museum is operated by Parks Canada and is interpreted bilingually. Well worth a visit (1000 rue du Phare, Pointe-au-Père; 418-724-6214; www.shmp.qc.ca; open daily late May to mid-Oct; $9 adults, $6 children eight to fifteen).

The narrow strip of coast boasts a line of restaurants, homes, inns, and campgrounds. To your right are farms with their fields stretching as far as you can see. It's touristy here, and you can see why: It's lovely. Beaches are rocky but beg for exploration, picnicking, and wildlife observation.

You can taste bee products like mead (honey wine) and *la gelée royale* (royal jelly) in the museum section of the **Vieux Moulin** near Sainte-Flavie; inexpensive tours and free tastes of mead (141 rte. de la mer, Sainte-Flarie; 418-775-8383; www.vieuxmoulin.qc.ca).

Just inside the village limits of Sainte-Flavie, stop at the Tourism Information Center on your right before leaving the south shore of the St. Lawrence. Find out about the **Centre d'Art Marcel Gagnon** (564 rte. de la Mer, Sainte-Flavie; 418-775-2829; www.centredart.net; open daily May 1 through Oct 14; free), where more than eighty life-size statues and several boats are exhibited on the St. Lawrence shores—perhaps a fitting goodbye to the coast?

A bit farther along, the aquariums, video presentation, and a humorous "play" at the **Centre d'interprétation du Saumon atlantique (Atlantic Salmon Interpretation Center)** explains the importance of protecting this resource. During the July/August spawning season, a minibus will take you to view the salmon jumping upstream (900 rte. de la Mer, Sainte-Flavie; 418-775-2969; daily end of June to start of Sept, 9 a.m. to 5 p.m.

A bit about the salmon . . . Did you know that Atlantic salmon differ from Pacific salmon in a very important way? Unlike their west-coast cousins who die after spawning, Atlantic salmon return for many years to the river where they were born to lay their eggs. How do salmon know where to return? Their birthplace is held in memory by smell and taste, which they can detect as water swirls in their mouth. Atlantic salmon can return to where they were born—or at least where they lived during their early development—by following the "track" of the scent and taste of water.

Wave good-bye to the coast as you ascend Route 132 Sud through **Mont Joli.** It's 155 kilometers to our eventual destination, Matapédia, on the Baie de Chaleurs.

Now we enter rural hinterland punctuated by pretty parishes. After 35 kilometers, you pass by the village of **Saint-Moïse,** the oldest region along the Matapédia River. In August 1998 the whole community celebrated its 125th anniversary. We took a short diversion off the highway to drive through the village. People had decorated their homes and front lawns with statues and scenes of pioneer days. It was a grand example of how a community can display its pride. It's interesting to note that north of Saint-Moïse, water flows from here to the St. Lawrence River; south of Saint-Moïse, it flows to the Baie des Chaleurs.

Four kilometers beyond Saint-Moïse, on the left side of the highway, your attention will be riveted by an abandoned slate mine that reveals oxblood red and gray slate, as well as some intriguing conglomerate. It reminded us of our trip to the slate museum at Melbourne in the Eastern Townships.

As you drive, there are pick-your-own farms where you can harvest luscious *fraises* (strawberries) in June, *framboises* (raspberries) in mid-July, and *pommes* (apples) starting in late August. Look for the signs: *framboises auto-ceuillére,* for example, means "pick-your-own raspberries."

Continue south through large, prosperous-looking dairy farms. This is the start of the famous Matapédia Valley, renowned for its picturesque, tranquil scenery. Continue through Sayabec to Val Brilliant, where there's an excellent lakeside lookout and picnic ground. Lac Matapédia is the headwaters of the famous salmon river of the same name. Amqui, the commercial heart of the valley, is at the south end of the lake.

Farther south on Route 132 at **Causapscal**, just beyond the bridge spanning the Causcapal River, is the **Site Historique Matamajaw** across from the tourist information office. In 1870 Lord Mount Stephen discovered this superb salmon fishing site and immediately purchased tracts of land beside the confluence of the two rivers, Causcapal and Matapédia. During the early 1900s, wealthy Americans and Canadians purchased his estate, founding the elite Matamajaw Fishing Club. Today the club still stands; part of it is a gift shop. Wander down to the river, and in July and August you will probably see fly fishermen casting here. A tranquil setting for a tremendous sport. There's a little suspension bridge over the river and also a pool with glass windows where you can view salmon (53 rue Saint-Jacques Sud, CP 460, Causapscal; 418-756-5999; www.sitehistoriquematamajaw.com). The Matamajaw Historical Site comprises five buildings, of which the canoe hut is perhaps the most interesting. Several different types are displayed here, showing the different types of materials used over the centuries, from birch bark to cedar strip, to modern-day innovations. The site is open from late June to early Sept daily except Mondays from 9:30 a.m. to 5 p.m.; admission is $5.70 for adults, $4.85 for senior citizens and students, $17.10 for families.

Continue south toward Matapédia, passing through the **Reserve faunique Matapédia,** the game preserve that protects the river. Lovely views of the tumbling waters draw you to the coast. Turn left to follow Route 132 Est as it curves toward Restigouche and the start of this trip, Pointe-à-la-Croix.

On your left opposite the bridge to Matapédia, you'll see a sign leading to a *belvédère,* or lookout, that is 210 meters up the hill. It affords a good prospect of the confluence of the Matapédia and Restigouche Rivers and the Baie des Chaleurs—and lets you stretch your legs one last time on this route.

On the Road to Newfoundland

Most people turn west after crossing the St. Lawrence by ferry from Matane. However, there is lots to see to the east—and not many people know it is possible to get to Newfoundland from here. In fact, you can circumnavigate the Gulf of St. Lawrence and see Canada's Maritime provinces without having to retrace your route. (A few years ago Eric had the opportunity to travel on a supply ship servicing the coastal villages of the lower north shore region from Sept-Îles to Blanc-Sablon on the Labrador border. Although we had to push through pack ice in places, it was fascinating: small isolated villages eking a living out of what few resources are available from the barren land and cold waters.)

Follow Highway 138 Est to **Sept-Îles,** Québec's largest deepwater port, named for the seven islands around the mouth of its large circular bay. Plan to spend at least a day at the **Mingan Archipelago National Park Reserve,** about 175 kilometers farther along the coast near Havre-Saint-Pierre. This federal park has well-organized water transportation to take visitors to many of its nearly forty limestone islands. Hiking and camping are available on some islands. Particularly impressive are the facilities on Quarry Island. Each very private site is well separated from the others, but all are within a short walk of a centrally located shelter with a wood stove. Sites 1 and 2 are the nicest. There are a total of only forty sites in ten locations on six of the islands, and you must make reservations (1010 Promenade des Anciens, Havre-Saint-Pierre; 418-538-3285; www.pc.gc.ca/mingan/; June through Sept).

You can arrange to catch the coastal boat at **Havre-Saint-Pierre** or continue east on Highway 138 along the coast. The road ends at **Natashquan,** birthplace of beloved Québec singer Gilles Vigneault. After getting off the boat here, you can enjoy a hearty breakfast at **Auberge La Cache** (183 chemin d'en Haut, Natashquan; 418-726-3347; www.aubergelacache.com; rooms from $70 double). Ask to see the restored shipwreck table.

You'll need to have arranged passage on the **MV Nordik Express** to continue east from here. Your car will be loaded into a container, and you can enjoy the comfortable but fairly frugal accommodations aboard ship. There are sixteen cabins, with sixty berths, but you can also sleep in seats in the lounges. The food is surprisingly good, but because some of the staff needs to help during dockings, the restaurant sticks zealously to its posted schedule. (For fare information and reservations, contact Relais Nordik Inc., 17 Lebrun Ave., Rimouski G5L 2T5; 800-463-0680 or 418-723-8787; www.groupedes gagnes.com; Apr through Sept.) The company requests a 50 percent deposit thirty days in advance. Fares for vehicles depend on the weight: A typical car is about $400 from Natashquan to Blanc-Sablon on the Labrador border. We'd suggest booking passage only from Natashquan to Vieux-Fort; you can drive the last 50 kilometers to Blanc-Sablon.

The coastal villages are all quite different, although most depend on fishing. A favorite is Harrington Harbour, where sturdy wooden sidewalks link buildings together. For a stay between ferries to explore the many nearby islands, a great choice is **Amy's Boarding House** (Harrington Harbour; 418-795-3376), a delightful B&B with a sunny, plant-filled dining area and comfortable rooms.

In 1534 the present site of Vieux-Fort (Old Fort) was known as Brest and was the "capital" of the New World. Then it was a busy fishing harbor where Basque fishermen prepared salt cod to be sent back to Europe. Now home to only a few hundred people, it is the westernmost end of the road that can

natashquan

This community is one of nine making up the Montagnais Nation in Québec, and this site was a traditional summer meeting place for these Natives. In the eighteenth century, the North West Company Trading Post erected near the mouth of the river was taken over by the Hudson's Bay (1821).

take you to Blanc-Sablon and into Labrador. The road is good, and you'll get a chance to see what is behind the rugged shore you've been seeing.

A daily two-hour ferry, the *MV Apollo*, crosses the Straits of Belle-Isle from Blanc-Sablon to Sainte-Barbe, Newfoundland. (Call 866-535-2567 for reservations; $7.50 adults, $6 seniors and children over five; $22.50 for a car and driver; www.tw.gov.nl.ca/ferryservices/).

Places to Stay in the Coastal Region

BAIE COMEAU

Hôtel le Manoir
8 Cabot, G4Z 1L8;
(418) 296-3391
www.manoirbc.com

LE BIC

Gite La Maison de L'Irlandais
182 Premier rue Est,
St-Fabien, G0L 2Z0;
(418) 869-2913

CARLETON

Hostellerie Baie Bleue
482 blvd. Perron,
G0C 1J0;
(800) 463-9099 or
(418) 364-3355
www.baiebleue.com

MATANE

Hôtel-Motel Belle Plage
1310 rue Matane-sur-Mer,
G4W 3M6;
(888) 244-2323 or
(418) 562-2323
www.hotelbelleplage.com

NOTRE-DAME-DU PORTAGE

Auberge du Portage
671 rte. de Fleuve,
Notre-Dame-du Portage,
G0L 1Y0;
(418) 862-3601
www.aubergeduportage
.qc.ca
Resort spa with many
treatments, massages, and
diets available.

POINTE-AU-PÈRE (EAST OF RIMOUSKI)

L'auberge La Marée Douce
1329 blvd. Sainte-Anne,
Pointe-au-Père;
(418) 722-0822
www.aubergelamaree
douce.com
Mansard-roofed heritage
home built as master-pilot's
house in 1860s with pretty
wrap-around porch.

Places to Eat in the Coastal Region

BAIE COMEAU

**Les Trois Barils
(The Three Barrels)**
200 rue la Salle;
(418) 296-3681

BERGERONNES

Auberge la Rosepierre
66 rue Principale;
(418) 232-6543
www.rosepierre.com
10 rooms plus superb din-
ing room.

LE BIC

Auberge du Vieux Bicois
134 rue Sainte-Cécile,
G0L 1B0;
(418) 736-4344 or
(888) 418-5518
Regional cuisine.

LES ESCOUMINS

Le Petit Régal
307 rte. 138;
(418) 233-2666
Fish, seafood.

TADOUSSAC

Restaurant Chez Mathilde
227 Rue Des Pionniers,
G0T 2A0;
(418) 235-4443

French–English Glossary

Here is a short list of French words and their English meanings that might be useful. If your car has a CD player, consider buying an audio course that you can listen to as you drive.

Accommodations

Auberge—Country inn
Gîte du passant—Bed-and-breakfast (usually reduced to gîte)
Hôtel/Motel—Hotel/motel
Où sont les toilettes?—Where is the bathroom (toilets)?
Toilette—Bathroom/toilet

Courtesy

À bientôt—See you soon
Au revoir—Good-bye; see you soon
Avec plaisir—With pleasure
Bonjour—Hello (literally, good day)
Bonne journée—Have a nice day
Bonsoir—Good evening
Excusez-moi—Pardon me
Salut!—Hi, or good-bye

Dates and Time

Aujourd'hui—Today
Demain—Tomorrow
L'année dernière—Last year
La semaine dernière—Last week
La semaine prochaine—Next week
Le mois prochain—Next month
Janvier—January
Février—February
Mars—March
Avril—April
Mai—May
Juin—June
Juillet—July
Août—August
Septembre—September

Octobre—October

Novembre—November

Décembre—December

Printemps—Spring

Été—Summer

Automne—Autumn

Hiver—Winter

Dimanche—Sunday

Lundi—Monday

Mardi—Tuesday

Mercredi—Wednesday

Jeudi—Thursday

Vendredi—Friday

Samedi—Saturday

À quelle heure?—At what time?

Quelle heure est-il?—What time is it?

Food and Restaurants

À la carte—From the regular menu of a restaurant

Apéritif—A pre-dinner drink

Bière—Beer

Boisson—Drink

Café au lait—Coffee with frothed milk

Déjeuner—Breakfast

Dîner—Lunch

Entrée—An appetizer (not the main part of a meal)

Frites—French fries

L'eau—Water

Menu du jour—Daily specials menu

Potage—Soup

Quelle est votre spécialité?—What is your specialty?

Repas—A meal

Salle à manger—Dining room

Souper—Dinner

Table d'hôte—Daily specials; usually a fixed price for a complete meal

Veuillez m'apporter la facteur—Please bring me the bill

Vin—Wine

Est-ce qu'il y a un bon restaurant près d'ici?—Is there a good restaurant near here?

General

Allumettes—Matches

ATM—Automated Teller Machine (same as English)

Centre d'achats—Shopping center

Dépanneur—Convenience store

Guichêt—Kiosk or wicket (where ATM is located)

Je ne comprends pas—I don't understand

Librairie—A bookstore (not a library)

Magasin—Store

Mécanicien—A motor or car mechanic

Météo—Weather report

Parlez lentement, s'il-vous-plaît—Speak slowly please

Pâte dentifrice—Toothpaste

Québec—the largest province of Canada (pronounced *kay-bek*)

Québécois—From Québec (pronounced *kay-bay-KWAW*)

Quels sont vos prix? What is the price (or rate)?

Quincaillerie—Hardware store

Timbre—Postage stamp

Landforms

Île—Island

Lac—Lake

Mont or *Montagne*—Mountain

Municipalité—Municipality

Parc—Park

Pont—Bridge

Réserve faunique—Wildlife reserve

Rivière—River (the St. Lawrence is sometimes referred to as a *fleuve*, a large river)

Ruisseau—Stream, creek

Driving and Road Signs

À quelle distance sommes-nous de . . . ?—How far are we from . . . ?

Arrêt—Stop

Autobus—Bus

Autoroute—Major highway, expressway

Chemin—Road

Cul de sac—Dead end

Départ de croisière—departure point for cruise

Départ de traversier—departure point for ferry

Droit—Right

En bas—Down

En haut—Up

Entrer—Enter

Est—East

Estationnement—Parking

Fin—End

Gare—A ferry dock (or train station)

Gauche—Left

Impair—Odd

Nord—North

Où conduit cette route?—Where does this road go?

Ouest—West

Pair—Even

Plein—Full

Route des baleines—Whale Route

Routes principales—Main highways

Routes secondaires—Secondary highways

Rue—Street

Sortie—Exit

Sud—South

Traversier—A ferry (a seasonal ferry is *traversier saisonnier*)

Vérifier l'huile, s'il-vous-plaît—Check the oil please

Virage à droit—Right turn

Virage à gauche—Left turn

Index